PLANNING AN APPLIED RESEARCH PROJECT IN
HOSPITALITY, TOURISM, &SPORTS

Frederic B. Mayo

Clinical Professor
Preston Robert Tisch Center for Hospitality,
Tourism, and Sports Management
New York University

WILEY

Library of Congress Cataloging-in-Publication Data

Mayo, Frederic B.

   Planning an applied research project in hospitality, tourism, and sports / Frederic B. Mayo, Clinical
Professor Preston Robert Tisch Center for Hospitality, Tourism, and Sports Management, New York
University.
      pages cm
   Includes bibliographical references and index.
      ISBN 978-1-118-63722-7 (pbk.)
      1. Hospitality industry—Research—Methodology.   2. Tourism—
Research—Methodology.   3. Sports—Research—Methodology.   I. Title.
   TX911.5.M38 2014
   338.4'7910072—dc23

                                                                          2013021885

Printed in the United States of America
10   9   8   7   6   5   4   3   2   1

This book is dedicated to:
Bobbie and Pinky, my parents,
whose belief that I could do anything converted
mountains and obstacles into friendly challenges
and
Maurice Wayne Dorsey whose sensitivity, integrity, passion for life,
and caring inspire me every day

Contents

Preface

WELCOME

Welcome to a planning book written to assist you in thinking about the process of academic research. For those in a course on research methods, *Planning an Applied Research Project in Hospitality, Tourism, and Sports* covers the process from developing and researching a topic to completing a coherent and well-argued proposal. This book also provides guidance for individuals writing proposals to support their research, whether the proposal is a request for funding, approval, or access to particular individuals and organizations. In addition, because of its scope, the book contains information for practicing professionals who are asked to conduct a piece of research or who will be hiring consultants to conduct research.

Planning an Applied Research Project in Hospitality, Tourism, and Sports is written for you, the student or practitioner of research, in a friendly easy-to-read tone to demystify the exciting process of planning all of the steps involved in conducting research.

The book can be read as separate chapters or as an integrated whole, depending on your goal. For example, the information on conducting and writing a literature review can be useful to any graduate student in a master or doctoral program. It can also help undergraduates who are starting to read scholarly research since **Chapter 1, Reading and Analyzing Research** focuses on how to sort through the information in a published research article.

The entire book covers the many stages of research, including developing a topic, creating a purpose statement and research questions, developing a research design, using various research techniques, and presenting a proposal. Using all of this information, you should be able to plan and conduct a coherent and carefully designed research project.

RESEARCH DEFINED

Research is a stimulating process of investigating or discovering something, an activity that you carry out all the time in your everyday life. Purchasing a present for someone you love, finding the right job, selecting a destination for a vacation, or deciding what restaurant to visit all involve research of a sort; these tasks require establishing a goal, defining criteria, developing options, finding out what others have said, trying out various suggestions, analyzing the information, and deciding what to do based on what you expect to find. Academic research is not that different. It may involve more steps and engage a longer and more complex thinking process, but it is still a matter of careful planning and deciding among a range of options based on what you find that others have done or recommended for future research.

Formal research is typically divided into three categories—theoretical, applied, and action research. Theoretical research involves the search for new knowledge for its own sake; it does not necessarily contribute to changes in practice. Applied research is the investigation of activities, events, behavior, practices, and programs in order to make a difference in business operations or organizational effectiveness. Action research involves making changes and then learning from them by using a carefully structured and disciplined process of reflection and analysis. All three types of research are valuable and make a significant contribution to a better world. This book focuses on applied research, the type of research that aims to improve the operation of businesses in hospitality, tourism, and sports. It is a manual for how to plan and conduct applied research.

RATIONALE FOR THE BOOK

Although there are a number of books about business research, most of them focus on business problems and emphasize the problem solving approach to addressing those challenges. They are excellent resources, and you may find good information in many of them. However, there are precious few that analyze the research planning process in detail starting with ways to read and analyze scholarship. Many of them do not provide advice about how to conduct and prepare a literature review.

Planning an Applied Research Project in Hospitality, Tourism, and Sports is designed to help students at the graduate or upper-level undergraduate level consider all of the issues involved in planning significant research that extends beyond the scope of analyzing materials in libraries, in publications, and on the web. This book takes seriously the notion that you can and should conduct your own field research, using interviews, questionnaires, observations, and other research techniques. It invites you to engage with the real processes of research and learn from the experience of designing all of the aspects of a research project before conducting it.

STRUCTURE OF THE BOOK

The book is organized into fourteen chapter and five appendices, four of which are online and one of which is included with this printed book. Each chapter contains a list of Key Terms to ensure that you understand the concepts as well as a Works Cited section at the end of each chapter. Each chapter begins with an Introduction that orients you to the main concepts and places them within the context of the entire book, and ends with a Summary that reviews the key ideas in the chapter. You will also find references to other chapters to help you pursue areas that might interest you more or to refresh your memory on past reading.

Since the book focuses on three related fields—hospitality, tourism, and sports—each chapter contains examples from the practices and scholarship of all three areas. In that way, the book can be useful in all three programs and help students consider issues in fields related to their major but not identical to it. In the current business climate, hospitality, tourism, and sports encompass disciplines such a management, service, law, planning, marketing, development, operations, finance, and more.

The sequence of chapters follows the notion of analyzing and developing research questions (Chapters 1–5), forms of qualitative and quantitative research (Chapters 6–7), key research design factors (Chapters 8–9), research techniques (Chapters 10–13) and developing a written proposal (Chapter 14). The appendices provide resources to help you with the details involved in planning and conducting a research project.

WAYS TO USE THIS BOOK

There are many options for making this book a productive learning experience. If you are interested in the full range of issues involved in planning an applied research project, then the whole book makes sense in the way it was written.

If you are only interested in learning how to write a literature review and you already know what your topic is or might be, then you might want to read the following chapters as a group:

Chapter 3 – Conducting a Literature Review

Chapter 4 – Reviewing and Revising your Purpose Statement

Chapter 5 – Writing a Literature Review

The separation of the two chapters on literature reviews recognizes that reading about scholarship on a chosen topic often leads to refocusing research questions and, sometimes, a refined purpose statement. However, you can drop Chapter 4 – Reviewing and Revising your Purpose Statement if you do not think it makes sense or read the first four chapters in a slightly different order than they appear in the book. For example, try reading them in the following order:

Chapter 2 – Developing an Interest or Topic

Chapter 4 – Reviewing and Revising your Purpose Statement

Chapter 1 – Reading and Analyzing Research

Chapter 3 – Conducting a Literature Review

Chapter 5 – Writing a Literature Review

If you are interested primarily in conducting research and using various tools, then you might want to isolate and read only the following chapters:

Chapter 8 – Sampling Issues in Research

Chapter 10 – Research Techniques: Interviews

Chapter 11 – Research Techniques: Questionnaires

Chapter 12 – Research Techniques: Observations, Focus Groups, and Other Techniques

Chapter 13 – Analyzing Data and Other Information

To provide an orientation to the field of scholarly research and to defuse its complexity, you might want to read the following group of chapters as a unit:

Chapter 1 – Reading and Analyzing Research

Chapter 6 – Forms of Qualitative Research

Chapter 7 – Forms of Quantitative Research

When you want to focus on developing a proposal and making an argument to support your research, you might want to emphasize reading the cluster of:

Chapter 5 – Writing a Literature Review

Chapter 9 – Validity, Reliability, and Credibility

Chapter 14 – Writing a Research Proposal

Of course, the entire book is useful, but if you have limited time and need to focus, these suggestions may be helpful. While the structure of the book is my own, many people helped me develop it.

ADDITIONAL RESOURCES

A comprehensive online *Instructor's Manual* with *Test Bank* accompanies this book and is available to instructors to help them effectively manage their time and to enhance student learning opportunities. In addition, there are several Appendices available online: **Appendix B, List of Scholarly Journals, Appendix C, Websites, Appendix D, Bibliographic Tools**, and **Appendix E, Popular Databases**.

The *Test Bank* has been specifically formatted for *Respondus*, an easy-to-use software program for creating and managing exams that can be printed to paper or published directly to Blackboard, WebCT, Desire2Learn, eCollege, ANGEL, and other eLearning systems. Instructors who adopt this book can download the Test Bank for free.

A password-protected Wiley Instructor Book Companion Web site devoted entirely to this book (www.wiley.com/college/mayo) provides access to the online *Instructor's Manual* and the text-specific teaching resources. The *Respondus Test Bank* and the *PowerPoints* are also available on the Web site for download.

ACKNOWLEDGMENTS

In the process of writing this book, many people assisted me, especially the five graduate students who helped with research, focus, and editing. My thanks to Brian Tritt, Laura Arneson, Eric Ricuarte, Nancy Huang, and Annika Anand. Without their help and dedication to the dream, this book would not be as thorough nor as clear. The questions posed by students in various applied research methods courses that I have taught at New York University have also clarified my thinking and broadened my approach to this topic. And my thanks to Javier Ceppi, Diana Ditto, Rachel Hahnraths, Kate McDowell, Shannon Shae Spalten, and Andrew Zenker who gave their permission to share their papers and ideas with other students and to use some of their work in this book. Without the support of Dr. Lalia Rach, founding dean of the Tisch Center for Hospitality, Tourism, and Sports Business, and Dr. Bjorn Hanson, Divisional Dean of the Center, I would not have completed this work. To all of them, I offer my humble thanks and hope that I have lived up to their hopes for what I could create.

Thank you also to the book reviewers:

Carol B. Brown, Roosevelt University

Sheryl Kline, University of South Carolina now University of Delaware

Amit Sharma, Pennsylvania State University

Enjoy the book. Read sections and take notes. Mark it up and make it yours. Research can be exciting and fun—it is not linear, it creates challenges, it frustrates, and it provides energizing activities and insights.

Read, write, research, and enjoy!

Frederic B. Mayo
Preston Robert Tisch Center for Hospitality,
Tourism, and Sports Management
New York University

CHAPTER 1

Reading and Analyzing Research

INTRODUCTION

Research is important and useful for several reasons. Industry publications, white papers, and *scholarly articles* provide managers and serious students with information about the kind and variety of research being conducted and the applications of that research. They show what topics and methods of research are being investigated, indicate what old theories or models are no longer relevant or useful, and make recommendations for improvements in practice. Industry publications generally focus on information that is immediately useful, and they sometimes lack detailed support for their recommendations. White papers—often the result of intensive study—cover the topic in a detailed and thoughtful manner and may provide applicable information or not, depending on the purpose of the paper and the publishing organization. Scholarly articles in refereed journals tend to advance the base of knowledge in a subject even if they do not provide immediately useful suggestions for practice. Books provide a broad range of information about an area or topic.

Whatever the format, the information can be useful if you know what to look for and how to read it. This chapter will provide information about the differences among kinds of research, the purposes of scholarly journals, the ways to read them, and their usefulness.

If you are going to conduct research or are planning to develop a research career, it is important and useful to know about the range of topics being researched and the types of research being conducted. The formats include industry articles and reports, white papers, and scholarly articles.

INDUSTRY ARTICLES AND REPORTS

Although scholarly journals are the major source of research information, industry publications often contain research as well. Professional associations, private firms, governmental and nongovernmental agencies, and trade magazines often publish very useful research information. For example, the American Society for Training and Development publishes the *Annual Review of Training*, the American Hotel and Lodging Association publishes *Lodging, Lodging HR*, and *Lodging Law*, among others; and the National Restaurant Association publishes *SmartBrief* and *Restaurant Industry Operations Report*.

In addition, a number of industry publications—which do not use the blind editorial review process associated with scholarly journals—provide insightful information to their respective industries. Many industry associations such as the Travel Industry Association (TIA), U.S. Travel Association, and The Business Roundtable, or private firms such as Smith Travel Research (STR) and Hospitality Valuation Services (HVS), also publish regular reports based on a significant amount of research pertinent to their industries. The material contributes dramatically to the knowledge base upon which industry professionals and researchers build. For example, John O'Neill used Smith Travel Research data to analyze the value of brand equity (O'Neill and Xiao 212).

Common research reports in the hospitality, tourism, and sports industries include *Hospitality and Leisure: Manhattan Lodging Index* by PriceWaterhouseCooper, *Hotel Valuation Index* by HVS, hotel market and forecasting reports by STR, and *The Consumer Travel Trends Survey* by PhoCusWright. Other publications include: *Hotel and Motel Management's* Top U.S. Hotel Companies Survey, PKF *Hotel Horizons*, YPartnership, *Insights*, CMI Green Annual Green Traveler Study, Mintel reports, Sports Business Research Network reports, and National Sporting Goods Association research reports.

GOOD REPORTS TO CHECK OUT

Mintel. "Marketing to Sports Enthusiasts—US." *Mintel*, June 2011. Web. 13 September 2011.

World Travel & Tourism Council. "Progress and Priorities 2009-10" *WTTC*, 2010. Web. 13 September 2011.

Mandelbaum, Robert. "Price Begets Profits." *PKF Hospitality Research*, Aug 2011. Web. 13 September 2011.

Giza, Christopher C., Jeffrey S. Kutcher, Stephen Ashwal, et al. "Summary of Evidence-based Guideline Update: Evaluation and Management of Concussion in Sports: Report of the Guideline Development Subcommittee of the American Academy of Neurology." *Neurology*. 80 (2013): 2250–2257.

Lund, Neel M. "No Longer a Gentleman's Sport: The Changing Format of Cricket and Its Impact on Sport Tourism." *HVS Global Hospitality Services*, September 2008.

WHITE PAPERS

White papers are carefully written and researched reports addressing specific topics that may or may not involve prior research and that typically are not blind reviewed by outsiders. Governmental agencies, nongovernmental organizations, and businesses generally publish white papers. The term *white paper* originated as a phrase to describe governmental documents written for the purpose of outlining a new direction for policy, a strategy to implement a policy, or a specific set of guidelines for implementing a program. Often, they are written to advocate for change in a policy or program and, therefore, tend to focus their evidence in the direction of persuading the reader to adopt the policy or program. Examples of white papers include:

South African Government Information." National Department of Sport and Recreation White Paper." *South African Government Online*. 2003. Web. 18 September 2010.

The Department of Conservation and Natural Resources (DCNR), the Department of Community and Economic Development (DCED), the Pennsylvania Historical and Museum Commission (PHMC), and the Center for Rural Pennsylvania. *Moving Heritage Tourism Forward in Pennsylvania*. 2001. The Center for Rural Pennsylvania. Web. 3 October 2010.

In business, white papers have come to mean works produced by private firms or individuals with the purpose of marketing their services to the audience based on the paper topic, proposed solution, or perceived credentials. While commercial white papers may contain pertinent data, viewpoints, and references, you should always remember that they ultimately are produced with a marketing or advocacy purpose in mind. Some examples of business white papers include:

Gupta, Saurabh, and Manav Thadini. "Critical Issues Facing Indian Hospitality: An HVS White Paper." *HVS*. 10 January 2009. Web. 18 September 2010.

"The Restaurant of the Future: A Hughes White Paper." April 24, 2013. http://hospitalitytechnology.edgl.com/white-papers

"The 2010 American Pantry Study: The New Rules of the Shopping Game." Deloitte Development, LLC and the Harrison Group, 2010. Web. 3 October 2010.

Rosenberger, Scot et al. "Traveling Through the Recovery: Ways THL Companies should Consider Navigating the Upturn." *Deloitte Development LLC*. 2010. Web. 18 September 2010.

Talbott, Barbara M. "The Power of Personal Service: Why It Matters, What Makes It Possible, How It Creates Competitive Advantage." *CHR Industry Perspectives: A White Paper Series from Cornell University* 1 (September 2006) 4–14.

In addition, industry associations may produce white papers, as well as private firms or individuals in partnership with academic institutions or industry associations. United States Travel Industry of America has produced a report each year on the status of the travel industry in the United States. Other examples include the various Mintel Reports on various countries and specific topics.

Houdré, Hervé. "Sustainable Hospitality: Sustainable Development in the Hotel Industry." *Cornell Industry Perspectives* 2. Cornell University School of Hotel Administration Center for Hospitality Research, 2008. Web. 18 September 2010.

U. S. Travel Association, "Outlook for Travel and Tourism 2011 Edition." 27 October 2010. Web. 5 September 2011.

Although white papers are valuable, they tend to collect current research and do not advance knowledge in the same manner as scholarly articles.

DEFINITION OF A SCHOLARLY JOURNAL ARTICLE

Scholarly articles have been published in journals that focus on discovering, adding, and revising new knowledge and sharing it with academicians, practitioners, and other interested researchers. A scholarly article—often called a peer-reviewed article or a blind-reviewed article—is one that has been developed to move the research forward in a particular area or to expand an understanding of certain practices. Scholarly articles can be conceptual, empirical, qualitative, rhetorical, or meta-theoretical, and they cover an area and provide a new perspective to the research that has already been conducted.

Many of these journals are published by universities or professional organizations. Decisions about what to publish are made by an editorial board of colleagues and fellow researchers. The purpose of the editorial board is to ensure that only quality research gets published and that the insights from the research are well presented to a broader audience. That goal means that the review process is conducted blind—the individuals reading and reviewing an article do not know who the article's author or authors are.

A *blind reviewer* is a person who reads an article, assesses its merits, decides about publishing it, and recommends possible revision without knowing who wrote the article. They are typically individuals who know the field and have conducted research on their own or with other colleagues. The recommendations of a blind reviewer can include:

- accept the article as is;
- accept the article with modifications;
- suggest major changes and resubmit; or
- reject the article.

The purpose of the blind review is to provide a quality check of the research done, its significance, and its merits, as well as determine the match between the article and the journal's own perspective and style.

While this blind review process is not typical of most industry publications, in the realm of scholarship, it ensures a more honest and fair reading of current research and provides a way to make sure that the research fills a lacuna in already published research or advances a significant area of research. The process also provides scholars with feedback and suggestions for improving their research and writing.

Often an article can be well designed, well researched, and carefully and thoughtfully written. However, the article may not fit into the range of topics published by that particular journal or, a specific issue focused on a particular topic. Sometimes, the article may be valuable but not particularly appropriate for the audience of the journal to which it was submitted, or the article may represent a different kind from what the journal regularly publishes. For example, the *Journal of Hospitality and Tourism Research* rarely publishes conceptual articles; the *Sports Marketing Quarterly* generally publishes empirically based research; and the *International Journal of*

Hospitality Management tends to focus on hotel issues in England, Australia, and New Zealand. The *Journal of Hospitality and Tourism Education*, for example, only publishes articles about teaching, learning, or the state of hospitality and tourism education in the United States and abroad. Journals such as *Journal of Hospitality and Tourism Research* or the *Journal of Sports Management* remain open to a wide range of topics and subjects. One particularly broad publication, the *Journal of Hospitality, Leisure, Sport, and Tourism Education*, includes sections for Academic Papers, Practice Papers, Perspectives, Comments and Rejoinders, Research Notes and Reports, and Education Resource Reviews. Each journal is different.

Most journals are clear about their focus and scope. For example, the *International Journal of Contemporary Hospitality Management*

> *Aims to communicate the latest developments and thinking on the management of hospitality operations worldwide. A multidisciplinary journal, it publishes double-blind reviewed papers covering issues relevant to operations, marketing, finance and personnel. . . . It is the* Journal's *intention to encourage an interchange between hospitality managers, educators and researchers.*

- Contributors are encouraged to identify the practical implications of their work for the management of hospitality across the range, from single unit concerns to large organizations.

- Articles based on experience and evidence—rather than philosophical speculation—are encouraged.

- Co-authored contributions from educators and managers on collaborative work are particularly welcome" (Emerald Group Publishing Limited).

If an article is accepted for publication, often the author (or authors) is asked to develop some part of the argument more thoroughly or rewrite parts of it to fit the style of the particular journal. There are often significant differences in the structure and format of various journals, and authors may not be aware of the differences.

Scholarly journals are typically published by universities, professional organizations, or, increasingly, private publishing houses. Some examples of the different types include:

- A publishing company for an association: *Journal of Sport Management*, published by Human Kinetics for the American Society for Sport Management

- A private publishing company: *Journal of Culinary Science and Technology*, published by The Haworth Hospitality and Tourism Press

- A university for the university: *Harvard Business Review*, published by the Graduate School of Business Administration, Harvard University

- A private publisher for a college or university: *Cornell Hotel and Restaurant Administration Quarterly*, published by Elsevier for School of Hotel Administration at Cornell University

Perusing a table of contents can be a great way to review quickly the kinds of topics being published and the range of issues being investigated. (For a sample of several different types of tables of contents, see the box **Sample Tables of Contents**.) The following tables of contents indicate the range of article topics that one can find in many of the scholarly journals in hospitality.

SAMPLE TABLE OF CONTENTS

Table of Contents for a Special Issue on the Hospitality Industry in India, *International Journal of Contemporary Hospitality Management*. 19.5 (2007).

Kirti Dutta, Umashankar Venkatesh, H.G. Parsa, "Service Failure and Recovery Strategies in the Restaurant Sector: An Indo–US Comparative Study"

Kamal Manaktola, Vinnie Jauhari, "Exploring Consumer Attitude and Behaviour Towards Green Practices in the Lodging Industry in India"

Gunjan M. Sanjeev, "Measuring Efficiency of the Hotel and Restaurant Sector: The Case of India"

Swati Dabas, Kamal Manaktola, "Managing Reservations Through Online Distribution Channels: An Insight into Mid-segment Hotels in India"

Kirti Madan, "An Analysis of the Debt-Equity Structure of Leading Hotel Chains in India"

Mridula Dwivedi, T.P. Shibu, Umashankar Venkatesh, "Social Software Practices on the Internet: Implications for the Hotel Industry"

Table of Contents for *Journal of Sustainable Tourism* 18.1 (2010)

Bramwell, Bill; Lane, Bernard, "Sustainable Tourism and the Evolving Roles of Government Planning"

Beaumont, Narelle; Dredge, Dianne, "Local Tourism Governance: A Comparison of Three Network Approaches"

Brunnschweiler, Juerg M., "The Shark Reef Marine Reserve: A Marine Tourism Project in Fiji Involving Local Communities"

Weaver, David, "Indigenous Tourism Stages and their Implications for Sustainability"

Wearing, Stephen Leslie; Wearing, Michael; McDonald, Matthew, "Understanding Local Power and Interactional Processes in Sustainable Tourism: Exploring Village-Tour Operator Relations in the Kokoda Track, Papua New Guinea"

Mair, Judith; Jago, Leo, "The Development of a Conceptual Model of Greening in the Business Events Tourism Sector"

Park, Eerang; Boo, Soyoung, "An Assessment of Convention Tourism's Potential Contribution to Environmentally Sustainable Growth"

Schellhorn, Matthias, "Development for Whom? Social Justice and the Business of Ecotourism"

Chang, Liang-Chih, "The Effects of Moral Emotions and Justifications on Visitors' Intention to Pick Flowers in a Forest Recreation Area in Taiwan"

Wilson, Erica, "A Review of 'Handbook of Sustainable Development'"

Biggs, Duan, "A Review of 'International Handbook of the Economics of Tourism'"

Table of Contents for *Journal of Travel Research* 43.1 (August 2004)

Jeffrey Sasha Davis and Duarte B. Morais, "Factions and Enclaves: Small Towns and Socially Unsustainable Tourism Development"

William S. Reece, "Are Senior Leisure Travelers Different?"

Yaniv Poria, Richard Butler, and David Airey, "Links between Tourists, Heritage, and Reasons for Visiting Heritage Sites"

James F. Petrick, "First Timers' and Repeaters' Perceived Value"

Yong K. Suh and William C. Gartner, "Perceptions in International Urban Tourism: An Analysis of Travelers to Seoul, Korea"

Mathew Ismert and James F. Petrick, "Indicators and Standards of Quality Related to Seasonal Employment in the Ski Industry"

Rex S. Toh, Habibullah Khan, and Lay-Ling Lim, "Two-Stage Shift-Share Analysis of Tourism Arrivals and Arrivals by Purpose of Visit: The Singapore Experience"

Jay G. Beaman, Tzung-Chen Huan, and Jeff P. Beaman, "Tourism Surveys: Sample Size, Accuracy, Reliability, and Acceptable Error"

Margaret J. Daniels, "Beyond Input-Output Analysis: Using Occupation-Based Modeling to Estimate Wages Generated by a Sport Tourism Event"

John C. Crotts, "The Effect of Cultural Distance Overseas Travel Behaviors"

Table of Contents for *Journal of Sport Management* Volume 22.4 (July 2008)

Research and Reviews

"Mega-Special-Event Promotions and Intent to Purchase: A Longitudinal Analysis of the Super Bowl" by Norm O'Reilly, Mark Lyberger, Larry McCarthy, Benoit Seguin, and John Nadeau

"The Impact of Brand Cohesiveness and Sport Identification on Brand Fit in a Sponsorship Context" by Kevin Gwinner and Gregg Bennett

"Destination Image and Intent to Visit China and the 2008 Beijing Olympic Games" by Heather J. Gibson, Christine Xueqing Qi, and James J. Zhang

"Mega Events, Fear and Risk: Terrorism at the Olympic Games" by Kristine Toohey and Tracy Taylor

"The Economic Impact of the Olympic Games: Ex Ante Predictions and Ex Poste Reality" by Philip K. Porter and Deborah Fletcher

SPORT MANAGEMENT MEMOS

Occasionally, the editor or editorial board of a particular journal will issue a request for articles about a special topic—such as technology or branding or sponsorship—or encourage regular submissions of scholarly merit. Generally, most published scholarly journals—whether online or in print—remain open to and encourage submissions from anyone who has a scholarly article to submit. The types of articles include *quantitative*, *qualitative*, or *mixed methods approaches*. Quantitative articles are usually empirical examinations or tests of a hypothesis or hypotheses using survey research or analyses of databases while qualitative articles are focused on exploring and discovering new information. (For more information on the differences between quantitative and qualitative research, see the following section on "**Quantitative vs. Qualitative Research**.")

LOCATIONS OF SCHOLARLY ARTICLES

Often you can tell what can be found in a particular journal by reading the title or a typical table of contents of that journal. It shows the range of topics, the structure of the articles, and the type of articles and research notes or book reviews. Journals also have a section inside the front cover explaining the editorial policies of the journal, the range of articles accepted, and information about the process of submission.

The most common way to find scholarly articles on a topic of your interest is through searching the database services provided by your library. Most college and university libraries have subscribed to a number of databases that contain vast collections of journals for you to access electronically. Scholarly articles can be found in scholarly journals, e-zines, reference databases, search engines, book collections of articles, library collections (online and hard cover), and other locations as well. Your college or university library will have a collection or subscribe to database services or online collections that enable you to access a wide range of scholarly journal articles. Although the journals are changing all the time—with new ones starting and some older ones disbanding or moving to exclusive electronic publishing—journals that have been around for a while are the ones with the most depth and range of articles and the ones you probably want to check out first.

Some of the most common scholarly journals in hospitality, sports, and tourism are the following:

Annals of Tourism Research

Consortium Journal of Hospitality and Tourism Management

Cornell Hotel and Restaurant Administration Quarterly

Harvard Business Review

International Journal of Contemporary Hospitality Management

International Journal of Hospitality Management

International Journal of Hospitality and Tourism Administration

International Journal of Sports Marketing

International Journal of Sports Marketing and Sponsorship

International Journal of Sports Psychology

Journal of Applied Business Research

Journal of Applied Sport Psychology

Journal of College and University Foodservice

Journal of Conventions and Event Tourism

Journal of Culinary Science and Technology

Journal of Ecotourism

Journal of Foodservice

Journal of Hospitality and Leisure Marketing

Journal of Hospitality Financial Management

Journal of Hospitality, Leisure, Sports and Tourism

Journal of Hospitality Marketing and Management

Journal of Hospitality and Tourism Education

Journal of Hospitality and Tourism Research

Journal of Human Resources in Hospitality and Tourism

Journal of Personality and Social Psychology

Journal of Product and Brand Management

Journal of Quality Assurance in Hospitality and Tourism

Journal of Sport Behavior

Journal of Sports and Social Issues

Journal of Sports Economics

Journal of Sports Management

Journal of Sports Sciences

Journal of Sports Tourism

Journal of Sustainable Tourism

Journal of the International Academy of Hospitality Research

Journal of Tourist Studies

Journal of Travel Research

Journal of Travel and Tourism Marketing

Sports Marketing Quarterly

Travel and Tourism Marketing

Tourism Management Journal

Tourism Review

UNLV Gaming Research and Review Journal

(An annotated list of them can be found in **Appendix B**).

Among the range of journals, there are a wide variety of categories of articles. Some of them are quantitative, some are qualitative; some provide extensive analysis of the state of research on a particular topic; others provide a conceptual point of view or new suggestions for research.

QUANTITATIVE VERSUS QUALITATIVE RESEARCH

Both quantitative and qualitative research methods provide valid ways to discover knowledge and improve our understanding of the world, whether it pertains to eco-tourism, brand loyalty, fan avidity, or coaching athlete's behavior. However, there is often a subtle bias toward quantitative research since it seems more valid and reliable—and more common—than qualitative research. It may not necessarily be more insightful or more significant in its findings; it is just a different type of research. Increasingly, many authors are using both qualitative and quantitative research methods in a mixed-method approach due to the complexity of the issues being examined and the richness obtainable by combining methods (Reece 17). For example, asking a set of standard questions about coaching behavior may provide information that can be compared across cohorts of respondents, but open-ended questions might bring even more richness of information and additional insights.

Typically, quantitative research takes a broad view of behavior—often looking for patterns among groups and cohorts—while qualitative research examines individual responses and takes a more focused, limited, and depth-oriented approach to the study of a phenomenon or behavior. While it is too simplistic to say that quantitative research focuses on crowds and large patterns and qualitative research focuses on individuals and situations, there is some truth to clarifying the difference in this manner.

Comparison of Quantitative and Qualitative Research

Quantitative Research	Qualitative Research
Large sample size with very few variables	Small sample size with many variables
Tests hypotheses, models, concepts, and ideas about the world	Discovers and explores what might be happening or what might be true
Contrived or controlled settings to limit the influence of outside factors on the information gathered	Natural setting that may contribute to the information gathered
Statistical tools to demonstrate that differences and correlations are significant	Analytical tools to determine the patterns and significance of various information

Quantitative research tends to focus on few variables over many cases or individuals sampled, while qualitative research tends to emphasis fewer cases but analyzes more variables. For example, quantitative research on brand loyalty will ask a few questions (beyond the demographic data) of many people while qualitative research would ask many questions of just a few individuals. In either case, the research can provide some powerful insights into brand loyalty; they just use very different methods for different reasons.

Quantitative and qualitative research can be compared on a variety of criteria—sample size, purpose, setting, and method of analyzing data. In terms of sample size, quantitative research tends to focus on large sample size and examines primarily a few issues or variables. Although there might be several items on a questionnaire or many questions in an interview, the purpose of gathering these data is to compare responses over a large sample or population so that the researcher can draw conclusions that have real merit and can make some statements about the significance of the insights. On the other hand, qualitative research usually involves far fewer subjects but each one of them provides greater depth of evidence or information about a wide range of topics. Gathering this breadth of information and analyzing it—carefully and appropriately—can be a challenge in qualitative research, but it does not mean that the research is any less valid.

A second difference involves the purpose of the research. Quantitative research is primarily oriented around and conducted to test or prove a particular hypothesis or assumption about the nature of things. It means that the researcher—or the team—has thought about and analyzed the issues from several perspectives and has developed a theory or set of assumptions about how things work. From thinking about the topic and reviewing the literature, the researcher has produced and refined a set of hypotheses that requires a large sample to test. The research process then involves operationalizing the variables and refining the hypotheses so that the researcher can prove—or disprove—them in some legitimate and statistically significant manner.

In qualitative research, the issue of number of samples or candidates does not arise since the goal does not involve proving something in a statistically significant manner; it is a matter of discovering something or exploring the possibilities that exist. Since there is no need to prove a hypothesis, the number of variables need not be limited—they can be endless. In fact, in some interviews, the open-endedness of the process provides the opportunity to discover a great deal of information that might not have been planned or even considered in the research design process. That difference does not mean that analyzing the data does not involve a lot of careful work and the application of rigorous scientific method. Qualitative research is often harder to conduct because the analytical tools are less commonly used and less well understood.

A third difference involves the setting for the research. Most quantitative research involves a created, artificial setting in which an experiment takes place or in which survey research is conducted. This situation enables the researcher to influence the conditions under which the information was gathered. In qualitative research, the setting is normally a natural environment over which the researcher has little or no influence. Sometimes the setting can play a role in helping a researcher gather the data and make the person being interviewed or observed more relaxed and willing to talk.

The fourth difference involves the methods of data analysis. Since the purpose of quantitative research involves proving something, the data and numbers need to be carefully and thoroughly analyzed for significance, validity, and reliability. There needs to be a level of confidence in saying that the difference in responses among varied cohorts constitutes a significant difference. Otherwise, you cannot make a statement about how things correlate and what has been proven. On the other hand, while the data in qualitative research need to be analyzed, the need for statistical tools diminishes, depending on the purpose of the research.

When the gathered data are analyzed, most often quantitative research requires a sophisticated set of analytical techniques to ensure that the findings have some significance and that the differences found are not ascribable to nature or random events. The tests of validity and significance are especially important if the researcher wants to be able to make statements that can prove, disprove, or modify the hypotheses being tested. In qualitative research, there are no ideas being tested; instead, they are being discovered; consequently, the burden of proof and significance is slightly different.

STRUCTURE OF SCHOLARLY ARTICLES

Most scholarly articles follow a common structure that may differ according to the requirements of a particular journal. They start with an abstract, followed by an introduction to the article, a review of the literature, some discussion of the research methods, the findings and conclusion. At the end of the chapter, you will find a comprehensive bibliography of the sources consulted and which you can use to learn more about the topic.

TYPICAL STRUCTURE OF SCHOLARLY ARTICLES

- Abstract
- Introduction
- Review of the Literature (often broken up into sections)
- Research Method or Research Design
- Findings or Discussion (often divided into sections reporting on various categories of findings)
- Limitations and Suggestions for Future Research
- Conclusions
- Bibliography

Some journals request the abstract to be prepared by the author or authors of the articles, while others prepare it using a common format that the editor prefers for that particular journal. In some situations, there is an Executive Summary and an Abstract for the article; for example, the *International Journal of Sports Marketing* and the *Journal of Product and Brand Management* carry both.

As part of the introduction to most articles, you can find three parts—context, purposes, and research methods or results (CPR)—that help you organize your understanding of the article.

1. The first element is the *context* of the article—why is this particular research being conducted, what gaps does it fill, how does it relate to other research already conducted?

2. The second is the *purpose* of the article—what is it focused on, what problem is it intended to solve, what questions is the research designed to answer?

3. The third is the *research design*—what method is being used to answer the questions, what constitutes the research design, what techniques are being used in this research?

Sometimes, the abstract and/or introduction does not focus on research design but actually provides a foreshadowing of the *research results*, but either way, these three pieces provide you with some perspective about the article and make it easier to figure out what the article is about.

Another way to focus on an article is to consider the information normally found at the end of the article and focus on the *limitations*, *opportunities* for further research, *applications*, and *findings* (LOAF). Once you have a sense of what the article is about by considering **CPR**, then look for **LOAF**. What did the researcher actually find? What insights have been gained by the projects and does it have applicability for the industry. Using these tools will help you approach reading scholarly articles with more ease.

In most cases, the research being conducted in culinary, hospitality, sports, and tourism is aimed at making a difference in these industries. Therefore, it is useful to consider what applications can be drawn from the careful research conducted. Are there suggestions for new marking approaches? Recommendations for training programs? Insights about investment or valuation strategies? Implications for new menus, new software, new ways of organizing staffing patterns? Sometimes the authors are explicit about the applications and sometimes you need to deduce the applications from the findings. However, examining applications is one way to assess the merits of the article. After all, if there are no implications and insights for the industry or for further research, then why was the research conducted?

FROM INTRODUCTION TO CONCLUSION: HOW TO READ A SCHOLARLY ARTICLE

BEGINNING

C—Context

P—Purpose

R—Research method or research results

END

L—Limitations

O—Opportunities

A—Applications

F—Findings

Most articles are very explicit about their limitations. They mention that the population was limited in size, or affected by cultural background; they point out that generalizations cannot be made for leisure travelers when the research was done exclusively on business travelers. Or the research on college students needs to be replicated in other settings to see if the findings are applicable to other population cohorts. Closely connected to the limitations are the opportunities for further research. Most articles that mention limitations also provide explicit suggestions for further research or lines of inquiry that need to be expanded to continue the research started in the article.

STRUCTURE OF QUANTITATIVE ARTICLES

Articles that are focused on empirical studies or that use quantitative methods normally have a particular structure driven by the type of research. The structure begins with an abstract and an introduction, followed by an extensive literature review that provides the detailed background for the research, places the importance of this article within current research, and provides support for the choice of research method. Then the findings are provided along with details about the statistical methods used and the significance of the numbers. The last parts of the article are the findings, applications, and the conclusions. Typically, the conclusion also contains suggestions for future research and limitations of the research conducted.

The limitations section becomes important in quantitative articles since the narrow focus raises questions about the extent to which the findings can be generalized. The range of suggestions for next steps also contributes to the credibility of the article and provides suggestions for others—sometimes the researcher and his or her colleagues—to follow.

STRUCTURE OF QUALITATIVE OR THEORETICAL ARTICLES

Qualitative articles follow the same basic structure as quantitative articles but often have a more extensive literature review, research design section, and analysis of findings. The importance of the method section derives from the fact that the options are more extensive and the choices that the researcher makes may have more impact on the validity of the findings. In addition, the findings and how they were developed often takes extensive explanation to provide the reader with an understanding of their merit.

Conceptual articles do not have a research design section but are extensively based on the reading of other literature and the explanation of the new model, framework, or concept and its power and applicability. These articles often move the field ahead quite measurably, but they depend heavily on an extensive knowledge of the literature, and they are very challenging to write. They also have an abstract, introduction, and conclusion, which contain suggestions for future research and indicate the limitations or applicability of the conceptual model being suggested. Like scholarly articles, most unpublished research studies have a common structure and format as well.

STRUCTURE OF RESEARCH REPORTS OR STUDIES

In preparing to conduct research, you may want to remember or realize that most research reports follow a common structure not unlike most published articles. However, editorial policies of some publications and restrictions of space often limit the depth and extent of the sections. In a bachelor's, master's, or doctoral thesis, these sections contain a great deal of depth and are often titled chapters in recognition of the size and scale of the document created. In other undergraduate research projects, these sections are typically included although they may be shorter and less thorough, and titled sections are separated by bold headings, depending on the assignment, course, or situation. What is important is to understand the range of the areas covered in research studies, whether called theses, dissertations, published studies, or published reports. Knowing the different sections makes it easier to read and less stressful to understand what the scholar or student has done and why.

Most studies begin with an introduction that sets the stage for the research, explains the need for this particular research given industry realities, the state of scholarship on the topic, and the importance or significance of the topic. It also typically describes the purpose statement and the research questions. (For more information on purpose statements and research questions, see **Chapter 2, Developing an Interest or Topic**.)

The second chapter or section—depending on the size and scope of the project— contains the review of the literature that indicates what scholarship has been completed on this topic and how useful it has been and where there are gaps that this study can fill. This section is most important to build the credibility of the researcher and to provide a context for undertaking the study.

Section three is typically a discussion of the research design, including information about ways it was conducted, the sampling strategy used, a demographic profile of the sample (if used), the details of any applied research methods used, and the hypotheses tested (if a quantitative study). (For more information on research designs, see **Chapter 6, Forms of Qualitative Research** and **Chapter 7, Forms of Quantitative Research**.) It provides the background information necessary to understand the next chapter or section analyzing the results.

The fourth chapter, or section, contains the analysis of the results, using statistical data if testing the significance of the results or other methods of analyzing the information collected. (For more information, see **Chapter 13, Analyzing Data and Other Information**.) Following the analysis of the results is a chapter or section discussing the results and their significance. This discussion of findings represents the heart of the entire study since it contains the results of the work and implications for practice.

TYPICAL STRUCTURE OF RESEARCH STUDIES

Abstract

Chapter One—Introduction

Chapter Two—Literature Review

Chapter Three—Research Design (often called Research Method)

Chapter Four—Research Results

Chapter Five—Discussion

Chapter Six—Findings

Conclusion

Bibliography

The final chapter or section contains the conclusion including a summary of the entire study and information about how it can be applied and what future research should be undertaken to supplement these findings. Typically, it contains a section that describes the limitations of the study that qualifies the findings and supports the validity of the insights.

Now that you know the structure of most articles and unpublished studies, you are ready to consider how to evaluate scholarly articles.

EVALUATING SCHOLARLY ARTICLES

In reading an article, you should consider several factors when assessing the merits of the research purpose, design, and findings. Those three components or elements are the core of the article and focus on the contribution—or potential contribution—to the knowledge being built about the industry. However, there are a number of other parts to consider as well:

- Introduction
- Review of the literature
- Theoretical framework for the research
- Data collection methods
- Data analysis
- Conclusions

To ensure that you consider all the elements of a published article, there are a number of questions that you can ask about each part. Remember, however, that not all journals follow the same format, and not all articles are written in the same

structure. If an article does not have these sections, it does not mean that it is
article. There are various types and foci, and each article should be interpreted within
the context and structure the authors provide.

QUESTIONS TO ASK IN READING AN ARTICLE

FOR THE INTRODUCTION

- Is it clear to you? To industry experts? To what audiences?
- Does it contain all three parts of CPR (context, purpose, and research method)?

FOR THE PROBLEM STATEMENT OR PURPOSE STATEMENT

- Is it clearly stated and understandable to the reader? Does it make sense to you?
- Is it narrow enough for a researchable problem?
- What is the significance of the purpose/problem? How is it related to other issues in the field (or industry) or the topic? How is it connected to other research?
- Would it make sense to industry professionals? Scholars?
- To what extent is it worth pursuing?

FOR THE LITERATURE REVIEW

- To what extent is it logically organized?
- In what ways are the sources and information relevant or not relevant?
- How many of the comments contain critiques of other content studies? Other relevant research methods?
- In what ways are gaps in knowledge identified and explained? Gaps in method identified and explained?
- Does the review indicate mastery of a particular area?
- At what level is the review written? From what perspective?
- Are the references and sources recent, relevant, and related to each other?
- Are key scholars in this topic included?

FOR THE RESEARCH DESIGN

- What is the overall research design? Can you explain it in three or four sentences?
- Is the design clear? What is being examined, investigated, or tested?
- Was it adequately developed and described?
- How does the design address issues of internal and external validity?
- Are all the elements of the research design explained?

(Continued)

FOR THE THEORETICAL OR CONCEPTUAL FRAMEWORK

- In what ways has the framework been explained? How was it linked to the research problem(s)?

- Are the concepts carefully and adequately defined? Are the relationships among various components clear?

- Are the limitations mentioned? Clear?

- Does the framework come from a research tradition? A particular body of knowledge? A specific perspective?

- Is there a conceptual framework behind the research?

- Does it seem appropriate?

FOR THE HYPOTHESES (IN QUANTITATIVE RESEARCH METHOD)

- Are they clear and testable? Can they be proven or tested by the design of the research?

- To what extent were they proven or disproven?

- How did they relate to the variables? Did the design address the hypotheses?

- To what extent are the hypotheses clear? Can they be proven or tested by the design of the research?

FOR THE RESEARCH VARIABLES (IN QUANTITATIVE RESEARCH METHOD)

- Are the independent variables operationally defined? Dependent variables defined?

- Are there other variables? Were they considered? Were there sufficient controls?

- What are the connections between the variables?

- Are they important? Significant?

FOR THE SAMPLE

- How was the sample chosen? To what extent are the sample selection criteria clear?

- To what extent is it adequate in size? Representative of the appropriate population?

- Was the method of sampling accurate and appropriate?

- Is there any sampling bias?

FOR DATA COLLECTION METHODS

- In what ways are they appropriate? Inappropriate? Well-designed?

- Have they been clearly described?

- Are the instruments being used appropriate and useful?

- Do the instruments have reliability? Validity?
- Do you trust the ways in which the information was collected?
- Were the sample size and structure appropriate to the research questions?

FOR THE DATA ANALYSIS

- In what ways are the results clearly organized?
- Is the type of analysis appropriate for the variables?
- Are the tables clear, well organized, and understandable?
- Are the figures clear and understandable?
- Are the statistical tests appropriate? Done correctly?
- Does the analysis address the purpose of the research?

FOR THE FINDINGS

- Are the actual findings different from interpretation?
- In what ways is the interpretation based on the analysis of the data? Other factors?
- In what ways are the findings related to previous research? To the conceptual/ theoretical framework?
- Are the results and generalizations warranted and defended?
- In what ways are the limitations and qualifications of the findings clear? Qualified? Contain parameters?

FOR THE LIMITATIONS, OPPORTUNITIES, AND APPLICATIONS

- Are the limitations of the research explained?
- Is it clear what qualifications need to be made about the conclusions?
- Do they add credibility to the article?
- Do they provide opportunities for further research?
- Do they repeat the study with different sample?
- Do they combine with other studies?

OVERALL

- Is the article well written?
- Is it well organized?
- Are the conclusions carefully and adequately supported?
- Does the design make sense?
- Does the article make a contribution to the industry?

From the perspective of criteria with which to assess an article, look for the clarity and coherence with which the whole topic, purpose, and significance is explained. Can a professional reader—who might not be an expert in this particular topic—understand the focus of the research: why it is being done, and what contribution it makes (often by proving or disproving a particular hypothesis)? There are more criteria to use; see the box **Criteria to Use in Reading Any Publication**.

CRITERIA TO USE IN READING ANY PUBLICATION

Clarity

Coherence

Comprehensiveness

Cogency

Currency

Credibility

Creativity

Contribution

There are also some other issues to consider when evaluating an article that does not fit into particular sections of articles. Just as the introduction and conclusion need to be coherent, congruent, and clear, the article must address questions of validity and reliability in the type of research methods used and the structure of the analysis of findings. (For more information on these issues, see **Chapter 9, Validity, Reliability, and Credibility in Research**.) Specifically, what is the validity of the article? Does it seem to focus on the topic it addresses or does it veer away from that clear focus? Does the article seem credible to you as a professional but not a researcher on this particular topic? And how reliable is the study?

Another dimension of evaluating the conclusion is an assessment of the recency and breadth of the sources used. Reading the bibliography, were the sources well documented and recent? What areas or topics were not included? Any key authors or theories not included? How recent or dated are the citations? What are the sources—industry reports, other scholarly journals, books, interviews, unpublished manuscripts?

A comprehensive evaluation means considering the overall significance and value of the article. It means assessing what aspects of the article were not clear, what were the major strengths, what improvements could be made—in short, what are its chief contributions. To whom would you recommend the article, and why?

SUMMARY

This chapter explained the types of publications available as resources for your research and the purpose and structure of scholarly journals. It also covered what scholarly journals are, where to find them, what they contain, and how to assess their merits. It has provided you with tools to find the journals, scan them, and analyze their perspective and contribution. The next chapter will focus on developing a topic for your research.

KEY TERMS

Applications	Opportunities	Research results
Blind reviewer	Peer review	Scholarly journal
Context	Purpose	White paper
Findings	Qualitative research	
Limitations	Quantitative research	
Mixed methods research	Research design	

WORKS CITED IN THIS CHAPTER

Bramwell, Bill, and Bernard Lane. "Priorities in Sustainable Tourism Research" *Journal of Sustainable Tourism* 16 (2008): 1–156.

Emerald Group Publishing Limited. *International Journal of Contemporary Hospitality Management Information.* Emerald Group Publishing Limited. Web. 16 Sept. 2010.

HVS Hotel Valuation Index.

International Journal of Contemporary Hospitality Management.

International Journal of Hospitality Management.

Jain, Abhishek, Caccamo, Molly, and Warren Marr. *Hospitality and Leisure: Manhattan Lodging Index.* PricewaterhouseCoopers LLP, 2010. Web. 23 October 2008.

Journal of Hospitality, Leisure, Sport and Tourism Education. The Higher Education Academy Hospitality, Leisure, Sport, and Tourism Network. 2009. Web. 3 October 2010. www.heacademy. ac.uk/johlste

Journal of Sport Management 22 (2008).

Journal of Sustainable Tourism 16 (2008).

Journal of Travel Research 43 (2004).

O'Neill, John, and Qu Xiao, "The Role of Brand Affiliation in Hotel Market Value" *Cornell Hospitality Quarterly* 47 (2006): 210–23.

PricewaterhouseCoopers, Hospitality and Leisure: Manhattan Lodging Index.

Reece, William. "Are Senior Leisure Travelers Different?" *Journal of Travel Research* 43 (2004): 11–18.

Talbott, Barbara M. "The Power of Personal Service: Why It Matters, What Makes It Possible, How It Creates Competitive Advantage" *CHR Industry Perspectives: A White Paper Series from Cornell University* 1 (September 2006): 4–14.

Teare, Richard, and Vinnie Jauhari, eds. "The Hospitality Industry in India." Special Issue of *International Journal of Contemporary Hospitality Management* 19 (2007): 351–63.

CHAPTER 2

Developing an Interest or Topic

INTRODUCTION

One of the intriguing challenges for individuals contemplating any research project—whether assigned or voluntary—involves finding a topic or area of interest and then focusing the topic into a researchable set of questions. Often individuals have an interest in some area such as sustainability, boutique hotels, condo conversions, fan avidity, new forms of tourism, unusual tourist groups, sports sponsorship, college athletics, or food safety but have no idea what to do with that interest. Sometimes they do not know what drives the interest or how to relate that interest to what is happening in the industries of hospitality, sports, or tourism. Other times, they do not know how to begin finding out more about their topic in order to develop several researchable ideas.

In many cases, identifying an area of interest can be easy and fascinating; in other situations, nothing seems to come to mind. However, if you are going to plan and conduct research, you need to start somewhere, and the journey starts with an area that both interests you and has some industry significance.

Finding that interest, clarifying it, and developing it into a coherent purpose statement and research questions is the main topic of this chapter. Once you have identified an area of interest, you need to develop it and refine the purpose and questions that will structure your reading about the topic and your plan for launching significant and feasible research.

In this chapter, you will learn what a purpose statement is, why it is important, and how you can develop, expand, and focus it into something that you can investigate or examine.

WAYS TO FIND TOPICS: YOUR MANAGER OR YOUR PROFESSOR

There are many ways to find topics: your work situation or your professor can provide some suggestions; perhaps reading a variety of industry materials can trigger interests. Some individuals have not had the chance to conduct real research on a topic of their interest; therefore, they have let those suggestions and potential ideas disappear. In that situation, there are ways to bring the ideas back.

Sometimes—especially in business settings—your boss, manager, professor, or the chair of a committee provides the topic of research to you. The topic is often pragmatic and current, such as the issue of mature customers, amenity creep in hotels, visa restrictions for international travelers, the cost of unhappy customers, personal seat licenses, collective bargaining agreements, or the effectiveness of loyalty reward programs. Then you get the assignment and some time frame or sense of resources.

Support for the research can be financial or academic, including the provision of a partially completed literature review, previous research results, or a situation in which you can easily conduct some serious research. That preparation can include access to individuals to interview, connections to a mailing list or group of people to whom you can administer a questionnaire, or copies of key databases you need for the project. In some cases, you must move quickly on research that has already been designed; in other situations, you have the luxury of time and will need to develop your own clear purpose statement and set of research objectives.

If you have been assigned a topic and need to begin planning out your research, then skip this section on developing your interests and move ahead to the section on **Importance of a Purpose Statement**.

If you do not have an interest or a topic, then the following sections will be helpful. If you need to develop a topic, there are several ways to proceed—reading broadly, listing, interviewing, and mapping. Each of these options is explained in more detail below.

WAYS TO FIND TOPICS: REVIEW OF PAST READING

One of the most common ways to identify an area of interest is to consider the issues that have fascinated you in previous courses or outside reading. Whether you have been reading industry reports, current events, scholarly articles, newspaper stories, blog entries, website notices, industry articles, analyses of trends, or new books, consider which of them may have triggered interesting ideas for you to consider. One technique involves making a list of what you have read; often writing the list will bring back the issues that fascinated you. It may also suggest other articles you wanted to read but have not had a chance to study. Write them down, because making note of the issues will help you to reflect on them and keep you intrigued by the possibilities.

If you have been making a list of issues that interest you, review that list and see what you think is important now. Are you intrigued by change in air travel? Do the trends in condominium conversion fascinate you? Are you interested in the newest trends in customer service? Have you examined player personnel practices? Does the controversy over bowl championships interest you? Do you want to examine sustainability factors in World Heritage sites? How has travel 2.0 changed tourism? What changes in branding have affected customers, franchisors, and asset owners? Have you determined what changes in media or sponsorship will affect sports revenue patterns? All of these questions—and many others—provide valuable areas to consider.

Write down any interesting questions and see if there is a pattern to them. Are there any common areas of interest, similar issues, or overlapping subjects? If so, consider following up on any of them as an area of research that you want to pursue.

WAYS TO FIND TOPICS: NEW READING

A second approach to developing topics on your own involves reading quickly among a wide range of industry publications—the ones on your desk, the websites you normally review, the publications at the library or in the research laboratory—that you can easily find. Skim them to ascertain any common challenges facing the industry or any patterns of topics that are being published. This quick review may prompt you to consider an aspect of a very current issue—such as branding, fan loyalty, sustainability, sponsorship, personal seat licenses, pay for amateur athletes, fantasy football, or revenue management—or it may help you develop other ideas in response or reaction to the topics that you are noticing.

The goals in this exercise are to help you consider what is current, what is important, what is worth doing, and what can be done. Chatting with fellow students can accomplish the same goal, but a review of several tables of contents of scholarly articles and industry publications can also indicate what topics are being examined and what experts in the field see as important.

As you come up with this list of topics, jot them down on a piece of paper—or on your computer, tablet, or smart phone—so that you do not lose the ideas and can come back to them and use them later to narrow down your options.

WAYS TO FIND TOPICS: INTERVIEWING

Among professional researchers, a more common way to develop research topics involves keeping a record of ideas for potential projects as they come up (Booth 38). The sources of these ideas often come in discussion with another industry professional or an interview with someone in a position to identify or comment on critical issues in the field. As part of the topic development process, you might consider identifying a person to interview and ask that person about some of the critical issues that need serious analysis or investigation. This approach will help you focus on a topic that needs attention and has significance.

The first challenge is deciding whom to interview—either a person or a position—and arranging access to that individual. Think about the industry professionals to whom you have, or can obtain, access: a hotel general manager, a director of sports marketing, the chair of the local hotel association or restaurant association, the manager of a destination marketing office, an officer in a player's union, an official in a professional league office, a college athletic director, or a national figure in the industry. Alternatively, you may want to interview faculty members in your department to obtain a sense of the critical issues in the industry. Besides having great ideas about what needs more investigation, they can often suggest resources to consult or other individuals to interview.

The second task is to prepare for the interview so that you use their time and your time productively. What do you want to ask them about? How can you learn the most from their perspective? What can the individuals contribute from their perspective about the trends or challenges in the industry? What would they suggest are the critical issues and who would be most interested in learning about them? Or where would they suggest you conduct your research? Often industry individuals can suggest a method for the research or a location that would yield good insights if investigated or analyzed. Don't forget to ask them the golden questions, the two most important questions, at the end of the interview: one, what questions have I not asked or what information do you want to share that I have not asked about, and two, who else would you suggest that I interview and can you make an introduction?

After you send the professional a thank you note, reflect on the notes from the interview since they will probably give you lots of ideas for research; there may be questions you want to answer or information that you think industry professionals would be intrigued to learn. They may also trigger your own thinking about other topics.

WAYS TO FIND TOPICS: BRAINSTORMING

A fourth approach to developing topics involves conducting an individual brainstorming session. *Brainstorming*—a creativity technique originally developed by Alex Osborn, who was frustrated by his employee's inability to develop creative ideas for advertising campaigns and products—can be a powerful way to unleash ideas (Osborn 139–149). To do it right, however, you need to give yourself a limited period of time, get several clean sheets of paper and good pens, and then start to think zany, bizarre, and open-ended thoughts about all aspects of your industry. Write each one down and add to them, making sure that you do not stop the flow of ideas; just keep writing them down until the time is up. Stop yourself from focusing on any one idea since the interruption will slow down your creative processes.

Once you have a list of possible topics and time has run out, then go back over each idea and find the real possibilities in each idea. Working on the positive aspects of each idea will encourage you to consider what would be involved in doing the research on that topic or in that area. Once you have found the possibilities in each idea, review the list and select the top two or three to consider more carefully.

Sometimes in this process, you will find ideas overlap and can be combined; other times, you may find that one idea turns into another. Honor that process and the journey in finding a topic you care about.

WAYS TO FIND TOPICS: CONVERSING

Perhaps the most common way to discover a topic or expand the germ of an idea involves discussing it with other people. Having to explain what you are interested in can help you think out loud about why it intrigues you. One way to begin this process involves talking with other students in the course or your program. They may be in the same situation and, therefore, more interested in talking about these topics. Another way involves chatting with your friends or your family members. They bring a different interest to hearing about the topic and having to explain it to them might help you determine what you really want to spend some time investigating. After all, if you cannot explain your interest in a topic to someone you care about, that situation raises some questions about your level of interest or your knowledge of the topic.

WAYS TO FIND TOPICS: FACULTY SUGGESTIONS

In some programs—often in doctoral programs—you will have no difficulty picking out a topic since your faculty advisor may suggest a few and urge you to do one or more of them. That decision is easy because you have heard about that topic or topics in various classes and your interest in it has been growing. Other times, the topic appeals to you because you will have a chance to work with a particular faculty member; the possibility of research support—in equipment, time, staff, or salary—makes it easy to select the topic being offered (Booth, Colomb, and Williams 41). In a long-term research project, being part of a team can also be very appealing since the design may already be selected and you know that you will be making a contribution by conducting this research. You can also see how your work fits into the work of others and would make a real difference.

Faculty members will sometimes suggest a process for you in locating a topic or area of research. They will recommend reading the last several years of a particular journal or reviewing several research lacunae that have been discussed in classes, or call your attention to the visiting speakers and professors in the program. They often point out exciting new areas of research or topics that need some disciplined research attention. Since your faculty members are doing research and collecting topics and ideas, they may just have a file of ideas that they may be willing to share with you as well.

CLARIFYING AND SELECTING AREAS OF INTEREST

Once you have all possible ideas written down, then you need to sort them out and select one that you think is worth your time to investigate and will be productive or useful to analyze. There are several ways to do that. One is to review the list and see what topic excited you. Then write a paragraph or two about what you want to learn or how you would investigate that topic. Begin to list what you know about this topic or who has written anything in this area. Do some initial research and see what kind of a bibliography you can build in this area as well. Don't spend a lot of time on this task now; a couple of hours should provide you with evidence of how much has been written and what has been done in this area.

Another way is to sort the list of possible topics by specific criteria, called *clarifying* (see **Clarifying Your List—An Activity**) so that you determine which topic or topics are worth investigating. When you have narrowed down the possible topics, spend some time seeing what has been written in this area as well so that you know if the topic is worth pursuing or feasible for you.

CLARIFYING YOUR LIST—AN ACTIVITY

- Once you have a list of possible topics, write them on a lined sheet of paper with a very wide column on the left-hand side and three smaller-width columns on the right-hand side.
- Write the list of possible topics or areas of interest one per line, on the left-hand column. If any new ideas come up, feel free to add them to the list at this time.

- Once the list is complete, go back over it and put an **S** in the first column on the right if the topic is important or <u>significant to the industry</u>.

- Then put a **P** in the second column if you have some <u>passion for this topic</u>; are you really interested in it and will have fun doing it? Be honest with yourself and only give a **P** where it is appropriate. Showing passion where there is little will make it harder to stay with this project.

- Then put an **F** in the third column if the topic is <u>feasible</u>; do you have the skills or access to the information necessary to conduct decent research on this topic?

- Now review the list and see if there are any possible topics that have two or more letters beside them. Are any of them ones that you would like to pursue?

Based on either of these activities, you may have a clear sense of topics or areas you want to investigate. If this process of reading, conversing, and clarifying, however, does not work for you or if you want an alternative path, you might want to try cognitive mapping, which is explained in the next section.

COGNITIVE MAPPING

Another way to investigate a topic is to reflect on it and consider the widest dimensions of a topic or area of interest. Some persons find that talking about a topic with another person can help them expand their ideas and stretch their thinking. Others want a strategy that they can conduct alone; one of the most productive is cognitive mapping.

Cognitive mapping involves the process of expanding ideas and suggestions by using a chart or graph to record the results of a brain dump, an individual brainstorming activity that promotes creative and intriguing byways and sidelines of thinking (Downs 11). In many ways, initial and creative brain mapping follows some of the same rules as brainstorming—any idea is allowed, even encouraged, all ideas are written down, and there is no judgment or evaluation during the initial stages of the process. It differs, however, from brainstorming in that there is usually only one person working and the same person does all the writing. There is no prompting by others and no piggybacking on others' ideas; it is about circling back on your own ideas.

By writing down your ideas and making connections, you will trigger new thoughts and expand old ones. This dimension of cognitive brain mapping promotes additional thinking and gives you places to go back to as you review and expand your thinking.

Some individuals use a variety of images or designs in brain mapping, but starting from a square, circle, or polygon in the middle of a blank page is the easiest way to begin. The process is explained in the box on **Steps in Cognitive Mapping**.

STEPS IN COGNITIVE MAPPING

- Start with a blank piece of paper, at least 8½ × 11 or larger.
- Make a box, circle, or other geometric form in the center of the paper.
- Record the topic or area of interest in that form.
- Consider one aspect of that topic and draw a line—as in a branch from a tree—from the box and write that idea on it.
- If other ideas on that same line come, write down.
- If writing one idea suggests an idea in a different aspect of the original topic, write it down on another branch.
- Do so several times until you can see several branches emanating from the central box or circle at the center of the paper.
- Stop—when appropriate—and look at the overall diagram.
- See what you notice is missing or needs more ideas added to it.
- Write them down on the appropriate branch, or branches.
- Where appropriate, add branches to the main branches showing a variety of smaller aspects of the overall topic or area.
- Continue writing down ideas, aspects of the purpose, areas to investigate, and other ideas that arise until you reach an impasse or a natural stopping point.
- Then step back and review the entire page.
- If new ideas arise during this review, write them down and attach them to the appropriate branch in your brain map.

When your energy subsides or you have no more new ideas, stop and review the entire sheet. Look at what it shows you about how you are thinking about this topic. What parts intrigue you the most? Mark those topics by circling them, and then pick one that seems to have the most interest.

Using that smaller topic, write several questions that arise as you review that topic or write a few sentences that expand on that idea. Suggest aspects you want to learn about, or parts of the topic that really intrigue you.

Once you have a number of ideas about your topic, the next step involves developing a purpose statement for your research. Regardless of how you came up with the topics for your research, you should make sure that the topic—or some part of it—intrigues you since you will be spending some time on this project. It will be increasingly difficult to spend time reading, thinking, and writing about something that you find inherently uninteresting. Therefore, take some time to consider what aspect, or aspects, of the idea on the paper really intrigues you.

PURPOSE STATEMENTS

Good research begins with an interest in a topic and quickly moves to developing a purpose statement—a guiding phrase or sentence that provides direction for your research. Purpose statements drive the entire research process by giving direction to your reading and helping you focus on the research methods that may be most productive for you to pursue. While not difficult, it is important to prepare a purpose statement carefully. Make it as clear as you can at this time, knowing that it will change and shift over time as you begin to conduct some research into the area.

Consider the following issues in writing your purpose statement:

- What is the topic you want to understand?
- What do you want to know more about?
- What industry challenge(s) are you trying to examine?
- What policy, action, event, activity, or phenomenon are you trying to understand?

Once you have a clear sense of these questions, then it is valuable to consider the significance of your purpose or its importance to others. That inquiry involves answering these questions:

- What is important about your topic?
- To whom is it important, and why do they care?
- What is its industry significance?
- Why is it important today, and will it be important in several years?
- What difference will it make to investigate this topic?
- How will knowing more about this issue make a difference for the industry or for sectors of the industry?

The third step in this process involves considering how you might want to conduct this investigation. Although it is very early in the process, contemplate what form of research you might want to conduct, how you might focus a purpose statement, and what research questions interest you. (For more information about types of research, see **Chapter 6, Forms of Qualitative Research,** and **Chapter 7, Forms of Quantitative Research.**)

Once you have a certain sense of what your purpose statement might include, why it is important, and how you might address it, write it in a format that will help you focus it (see **Structure of a Purpose Statement**).

The format helps you focus on what you want to investigate, why you want to investigate it, and what other studies you might want to consult in your preliminary research.

STRUCTURE OF A PURPOSE STATEMENT

Writing a purpose statement can be intimidating and difficult. However, considering the following structure might help.

- Try the following sentence structure—**My purpose is to** . . . (what you want to learn—the questions).

- **The reasons it is important include** . . . (why it is significant).

- **Therefore, I will** . . . (what you will do to answer your questions and accomplish your goal).

Since a big part of establishing your research plan involves consulting other research, the purpose statement may help you consider how you will conduct a review of other studies and examine the range and depth of research already conducted—if any—on the topic that intrigues you. Depending on the level of your program—bachelors, masters, or doctorate—you may need to create a proposal for research (for more information, see **Chapter 3, Conducting a Literature Review,** and **Chapter 5, Writing a Literature Review**). Developing a purpose statement also helps you clarify what type of research you are considering.

TYPES OF RESEARCH

Most research in hospitality, tourism, and sports is applied research, but there is some basic research and much action research, the three common types of research. *Basic research*, also called theoretical or pure research, is primarily conducted to develop theories and a greater understanding of an activity, phenomenon, or situation without any regard for the applicability of the findings. The research focuses on discovering and inventing new knowledge as well as reflecting on new developments. Basic research provides great insights, sometimes moving the frontiers of knowledge forward in small doses, and sometimes in large, quantum leaps. It uses qualitative, quantitative, and mixed methods of research, most often true experimental methods, and the insights are transmitted through published articles, presentations, theses, dissertations, experimental reports, unpublished papers, notes, and correspondence.

Applied research, the second form of research, differs from pure research since it emphasizes solving specific problems through conducting careful research that has a direct industry connection; it tries to find out what is happening and what factors influence behavior in order to make recommendations for changes in practice. The principal perspective is on understanding behavior, diagnosing situations, and creating information using sound methods and careful analysis. The goal is to improve operations, policies, programs, and strategic plans.

At the far end of the spectrum is *action research*, the third type of research. Action research seeks to understand and change programs, operations, activities, and policies through participation in and reflection on the change processes. The principal perspective involves making organizational and programmatic changes and trying out new ideas while reflecting on the changes as they are being made. Most often this method of research involve case studies, analyses of change strategies, and reports of program and policy changes. The goal remains instituting significant changes in policy, procedures, and programs, the ways that people, department, and organizations do things while documenting and reflecting on those changes.

Whichever type of research you will be planning, developing a clear purpose statement remains the first and most important task. Without a clear goal, your efforts can produce a lot of activity but no impact or insight.

IMPORTANCE OF A PURPOSE STATEMENT

One of the most critical aspects of conducting serious research—and often one of the most difficult—involves creating a clear and focused purpose statement. The purpose statement needs to be clearly stated since it becomes the beacon by which you judge the appropriateness of what to do to learn more about the topic (Sekaran 69; Westmeyer 48).

A clear and useful purpose statement has several benefits for anyone doing research, the primary one of which is to structure the research process in a way that your effort will be used efficiently and effectively. A clear purpose statement frames the parameters for researching the literature—a critical aspect of well-crafted research—and helps focus your research on certain aspects of the purpose or categories of findings and methods. It also helps to increase your creativity in researching the literature. Knowing where you want to go can help you think about a range of ways to get there; not knowing what you are trying to do often channels your energy into unproductive pathways and sends you down bypasses and in irrelevant directions. While that process may be fun—and something that many of us did in our schooling (undergraduate programs or high school)—it is not very effective.

Clarifying your purpose statement enables you to actually do the research. It ensures that the work you do addresses the actual purpose and answers the key questions. It is, in some ways, the most critical aspect of your entire research process (Creswell 87).

Once you have developed and written a first draft of your purpose statement, it is important to think about your research questions.

DEVELOPING RESEARCH QUESTIONS

Once you have a purpose statement, your next task involves developing *research questions*, or research objectives, about the topic. These questions should indicate what you really want to know about the topic. Remember, curiosity is the hallmark of a good researcher, and good questions will help you broaden your focus rather than reduce it. In fact, the clarity and comprehensiveness of your research questions will dramatically affect your success in developing and implementing a coherent research project. As Stuart Blythe, Department of English & Linguistics, at Indiana University–Purdue

University Fort Wayne, says, "It's important to ask good questions because they point you in a specific direction while blinding you to other options" ("On Asking").

Good research questions will help you clarify what you want to do and how you want to do it. A good research question begs to be investigated and contains some suggestions about how to answer it. From the questions that you want to ask, write why that question is important and what else you already know about that area so that you can clarify what you may want to do as part of your continuing research (see **Chapter 3, Conducting a Literature Review**).

Research questions frame the lines of inquiry that you want to pursue. While many purpose statements are written in simple, declarative prose, a research question is interrogative and emphasizes action—what do you really want to know? It is almost like a hypothesis, but it is a bit more general and lacks the background to establish a set of hypotheses (Krippendorf 33). Often, an initial purpose statement will inspire a number of research questions, which then prompt more reading and refinement of the questions. That iterative process is part of the dynamic of research.

Developing research questions is the most important aspect of this phase of your research. The questions organize and establish the structure and scope of your research if they are well written. Research questions focus more specifically on the issues that you want to examine or the parts of the purpose that are the most critical. Some researchers like to focus on research objectives, while others focus on research questions. Either format makes sense (Krippendorf 343).

Research objectives are not as detailed as the questions that you might ask in a survey questionnaire or interview, but they are not as general as purpose statements. Research questions involve examining something that is not known.

> *Research questions are not like ordinary questions. They are somewhat inquisitorial in that they expect an answer (not necessarily a reply). A research question must be* answerable. *This means that it is not helpful in research to have a question that is so all-embracing that it would be impossible to answer it within the confines of a research project however large." (Andrews 2).*

If it is easy to find out the answer, then it does not need to be a research question. Remember that if you have a clear statement of the problem, then it is easy to write research questions or research objectives. In the process of conducting research, many investigators prepare an initial purpose statement and research questions and then refine them as they continue background reading in the area. Therefore, although you will go through this same process, start now to create some research questions. The following questions may help you:

- What do I really want to know about this topic?

- What aspects of it intrigue me the most?

- What is important to understand or analyze?

- What do I want to describe, determine, identify, compare, test, validate, or confirm?

What practices do I want to examine or analyze?

- What perspective do I want to take towards this topic?

You can see from answering these questions that doing a certain amount of background reading will help you write them. Another way of thinking about the research questions or research objectives is that they make clear the specific aspects of the purpose that interest you. In a way, they operationalize the purpose statements and start to establish parameters for the research that you will conduct. They also provide an early perspective on the research method that you are contemplating.

Remember, however, that these objectives will change over time; therefore, at this point, write them as preliminary and use them to structure your literature review. As you write them, remember research questions are not:

- Yes/no questions—Why spend time on investigating if you can simply answer yes or no?

- Easy to answer—Why develop a whole research design if the questions are easily answered? Just answer them.

- Of restricted interest—Why spend considerable time and energy on a limited area that is just valuable for you and not for others?

- Limited in their time frame—Why pick something that will not be important in another year?

As you can see from these four questions, research involves a lot of careful study and planning as well as analysis; it is not worth all that effort for questions that are not significant and useful to the industry. That does not mean that the issues need to be monumental and wide in scope; they just need to be worth investigating and analyzing.

(For examples, see the box on **Examples of Purpose Statements and Research Questions**.)

EXAMPLES OF PURPOSE STATEMENTS AND RESEARCH QUESTIONS

For a study of National Collegiate Athletic Association (NCAA) ways of handling violations in various schools, the purpose statement might be to identify the main causes of NCAA violations and to determine the steps that must be taken in order to help reduce the stresses on this system. In this situation, the research questions might be:

- What are the main causes of the increase in NCAA rules violations in college athletics today?

- Who are the central actors most influential in this issue?

- What changes need to be made to help decrease cheating and violations?

- What are the suggestions of each of the actors involved in this dilemma (coaches, players, athletic directors, NCAA)?

For a research project on self-service technology in hotels, the purpose might be to examine the factors that affect consumer use of self-service technologies in the hospitality industry and determine the factors that affect consumer willingness to pay more for the technology. The research questions might include:

- What are the benefits of using self-service technology in the hospitality industry?

- When are people willing to pay more to use self-service technology in the hospitality industry?

- What are the antecedents of willingness to pay for self-service technology in the hospitality industry?

For a research project on fans' perceptions of certain Olympic sports, the purpose statement might be to analyze what factors impact attendance and watching of "artistic" Olympic sports. The research questions might be:

- What are the most significant motivational factors for fans who watch the Olympic sports of figure skating, artistic gymnastics, track and field, and swimming?

- In what ways does gender play a role in the way men and women self-identify as fans of these Olympic sports?

- What aspects of Olympic television coverage positively or negatively influence fan's perception of Olympic sports?

For a research project on the factors that motivate independent travelers to visit certain destinations, the purpose statement might be to examine the connections between their reasons for traveling and the factors that attract them to a destination. The research questions would then be:

- What are the primary motivational factors for independent travelers?

- What is the relationship between particular motivational factors and pull factors when choosing destinations?

- What is the relationship between certain motivational factors and travel characteristics of independent travelers and their preference to plan his or her own trip?

To further the development of your initial research questions, consider the following:

- What do I know about this topic?
- Why is it important to me and to the industry?
- What made the policy or practice develop the way it did?
- What factors influence customers, consumers, and fans who make these decisions?
- What leads managers to make these decisions?
- What factors explain this behavior?

Writing questions is the first step of the journey to finding out something. As you write questions, other questions and topics may come to you; make sure that you also record them since they may provide suggestions of what and how you want to investigate them. One question may lead to another, and the more you write the better you will be able to focus the research when you actually start to plan it. Therefore, record all the questions that you consider.

Recording and writing clear research questions can help you refine your purpose statement and clarify if you have a purpose statement (more common in basic research or applied research) or a problem statement (more common in action research).

PURPOSE STATEMENTS AND PROBLEM STATEMENTS

In the literature on research, many authors use the two words—problem statement and purpose statement—in similar ways. However, more often a *problem statement* refers to a specific business or industry—sometimes an individual corporate or organizational—problem that a manager or team of managers wants to solve (Hemon and Schwartz 308). It has an urgency and an immediate application since the research is needed to find out how to solve the problem and increase the corporation or organization's effectiveness.

A *purpose statement*, on the other hand, typically refers to a concern or area of interest appropriate to the industry and not something that an individual company is necessarily trying to address immediately. The time frame and scale for it tends to be broader and longer lasting, and the research it triggers may contribute to a significant improvement in understanding what factors influence customer behavior or business practices.

For example, a person interested in researching sustainability issues in the hotel industry might focus on the *problem* of what a hotel should do to increase guest participation in a energy saving or towel reuse program or how to market the hotel's sustainability practices, while another person's *purpose* might be to examine the factors that foster guest attitudes and behavior practices about energy saving and towel reuse or their response to green marketing across a range of hotel categories. A problem statement in tourism might be what to do with overcrowding in a specific cultural heritage site and a purpose statement might examine the categories of visitors and their reasons for visiting that site. An analysis of fan behavior in minor league baseball would be a purpose statement, and developing new marketing and promotion strategies would be a problem statement.

Purpose Statement	Problem Statement
Determine service factors that foster guest satisfaction in luxury hotels	How to increase guest participation in towel reuse and other energy saving programs in luxury hotels
Examine categories of visitors at a specific World Heritage site	How to reduce overcrowding at particular World Heritage sites
Analyze fan behavior in minor league baseball stadiums	How to promote ticket sales to new customers of a minor league team

With the kind of applied research that is the focus of this book, you will be developing purpose statements.

CRITERIA FOR EFFECTIVE PURPOSE STATEMENTS

Once you have developed a series of research questions, then it is time to review your purpose statement again since it is so critical in guiding your literature review. As Creswell, the author of many good books on qualitative and quantitative and mixed methods of research, said, "The purpose statement is the most important statement in an entire study" (Creswell 87). Therefore, write it clearly and test it against a series of criteria.

Using the criteria as a standard will help you consider what is missing and what you can—or need to—do about the purpose statement. The criteria for a good purpose statement include:

- Usefulness
- Validity
- Focus
- Feasibility
- Significance

Usefulness refers to the utility of the statement. Is your purpose statement useful in guiding your research efforts and helping you decide what to read in your literature review? Does it help you decide what sources to consult? What fields of inquiry do you need to examine in developing an understanding of your topic?

Validity indicates the degree to which the purpose statement is authentic and sound. Does it aim at something real? Is it something that is worth doing? Are you aiming at what you want to focus on and is it something that you can measure or assess?

Focus refers to the clarity of direction you have from the purpose statement. Does your statement focus on one particular area or a broad topic or question? Does it help you eliminate extraneous areas of investigation? Does it show you what topics you want to read about in preparing a research design?

Feasibility refers to the reality of conducting the research. Can you actually do this project with the resources available to you? Can the purpose be investigated? What time will it take? Are the resources—access to people, software, analytic tools—available to you? What would be involved to really conduct this research?

Significance is one of the most important criteria to apply to a purpose statement—is this issue important to the industry? Will other professionals want to learn about your results? Will investigating this issue or topic make a difference? Is it worth investigating and analyzing? What kind of contribution would it make? (Booth, Colomb, and Williams 49).

As you answer these questions and read more about the areas that surround your purpose statement, you will review and revise your purpose statement to make it clearer and more understandable to yourself and to others. It will become a beacon while you develop your research proposal and conduct your research.

With your clear and well-written purpose statement, you are ready to move on to the next step in the research process—reading broadly and deeply about what has been written and discovered around your topic—which is the subject of **Chapter 3, Conducting a Literature Review**.

SUMMARY

This chapter has provided some suggestions for ways to locate and build a topic for your research and start you on the journey. While suggesting several critical and creative thinking methods, it has focused on developing, clarifying, and refining your interests into a clear purpose statement and researchable questions. It also differentiated between problem statements and purpose statements and suggested several criteria to use in evaluating your purpose statement.

The next chapter will focus on what to read and how to read it so that you build the background for your research.

KEY TERMS

Action research
Applied research
Basic research
Brainstorming
Clarifying
Cognitive mapping

Feasibility
Focus
Problem
Problem statement
Purpose
Purpose statement

Research questions
Significance
Usefulness
Validity

WORKS CITED IN THIS CHAPTER

Andrews, Richard. *Research Questions*. London: Continuum, 2003.

Booth, Wayne, Gregory G. Colomb, and Joseph M. Williams. *The Craft of Research*. New York: University of Chicago Press, 2003.

Blythe, Stuart. "On Asking Productive Research Questions." 17 July 2001. Web.

Creswell, John. *Research Design: Qualitative, Quantitative, and Mixed Methods Approaches*. Minneapolis: Sage Publications, 2002.

Downs, Roger M. *Image and Environment: Cognitive Mapping and Spatial Behavior*. Chicago: Aldine Publishing, 1973.

Hemon, Peter and Candy Schwartz, "What is a Problem Statement?" *Library and Information Science Research* 29 (2007) 307–309.

Iarossi, Giuseppe, *The Power of Survey Research; A User's Guide for Managing Surveys, Interpreting Results, and Influencing Respondents*. Washington: World Bank, 2006.

Krippendorf, Klaus. *Content Analysis: An Introduction to its Methodology*. 2nd ed. Thousand Oaks: Sage Publications, 2004.

Osborn, Alex F. *Applied Imagination: Principles and Procedures of Problem Solving*. 3rd ed. New York: Scribner, 1956.

Sekaran, Uma. *Research Methods for Business: A Skill Building Approach*. New York: John Wiley & Sons, 2002.

Westmeyer, Paul M. *A Guide for Use in Planning, Conducting and Reporting Research Projects*. New York: Charles C. Thomas Publisher, 1994.

CHAPTER 3

Conducting a Literature Review

INTRODUCTION

One of most important dimensions of research entails finding out what other people have discovered in the areas that you want to explore. Reading and analyzing what others have found will provide you with a strong background for your purpose statement and the topic you want to investigate. It will also help you consider ways to shape your purpose statement, foster ideas about conducting your research, and protect you from doing a study that has already been done. In addition, it remains the best way to ensure that you develop a coherent and comprehensive research design.

The process of reading the literature on your topic, digesting it, and analyzing it is called conducting a literature review. In this chapter, you will learn both why it is worth conducting a thorough literature review and how you can do it efficiently and effectively. The last section of the chapter contains tips on how to make the process easier, more effective, and more interesting.

DEFINITION OF A LITERATURE REVIEW

A *literature review* is a particular form of writing found primarily, but not exclusively, in scholarly articles, dissertations, theses, grant proposals, industry reports, and often special reports prepared for managers or other decision makers. Literature reviews are designed to provide readers with the central findings of various research studies as well as key ideas or conceptual models used to structure research. They include information about the work of scholars studying the topic, industry reports that shed light on the topic, and essays that further thinking about the topic. Literature reviews examine, in a thoughtful manner, the work of key authors; the classic studies in the field, the types of studies conducted; the demographics sampled; the statistical methods used; and other aspects of studies that have been done.

Good literature reviews are written as coherent essays that provide structure and logic to the often inchoate and unplanned ways in which a topic or area has been investigated. They are designed to provide an overview of what has been written and what needs to be examined in the future; they include information about key studies and topics of research; they should explain and highlight key studies and lines our research; and they should point out patterns among the various articles. A literature review should also point out clear gaps in the range of studies already conducted and suggest what areas of research need to be pursued, what topics need increased attention, and what research methods are most useful.

Well-written reviews have an introduction, a conclusion, and plenty of sections in between, each of them written from an analytical perspective. The introduction orients the reader to the perspective of the literature review as well as the structure, tone and style of the literature review. Therefore, the introduction must be written carefully. (For more information about preparing a literature review, see **Chapter 5, Writing a Literature Review**.)

Depending on the publication or the style requirements, literature reviews can be formal or informal. They are typically written from the third person point of view and provide an objective perspective about the nature of the research already conducted, the patterns—if any—and the gaps that need to be filled. Comments about research methods, conceptual frameworks, and researchers' perspectives are always appropriate.

Often, literature reviews carry a particular perspective, either due to the point of view of the author or publication, or because the field lends itself to certain ways of examining a topic. For example, early literature reviews of boutique hotels started out from the perspective of examining fads. Now they consider these hotels as a phenomenon unto themselves and one that is important to notice along with the proliferation of brands in the hotel industry (Aggett 169–77; McIntosh and Siggs 74–81). Previous studies of sports sponsorship examined consumer recognition and awareness as well as return on investment; now that companies have developed their own metrics, research on sponsorship has moved to new topics (Irwin et al. 131–39).

Literature reviews for grant proposals or doctoral dissertations are typically more comprehensive than those found in scholarly articles since there is more need in a dissertation to place the project within the context of all related research and to make a case for its originality and contribution to a specific body of knowledge as well as its significance. In a grant proposal, the literature review often focuses on other projects that have been successful or failed in order to make clear the need for this project and its applicability. In dissertation research, the need to make an original contribution requires a thorough mastery of all the scholarship in the area. For example, doctoral students in hospitality, tourism, or sports who are conducting a literature review need to consider not only the research on practices but also the theories, concepts, applications, phenomena, and historical context of the topics being investigated. In grant writing, the literature review places the topic within the context of other projects. For grant proposals, the case needs to be made for the need to support this project and its merit in light of other work in the field; therefore, the literature review needs to be more comprehensive since the audience of reviewers wants to read a thorough analysis of the field. Scholarly articles also have space strictures which limit the size of their literature reviews.

In all cases, the literature review is critical to the success of the research plan: "The centrality of relevance as a criterion for dissertation literature reviews also applies to literature reviews for funding proposals, research reports, and other forms of scholarly writing in which the primary purpose is not to summarize and synthesize some body of literature, but to use this literature to inform and support some decision or argument external to the review itself" (Maxwell 29).

Scholarly articles select more carefully among the information needed for that study and that publication. Very broad and comprehensive literature reviews provide a full review of the key studies, their methods, idiosyncrasies, historical context, funding support, connection to continuing research, nature of the publications in which the studies are found, patterns of research (qualitative, quantitative, mixed), dates of particular studies, demographics used in various studies, and the merits of various research designs.

The following articles provide examples of good literature reviews in hospitality, tourism, and sports:

Bauer, Hans H., Sauer E. Nicola, and Exler Stefanie. "The Loyalty of German Soccer Fans: Does a Team's Brand Really Matter?" *International Journal of Sports Marketing and Sponsorship* (October 2005): 14–22.

Cho, Seounghee, Robert Woods, SooCheong Shawn Jang, and Mehmet Eder. "Measure the Impact of Human Resource Management Practices on Hospitality Firms' Performances." *International Journal of Hospitality Management* 25 (2006); 262–77.

Morosan, Cristian, and Miyong Jeon. "Users' perception of Two Types of Hotel Reservation Web Sites." *International Journal of Hospitality Management* 27 (2008): 284–92.

Rivera, Manuel Antonio, and Randall Upchurch. "The Role of Research in the Hospitality Industry: A Content Analysis of the IJHM Between 2000 and 2005." *International Journal of Hospitality Management* 27 (2008): 632–40.

Snelgrove, Ryan, Marjike Taks, Laurence Chalip, and Christine B. Green. "How Visitor and Locals at a Sport Event Differ in Motives and Identity." *Journal of Sport and Tourism* 13 (2009): 165–80.

Torres, Edwin, and Sheryl Kline. "From Satisfaction to Delight: A Model for the Hotel Industry." *International Journal of Contemporary Hospitality Management* 18.4 (2006): 290.

Wagenheim, Matt, and Stephen Anderson. "Theme Park Satisfaction and Customer Orientation." *Managing Leisure* 13 (2008): 242–57.

Literature reviews in scholarly publications more often focus primarily on key findings and insights rather than all the aspects that you might find in other reviews, in part because of the limitations of space. Often, they analyze major conceptual models as well to provide a context for the study.

Whatever the structure of the literature review, it can serve many functions.

PURPOSES OF A LITERATURE REVIEW

There are many reasons to conduct a careful and thoughtful literature review, all of which build credibility for your research, including the purpose statement you have defined, its importance, and the method that you will select to accomplish your purpose. The reasons to undertake the breadth and depth of reading involved include:

- Assisting you in clarifying your purpose statement
- Providing background information for your research proposal
- Preventing you from doing work that has already been done
- Benefiting from the work of others
- Showing you what research designs have been used
- Introducing ideas that will help you analyze your findings

One of the ways to help think about your research design involves placing it within the context of other research done on the same topic or on related topics. The more studies you read in the general area you are focusing on, the clearer you will be about exactly what you want to do and how to do it. That means focusing your literature review on both findings and on methods. It means reading for suggestions of limitations, qualifications of findings, and indications for more research, often found at the end of scholarly articles. It also means taking careful notes as you read.

PURPOSES OF A LITERATURE REVIEW

- Build credibility for the research.
- Clarify the research goal or purpose statement.
- Give background information.
- Identify key issues which provide a context for your work.
- Save you from making errors by repeating others' work or not benefiting from their experience.
- Help you analyze what you find.

From this breadth of reading, insights will emerge that position your work within the context of other researchers and that clarify your thinking about your own purpose statement. The process of reading similar work gives you insight—sort of like a mirror—into what you want to do or what you think you want to do. It may also show you that your project cannot be done as planned. And it may suggest ideas you had not initially considered.

Since you can benefit from what others have found—in defining the problem, developing hypotheses to test, or identifying areas for future research—reading what others have written can only help you. To make this process work most effectively, however, take into account not only the topic, or area, that you are considering but also other fields and areas that are closely related. For example, if you are interested in customer service in hotels, that means reading about customer service in general, customer service in restaurants and other hospitality companies, customer service in retail sales, customer relationship management models, service recovery, service challenges and systems in restaurants as well as hotels, models of service delivery, training service staff, and a wide range of customer issues.

Providing background information for your proposal requires knowing a great deal of information, which you can obtain from reading broadly. You need to know:

- What others have done

- What key researchers in this field have found

- What major theories or conceptual models have been identified

- What designs have been used to conduct research

- What suggestions have been made for future research

- What topics are timely and new, as opposed to topics that have already been fully investigated

Reading widely will give you information about what others have done and prevent you from doing the same thing all over again in a way that is basically redundant. That form of protection involves reading to find out who the key people in your chosen area are, what they have found, and how they have discovered or tested their ideas.

Often, however, you can conduct research similar to what others have done or test their work by using a different population, a different instrument or research method, or a different geographical focus. In the casino world, there are so many types of gaming establishments that you can expand current research into different types of organizations, profiles of gambling customers, regional differences in gambling, and various gambling strategies. Doing this reading will help you expand the knowledge of your topic (Young et al. 276; Bernhard Dickens, and Shapiro 1; Noriega and Li-Chun 182). Examples of such studies include:

Bernhard, Bo J., Dickens, David R., and Paul D. Shapiro. "Gambling Alone? A Study of Solitary and Social Gambling in America." *UNLV Gaming Research & Review Journal* 11.2 (2007): 1–13.

Eadington, William R. "The Economics of Casino Gambling." *The Journal of Economic* Perspectives 13.3(Summer 1999): 173–92.

MacLaurin, Tanya, and Donald MacLaurin. "Casino Gaming and Tourism in Canada." *International Journal of Contemporary Hospitality Management* 15.6 (2003): 328–32.

Noriega, Pender B., and Li-Chun Lin. "A Comparison Study of the Behavior and Practices of Casino Gamblers as Compared to Those Gamblers of Sport Book Activities." *Journal of Hospitality and Leisure Marketing* 10.½ (2003): 181–93.

Another reason to conduct a literature review is to discover what other people have found about useful methods or ways of analyzing an issue. Have previous scholars used experimental designs, quasi-experimental designs, survey research, or observational methods, and if so, what does their experience suggest you should do? For example, articles may build on a previously published theory for their own models, such as BIRGing—basking in reflected glory—and CORFing—cutting off reflective failure—in sport fan psychology (Cialdini et al. 366–75; Campbell, Aiken, and Kent 151–56).

Reading the work of other people can help you consider a range of ways to focus your purpose statement, open your mind to alternative approaches to a research design, or decide on a different population to survey. It also might help you consider preparing a totally different type of research such as depth interviews of employees to explore what the real issues in customer services are instead of yet another survey of hotel general managers.

You can learn a lot about how to interpret the information you collect from interviews, survey questionnaires, or observations by reading broadly about how scholars have used content analysis models, statistical patterns of analysis, and other strategies to analyze data. Often just considering how you will analyze the data and interpret the findings helps you notice what others have done and how you could do things differently or more effectively given your purpose statement. You might also find that the insights other persons have gathered provide a context for interpreting the results of your research.

Since developing a literature review primarily involves reading a wide range of scholarly journals to ascertain what other researchers have found, the first step involves finding articles to read.

FINDING SCHOLARLY ARTICLES

Since you have worked on developing a purpose statement and a series of research questions, you have created a series of words that can be used to search for scholarly articles. These words and phrases provide a good start. Using your library's website or bibliographic tools, you can search for scholarly articles using key words in your purpose statement or research questions. (For a survey of common bibliographical tools, see **Appendix D, Bibliographical Tools**.) Remember to use cognates, similar words with slightly different meanings, as well. It is often surprising what you can find in this way.

Another way to find good research is to review the bibliographies of articles that you read; if you find several authors mentioned often, then use their names in the search engine and see what they have written about. You may find articles different than the ones in the bibliographies you read; sometimes the articles are newer; other times they are more relevant to your research than the one you were reading about. In addition, they may have co-authors; use those names to see what else the individuals have published. In this way, you will start to expand your search to include significant researchers and often you will find some classic studies on your topic or a related topic.

If you are planning to investigate a topic about which there is not much scholarship, you will have a more interesting challenge. The lack of scholarship directly focused on your topic might mean that it is important to do, no one has thought about it yet, it might be too complex to undertake, or conditions have now brought the topic to light, and it might be very timely. In any of these cases, you may not easily find much scholarship focused on the topic you want to examine. While that may feel very frustrating, it should not deter you. You just need to broaden your search for research on related topics or similar areas of investigation. For example, if you are interested in the impact of recognition—whether from nomination for an award or official designation—on a tourism site, there may be little research focusing on that site or the award, but there is a lot on the impact of UNESCO world heritage site designation, Olympic site designation, or Super Bowl site selection; consulting those studies may produce some interesting insights. Alternatively, reading about the positive and negative impact of official designation may also open your eyes to the range of literature that you need to consult.

As you find articles, be sure to read the abstracts carefully. They often suggest alternative words that you might use in searching for other articles. The key words listed after the abstract can trigger other ideas for you, and the words used in describing the article also provide you with good words to consider as useful search terms.

Another way of finding good scholarship includes thinking of parallel situations, reading a wide range of basic studies that may trigger new ideas about how to search, and interviewing persons who know something about the field so that they can alert you to articles you should read. You can also consult databases or indexes in hospitality, tourism, or sports to find articles or editorial notes about your topic. (For a list of scholarly journals and websites, see **Appendix B, List of Scholarly Journals,** and **Appendix C, Websites**.) All of these options require you to think more broadly about key terms to use in searching for articles and cast a wider net than you might possibly consider otherwise. In the early stages of building your bibliography, you cannot find too many articles since you never know which ones will be helpful until you read a wide range of scholarship.

If you find lots of articles but most of them are in trade publications and not in scholarly journals, you may need to modify the criteria that the search engine is using. Most of them have a button or drop-down box that enables you to request only citations for scholarly articles, also identified as academic journals. Sometimes the filter says scholarly articles; other times, it says academic articles. Whichever phrase is used in your library or firm search tools, select that filter since it will save you an enormous amount of time.

Now that you have thought about how to find articles, it is helpful to consider specific ways to read and methods of recording your insights while reading.

ORDER OF READING SCHOLARLY JOURNAL ARTICLES

One of the central ways that you can conduct a literature review with some ease is to develop the practice of reading scholarly journals in a particular order. Many people read these articles from the beginning to the end and typically follow the pattern of

- Abstract

- Introduction

- Literature review

- Research design, sometimes called research methods

- Research findings

- Analysis, sometimes called discussion or findings

- Applications

- Limitations

- Summary

Although not all articles have these sections as separate elements, most scholarly articles follow this structure, and many people read them in this manner. While many scholars read the articles in this order, it is often difficult for students not conversant with the literature in the field. Without any background, it is often challenging to make sense of the literature review and the need for this study. To overcome this difficulty, try reading scholarly journal articles in another order. (See the box **Order of Reading a Scholarly Journal Article**.)

Reading an article in this published format often causes problems for students new to a field since the literature review does not often make sense without some perspective about the importance of the research and the findings. This method also tends to let the mind wander and not keep focused on the results of the study. After all, the findings are the most important part of what you want to learn, followed by their application. Therefore, it makes sense to read the findings just after you have an overall perspective about the purpose and reason for the study. Reading the abstract or the summary first, the introduction and the conclusion second (and different scholarly journals have different titles for these sections) will help you get the overview. Then you should proceed to the findings and ask to what extent the investigators accomplished their objectives.

As soon as you are clear about the key findings—sometimes explained in the discussion or results of research or findings or conclusion sections (often differing due to editorial styles of publications and sometimes due to varying formats for different types of research) or other aspects of an article, you should record them. Then you can focus on other aspects of the article, such as the research design that produced the findings. Once you have a clear picture about what the article focused on and found, then it makes sense to review the literature section to see what case was made for conducing this research and how it fits into a pattern of other research or what gap it fills.

Quickly consulting and skimming the bibliography directly after the conclusion (or summary) provides you with a sense of the major names in the field, the number of studies done by one author or a combination of authors, the journals that have published articles around the topic, and the dates of some of the studies. This information will be valuable for you in conducting your literature review since there may be sources in the bibliography that you want to read yourself. Therefore, you should record them as you read the article and before getting involved in the details of the study.

ORDER OF READING A SCHOLARLY JOURNAL ARTICLE

- Abstract or executive summary (if there is one)
- Introduction
- Conclusion and bibliography
- Research results and key findings
- Limitations and applications
- Research design and method
- Literature review
- Introduction and conclusion (again)
- Full reading of entire article

Reviewing the research results and findings will enable you to ascertain what the investigators found and how they conducted their analysis of the data. (In the case of more conceptual articles, there may not be a section on research results and findings; often that section is replaced by a conceptual model that has been developed from the review or a set of insights derived from the research that was conducted.) Knowing the findings enables you to appreciate the limitations and applications a bit more and helps you read those sections more critically—or even notice that the scholars did not even indicate any limitations to their research method or their findings!

The next section is the overall research design, the methods of collecting data, that analysis of which you have just read. Reading backward this way keeps your mind nimble and focused on determining what the study found, why it was conducted, and how it was constructed and implemented.

Returning to the introduction and conclusion puts the article in perspective again and enables you to read it as a coherent piece of writing, knowing key elements already and, therefore, being more ready to notice important parts that you want to remember and use in your literature review.

Using this structure will help you sort out the most important parts of an article from less important ones and recognize that what might be minor in the article you are reviewing might be very important to your study.

WHAT TO LOOK FOR WHEN READING ARTICLES

When reading a wide range of scholarly articles or publications in preparing a literature review, you should remember that you want to acquire a clear vision of what the studies show from a viewpoint that examines the field. Imagine yourself looking at all the articles you will read from one hundred feet off the ground so that you can compare various studies with each other. Sometimes, you will notice common findings, methods, points of view, use of statistical methods, patterns of charts, tables, and graphs, and limitations. Other times, you will find very different research methods, a wide range of research questions, and dissimilar points of view. Bringing this overall perspective to your reading will help you realize that many of the tourism and hotel studies have been conducted in Australia and New Zealand or that a preponderance of studies use only college students (which can be very appropriate in certain situations) or that quantitative research seems to be the most prevalent model (Kandampully and Suhartanto 348; Matilla 76; Wann and Weaver 221; Matzler, Renzl, and Rothenberger 180–183). Noticing these patterns of similarities and difference will help you construct your literature review, and reviewing bibliographical citations may provide insights as well. For example, all the articles below had their research conducted in Australia or New Zealand:

> Buchmann, Anne. "Experiencing Film Tourism: Authenticity & Fellowship." *Annals of Tourism Research* 37.1 (2010): 229–248.

> Kandampully, Jay, and Dwi Suhartano. "The Role of Customer Satisfaction and Image in Gaining Customer Loyalty in the Hotel Industry." *Journal of Hospitality and Leisure Marketing* 10.1/2 (2003): 3–25.

> Kim, Samuel Seongseop, McKercher, Bob, and Hyerin Lee. "Tracking Tourism Destination Perception." *Annals of Tourism Research* 36.4 (2009): 715–718.

> McIntosh, Alison, and Anna Siggs. "An Exploration of the Experiential Nature of Boutique Accommodation." *Journal of Travel Research* 44.1 (2005): 74–81.

> Pearce, Douglas G. "Capital City Tourism: Perspectives from Wellington." *Journal of Travel & Tourism Marketing* 22.3/4 (2007): 7–20.

When reading the literature, you should consider several aspects of each article or study that you read. Consequently, when reading scholarly articles or theses for a literature review, you should look for the following information:

- Insights or findings
- Type of research—quantitative, qualitative, mixed
- Structure of the research design
- Use of pilot study
- Research techniques—survey, questionnaire, experiment, focus group, or content analysis
- Type of sample—convenience, purposive, random, nonrandom, cluster, etc. (see **Chapter 7, Sampling Issues in Research**)

- Demographics of the sample (if appropriate)

- Statistical methods of analysis

- Limitations of the study

- Suggestions for future research

- Dates of works cited in the bibliography

Reading industry reports or conceptual pieces requires a different approach. It means that when you read these materials, you should look for the following information:

- Insights or findings

- Support—financial or otherwise—for the research

- Goal of the publication

- Audience for the publication

- Type of research—quantitative, qualitative, mixed

- Structure of the research design

- Type of sample—convenience, purposive, random, nonrandom, cluster, etc. (see **Chapter 7, Sampling Issues in Research**)

- Dates of sources used to prepare the report

- Sources consulted

Considering this range of information, you will need to learn to read articles and other studies quickly and carefully. However, using a Columbus or Sherlock Holmes method of reading—where you search for information in each article rather than reading it from the beginning to the end—will provide you with more useful data to use in compiling your literature review. It will also help you focus on the key elements you need to consider in preparing the analysis that is the key aspect of a literature review.

In this broad reading, look for common researchers, common issues, common methods, and patterns and gaps in what you read. The more similarities and patterns and gaps that you find, the better the quality of your research will be and the stronger your case for the validity and importance of your research design or project.

While reviewing each article for all aspects of content, one often-overlooked area can make a significant difference in the design of your research; the area that is most important after findings is research method.

RESEARCH METHODS

In the process of reading articles and taking notes, don't forget to examine and make notes about the methods that have been employed in the studies. The ways in which other investigators have conducted their research will provide you with great ideas for your research, and noting them in your literature review will help establish the background for what you want to do. Comments about methods may show you what people have done, when they have done it, what limitations they found, what suggestions they make for future research methods, and other ways to conduct significant research. However, mining the articles that you read for this information takes clear focus and intention.

One way to keep your mind focused on methods is to commit to take at least two sets of notes on methods in each article. One might focus on the elements of the design and any limitations that the author's found or that you can determine from reading the article and noticing the match—or lack of it—between what the authors said they wanted to examine and what they actually did. The second note might address the specific methods that the authors used to collect data—that might refer to sampling strategy, sample size, or type of sample. (For more information on sampling issues, see **Chapter 7, Sampling Issues in Research**.)

Taking these notes will help you build a reservoir of ideas about what methods have been used and to what purposes. Comments about methods that have worked will also give you ideas about what you can do and how you can do it.

Often, investigators have used standard questionnaires or interview protocols either because they are replicating other studies or are continuing a line of research that expands over time. For example, several studies have evaluated service quality using the SERVQUAL model developed by A. 'Parsu' Parasuraman (18). Wann used his earlier Sport Fandom Questionnaire in a study of motivational profiles of sports fans (Wann et al. 9) and Morais used his earlier Providers' Perceived Resource Investments (PPRI) and Customers' Reported Resource Investments in a study about tourism providers purchasing customer loyalty (Wann et al. 9; Morais, Dorsch, and Backman 238). These scholars were continuing significant lines of research and expanding the use of the instruments they had designed.

Building a collection of comments on research methods will help prevent you from making errors that others might have encountered, and it will also expand the range of methods you may want to consider.

Since all of this information is critical to remember and be able to refer to as you prepare your literature review, it might be helpful to consider ways to record your insights and take notes on them in a way that helps you prepare a careful and thoughtful literature review. They are explained in the next section.

TAKING NOTES AS YOU READ

While conducting a literature review, you will read a wide range of articles. Most of them are scholarly but some may be or might be industry reports, statistical data, and other forms of useful information. To make it easier, the following tips can save you time and aggravation:

- Record full bibliographical information as soon as you start to read an article, using Endnotes, Refnotes, or other bibliographical tools with which you are comfortable.

- Read discussion and findings sections carefully and write about them as you go.

- Build notes around the topics of your literature review and not around the articles themselves.

When you start to read an article, a book, or a publication of any kind, the first thing you should do is to record the full bibliographical information for that document. For an article, that means the full name of the author (or authors), the full title of the article (including the subtitle if appropriate), the name of the publication (in italics) and the volume and number, the date of publication, and the pages of the article. For books, the full information includes the full name of the author, the full title of the book (including the subtitle if appropriate), and the place of publication, the publisher, and the date of publication (Gibaldi 147). If the book has an editor (e.g., chapters might have different authors), note the book editor and the chapter titles, authors, and page numbers that are relevant to your work. You don't want to have to hunt these down after you have returned the book to the library.

As you read a section or get an insight, start to write a paragraph about that insight or finding or demographic. Do not worry about the length or style of the paragraph; you should, however, focus on accuracy as you write since you will use this paragraph as one of the building blocks of your literature review.

If you write in the third person, you will save yourself some time later and not have to edit all of the stuff that you write. Then make sure to cite the information using a parenthetical reference (Mayo 2007, 23) with the author's name inside it and the year of the publication—an APA style recommendation; if you are more comfortable with an MLA style, or your program requires it, then use the author's name and a page reference (Mayo 23; Hacker 129).

BIBLIOGRAPHICAL TOOLS

When performing your literature review, several resources and tools are available for keeping track of all the citations for your reviewed articles and publications. These range from web-based to downloadable software. Some are free of charge, others are available for purchase, and your academic institution may have acquired licenses for you to use them as a student.

These tools, as with the ever-evolving presence of technology, are becoming more prevalent, diverse, and helpful for your research. Some allow you to include your annotated bibliographical comments, and some tools have increased Web 2.0 capabilities for social networking. For a descriptive list of these tools available, see **Appendix D, Bibliographical Tools.**

After each paragraph, look for other elements of the article or statistical report and then write a paragraph capturing that insight or comment. While these suggestions may fly in the face of your previous experience in taking notes for term papers, you will find that this structure of note taking helps you to make the comparisons that are a critical aspect of a coherent and analytical literature review.

For each aspect of each article you read, you will end up with a paragraph or two. Once you have read five or six articles and have a number of paragraphs about each one, then you can place the paragraphs about findings together, the paragraphs about demographics together, and the paragraphs about statistical methods together in order to notice patterns, gaps, and distinctions that might otherwise be hard to see in traditional note taking styles.

Remember that these paragraphs need to be more than simple summaries. Think about the strengths and weaknesses of the findings or the limitation and advantages of particular statistical methods, or the unintended influence created by selecting a particular demographic population to sample. Write them as comments on what you are taking notes about; write your ideas in the third person point of view; and mention, in some detail, what the article has said. These notes become critical parts of what you will use to write your literature review. (For more information on writing the review, see **Chapter 5, Writing your Literature Review**.)

By taking these notes on a laptop or notebook computer, you can also print out several copies of the paragraphs so that you can see various patterns and use the paragraphs several times in order to make the points that are important to you. For example, you may want to use the paragraph about demographics in one section of your literature review when discussing populations studied and in another section when you point out gaps in the methods or tactics of research methods used. By having the paragraphs, you have a chance to use them several times. Combining them provides you with parts of your literature review already written in a draft form.

Revising, editing, and making transitions becomes the next step, and then you will have a literature review that provides the background information that you want or need for your research design.

EVALUATING ARTICLES

One aspect of conducting a literature review that intimidates some students is their lack of knowledge of a field and their belief that because something has been published, it cannot be criticized. In conducting your literature review, you will build a base of knowledge in the topics you read, and you will pretty soon discover that you can recognize key issues and find limitations. Building on this knowledge and bringing a critical—i.e. skeptical—attitude toward your reading will help you build your confidence in making assessment.

Remember that your focus should be to examine the findings and the methods used to develop those findings. These two elements of each article that you read or each study that you encounter should cause you to think about what the authors found and ask a few important questions:

- Did they have an appropriate way of drawing those conclusions from the data they collected and the ways they were analyzed?

- Are there qualifications to the statements that they can make from their research?

- What qualifications should they have made?

- What limitations did they mention?

- What limitations did they fail to point out or other limitations you identified?

- What generalizations (called applications in **Chapter 1, Reading and Analyzing Research**) did they draw and can they draw from what they discovered?

The more you bring this questioning approach to what you read, the easier it will be to develop a critical approach to what you read. Taking careful and thematic notes (see section on **Taking Notes as you Read** above) should also help you focus on assessing the value of the study.

Another way to build your confidence in evaluating what you read involves comparing the findings of the article you are reading with other articles. Often, you can begin to see a pattern of research and ways that this study might fit into that pattern or open new ways to consider the topic of the field. Research on sports fans has focused on spectator patterns, fan avidity, self-concept, and patterns of behavior. There is lots of research in each area and room for future research. Realizing where the article you are reading fits into that pattern, or set of categories, will help you read with an evaluative perspective.

As you review the contents of each article or study that you read and start to make some assessment of its merits, you are doing the work appropriate for building your annotated bibliography.

PREPARING AN ANNOTATED BIBLIOGRAPHY

After you have read each article completely, go back to the full bibliographical citation and add some comments about the value of the article, book, or industry report. Summarizing the article—in only a few sentences—and commenting on it will help you focus your critical thinking on what you are reading and help you later when you want to go back to certain articles and not others.

These three elements of an annotated bibliography—the citation, the summary, and the commentary—are good tools to develop and practice. They will provide you with resources for all your future research and help discipline your mind to read critically and always ask questions about what you are reading and analyzing. You may also be required to provide an annotated bibliography as part of your research proposal; taking notes toward that type of bibliography will help you complete your research proposal.

The following example of annotations may help you see the value of this form of taking notes:

> Ekinci, Yuksel, Philip L. Dawes, and Graham R. Massey. "An Extended Model of the Antecedents and Consequences of Consumer Satisfaction for Hospitality Services." *European Journal of Marketing* 42.1 (2008): 35–68. Print.
>
> This study tested five antecedents of satisfaction: actual self-congruence (self-concept), ideal self-congruence, desires congruence, and two dimensions of service quality: physical quality and staff behavior and explored the

consequences of dissatisfaction, including impact on overall attitude to the service firm, and the intention to return. They found that the multiple proposed antecedents were all related and significant, and that of the two dimensions of service quality, staff behavior more strongly affects satisfaction. A major implication of this study is that there are many different antecedents of customer satisfaction, including service quality.

A recent study that provided an alternative perspective toward customer satisfaction. Its treatment of conceptual frameworks and the use of a pilot study to test the instrument added to the validity of the study; the convenience sampling technique was a limitation. While the findings that staff behavior affects customer satisfaction more than physical quality is not new, the examination of how self-concept affects customer satisfaction (but may not be an element of service quality) opened new lines of thinking. A carefully done study, well worth returning to read.

McIntosh, Alison J., and Anne Zahra. "A Cultural Encounter through Volunteer Tourism: Towards the Ideals of Sustainable Tourism?" *Journal of Sustainable Tourism* 15 (2007): 541–55.

The researchers explored the connection between volunteer tourism and cultural tourism in the search for alternative and sustainable experiences. The study examined pre-, during-, and post-trip experiences of Australian visitors who participated in organized volunteer activities in an indigenous Maori community in the North Island of New Zealand. The findings revealed that the nature of cultural experiences was perceived as mutually beneficial and different from those gained from traditional cultural products. However, the findings cannot be generalized to all volunteer tourism experiences, as the interaction between host and volunteer might be different in various situations.

Twenge, Jean M. "A Review of the Empirical Evidence on Generational Differences in Work Attitudes." *Journal of Business and Psychology* 25.2 (2010): 201–210. *SpringerLink*. Web. 10 June 2010.

Twenge compared Silents, Baby Boomers, GenX, and GenMe by characteristic traits that lead to differences in the workplace. GenX and GenMe value leisure more than their predecessors, and have less of a work-centric life focus. However, there are no significant differences among GenMe, GenX, and Baby Boomers on altruistic values. Based on her findings, Twenge makes recommendations on how to effectively recruit and retain GenMe.

The survey of other research provided a good background to this topic and highlighted areas for future research. There was no empirical work in this article, but it was valuable background information. The bibliography was extensive and helpful.

Fink, Janet, Trail, Galen, and Anderson, Dean. "Environmental Factors Associated with Spectators Attendance and Sport Consumption Behavior: Gender and Team Differences." *Sport Marketing Quarterly* 11.1 (2002): 8–19.

The authors investigated the differences in factors that affect spectators' attendance to women's and men's games, and also between women and men. They conducted a study at two women's and two men's intercollegiate basketball games using three categories—environmental factors (ticket pricing, friends and family influence and advertising promotions), present behavior (merchandise consumption, media consumption and wearing team apparel), and behavior intentions (future loyalty, attendance intentions and merchandise consumption intentions). They found certain differences between both people who attend different gender games and those of different gender that attend games. Those who attend women's games are more influenced by environmental factors, remain loyal, attend future games and buy future merchandise. Those who attend men's games are more likely to follow teams in media, wear apparel and purchase merchandise. Women spectators purchase more apparel and pretend to purchase more merchandise, are more future loyal fans and remain loyal. Men spectators are more interested in statistics and in the promotion of the games through print media.

The study provides useful insights about differences in spectators of men's game and women's games but there were limits to the conclusions that can be drawn about gender differences. The focus on only college basketball focus may limit it its application as well but did not indicate any limitations.

With this kind of information, you know what articles to review again more closely and what references can make a great contribution to your literature review. (For more information about an annotated bibliography, see **Appendix A, Writing an Annotated Bibliography**.)

Making comments about the sources that you read as you read them can make the whole process of conducting a literature review easier and more effective. It is a way to organize your efforts to be more efficient as well. Making it interesting is the subject of the next section.

MAKING A LITERATURE REVIEW EFFECTIVE AND INTERESTING TO DO

Reading a wide range of literature can be interesting and enlightening if you make it an adventure in trying to find out what has been studied and why. If you simply follow a few key words that you match your purpose statement and the research questions, you might come up with a number of sources that are central to what you need to read. However, you might also not find very much that has been published in the areas of your interest. In that case, you might need to use a different approach.

The hardest part of finding studies for your literature review often derives from a lack of creative thinking about key words for search engines or bibliographical sources. Try to consider what aspects of the subject might be studied and what you think that the investigators might have found from their work. As you do so, you will develop a range of different ways to approach the subject. Clearly, you can start with the key authors that you find in bibliographies of the scholarly journal articles that you find. Searching by author may produce a record of scholarship in an area that shows the development of concepts and the breadth or depth of research in a field. It may also provide you with a number of articles whose sections on limitations give you other suggestions of what to research.

A second way to find related research that you might not consider to be relevant at first is to see if there are parallel organizations or situations to investigate. If you are interested in the impact of celebrity publicity on tourism in certain countries, you will probably find little research in this area, even though the topic is an important one. However, examining celebrity endorsements, sponsorship activities, impacts of sponsorship on attendance at entertainment events, branded celebrities, political endorsement, and other topics, you may come up with a range of articles and studies that will help you articulate the need for your research and suggest ways in which it can be conducted. It might still be difficult to fill in lacuna of studies.

To overcome this gap, try some creative thinking about your topic and imagine what other areas might be similar to the research you want to investigate. For example, if you are interested in adventure tourism, a growing niche area, you will find a paucity of sources, but if you consider related areas like hiking, biking, exploring, x sports, sporting trips, and voyages into new areas, you may discover several useful scholarly journal articles that might provide useful background. If you wanted to investigate self-service technology in hotels, you might have to look for studies of self-service technology in schools, airlines, cruise lines, gambling casinos, and travel sites since there have been few studies published about the use of kiosks and other self-service technologies in hotels and lodging sites. You might also look at issues such as resistance to technology, general differences in accepting technology, and technological anxiety. Considering these other areas opens up possibilities for exploring other topics and will broaden your review. You may find that some of the literature you uncover adds immeasurably to the information needed for your research.

Another way to expand your search involves playing with words that might serve as search terms. Try parallel situations, opposites from what you really want, first cousin ideas to what you need, and other techniques. If you cannot come up with these ideas by yourself, you may find that trying to explain your areas of interest—your purpose statement—to others will enable them to ask questions that trigger new search terms. Alternatively, they may come up with parallel areas of interest and suggest ways you can expand the scope of your review. Ask them; you may be surprised at the results.

The more you expand the words you consider and the ways that you search for articles, the more fun you will have with this adventure, and the more creative you can become about how to conduct the research that you will design.

SUMMARY

In this chapter, you have learned what a literature review is, why it is important, and how to conduct one in a way that helps you with your research. The key point to remember is that critical and fast reading as well as careful note taking can help you notice what you are reading. This process will start you on building an analysis of what has been found and how it has been found in the areas you are interested in investigating.

You have also learned that a good literature review will help you with your own work by suggesting research designs and ways to analyze findings—as much as building your credibility and protecting you from redoing something that has already been examined.

The next chapter will address revising your purpose statement in terms of the insights from your literature review.

KEY TERMS

Abstract	Literature review
Annotation	Order of reading a scholarly
Annotated bibliography	Perspective
Bibliographical tools	Purpose of a literature review

WORKS CITED IN THIS CHAPTER

Aggett, Mandy. "What Has Influenced Growth in the UK's Boutique Hotel Sector?" *International Journal of Hospitality Management* 19.2 (2007): 169–171. Web. 26 September 2010.

Barez, Arne, Michael T Manion, Kristi L Schoepfer, Joseph Cherian. "Global Cases Of Effective Sports Sponsorship: An Exploration Of A New Communications Model." *Innovative Marketing*. 3.3 (2007): 69–77,102. ABI/INFORM Global. ProQuest. New York University, New York, NY. 2 Feb. 2009 <http://www.proquest.com/>

Bauer, Hans H., Sauer E. Nicola, and Exler Stefanie. "The Loyalty of German Soccer Fans: Does a Team's Brand Image Matter?" *International Journal of Sports Marketing and Sponsorship* October (2005): 14–22.

Bernhard, Bo, David Dickens, and Paul Shapiro. "Gambling Alone? A Study of Solitary and Social Gambling in America." *UNLV Gaming Research & Review Journal* 11.2 (2007): 1–13.

Boote, David N., and Penny Beile. "Scholars Before Researchers: On the Centrality of the Dissertation Literature Review in Research Preparation" *Educational Researcher* 34.6 (2005): 3–15.

Campbell, Robert M, Jr. Damon Aiken, and Aubrey Kent. "Beyone BIRGing and CORFing: Continuing the Exploration of Fan Behavior 13 (2004): 151–157.

Cho, Seonghee, Robert H. Woods, Soo Cheong Shawn Jang, and Mehmet Erdem. "Measuring the impact of human resource management practices on hospitality Firms' performances." *International Journal of Hospitality Management* 25 (2006): 262–77.

Cialdini, R.B., Border, R.J., Thorne, A., Walker, M.R., Freman, S., and Sloan, L.R. "Basking in Reflected Glory: Three (Football) Field Studies." *Journal of Personality and Social Psychology* 34.3 *(1976):* 366–375. PsycARTICLES. PsycNET. Web. 26 September 2010.

Ekinci, Yuksel, Philip L. Dawes, and Graham R. Massey. "An Extended Model of the Antecedents and Consequences of Consumer Satisfaction for Hospitality Services." *European Journal of Marketing* 42.1 (2008): 35–68.

Fink, Janet, Trail, Galen, and Anderson, Dean. "Environmental Factors Associated with Spectators Attendance and Sport Consumption Behavior: Gender and Team Differences." *Sport Marketing Quarterly* 11.1 (2002): 8

http://hospitalitytechnology.edgl.com/white-papers.

Gibaldi, Joseph. *MLA Handbook for Writers of Research Papers*, 6th ed. New York: Modern Language Association of America, 2003.

Hacker, Diana T. *A Pocket–Style Manual*. Boston: Bedford/Saint Martin's, 2003.

Hart, Chris. *Doing a Literature Search: A Comprehensive Guide for the Social Sciences*. Thousand Oaks: Sage, 2001.

Hart, Chris. *Doing a Literature Review Doing a Literature Review: Releasing the Social Science Research Imagination* (Published in association with The Open University). Thousand Oaks: Sage, 1999.

Hart, Chris. *Doing a Literature Search: A Comprehensive Guide for the Social Sciences*. Thousand Oaks: Sage, 2001.

Irwin, Richard L., et al. "Cause-Related Sport Sponsorship: An Assessment of Spectator Beliefs, Attitudes, and Behavioral Intentions." *Sport Marketing Quarterly* 12.3 (2003): 131–39. *Business Source Premier*. EBSCO. Web. 24 Sept. 2010.

Kandampully, Jay, and Dwi Suhartanto, "Customer Loyalty in the Hotel Industry: The Role of Customer Satisfaction and Image." *International Journal of Contemporary Hospitality Management*. 12 (2000): 346–51.

Leedy, Paul D., and Jeanne E. Ormrod. *Practical Research : Planning and Design*. Upper Saddle River: Prentice Hall, 2004.

Matilla, Anna. "Emotional Bonding and Restaurant Loyalty." *Cornell Hotel and Restaurant Administration Quarterly*. (2001): 73–79.

MacLaurin, Tanya, and Donald MacLaurin. "Casino gaming and tourism in Canada." *International Journal of Contemporary Hospitality Management* 15.6 (2003): 328–332. ABI/INFORM Global, ProQuest. Web. 26 Sept. 2010.

McIntosh, Alison J., and Anne Zahra. "A Cultural Encounter through Volunteer Tourism: Towards the Ideals of Sustainable Tourism?" *Journal of Sustainable Tourism* 15 (2007): 541–55.

McIntosh, Alison, and Anna Siggs. "An Exploration of the Experiential Nature of Boutique Accommodation." *Journal of Travel Research* 44.1 (2005): 74–81. Web. 24 Sept. 2010.

Matzler, Kurt, Birgit Renzl, and Sandra Rothenberger. "Measuring the Relative Importance of Service Dimensions in the Formation of Price Satisfaction and Service Satisfaction: A Case Study in the Hotel Industry." *Scandinavian Journal of Hospitality and Tourism*. 6 (2006): 179–96.

Maxwell, Joseph. "Literature Reviews of, and for, Educational Research." *Educational Researcher* 35.9 (2006): 28–31.

Morais, Duarte B., Michael J. Dorsch and Sheila J. Backman. "Can Tourism Providers Buy their Customers' Loyalty? Examining the Influence of Customer–Provider Investments on Loyalty." *Journal of Travel Research* 42 (2004): 235.

Morosan, Cristian, and Miyoung Jeong. "Users' Perceptions of Two Types of Hotel Reservation Websites." *International Journal of Hospitality Management* 27 (2008): 284–92.

Noriega, Pender, and Li-Chun. "A Comparison Study of the Behavior and Practices of Casino Gamblers as Compared to those Gamblers of Sport Book Activities." *Journal of Hospitality & Leisure Marketing* 10.1 (2003): 181.

O'Connor, Stefanie. "Ambiguous Boutique Sector Set for Expansion." *Hotel Business* 16 (2007): 10–28.

O'Leary, Zina. *The Essential Guide to Doing Research* [Electronic Resource]. London: Sage, 2004.

Panasuraman, A., Valarie A. Zeithaml, and Leonard L. Berry, SERVQUAL; A Multiple-Item Scale for Measuring Consumer Perceptions of Service Quality *Journal of Retailing* 64.1 (1988): 12–40.

Rivera, Manuel Antonio, and Randall Upchurch. "The Role of Research in the Hospitality Industry: A Content Analysis of the IJHM Between 2000 and 2005." *International Journal of Hospitality Management* 27 (2008): 632–40.

Rose, I. "Casinos on Cruise Ships, Why Not on Airplanes?" *Gaming Law Review* 10.6 (2006): 519–20.

Snelgrove, Ryan, Marijke Taks, Laurence Chalip, and Christine B. Green. "How Visitors and Locals at a Sport Event Differ in Motives and Identity." *Journal of Sport & Tourism* 13 (2009): 165–80.

Young, Matthew, et al. "The Desire to Gamble: The Influence of Outcomes on the Priming Effects of a Gambling Episode." *Journal of Gambling Studies* 24.3 (2008): 275–93.

Wagenheim, Matt, and Stephen Anderson. "Theme Park Employee Satisfaction and Customer Orientation." *Managing Leisure* 13 (2008): 242–57.

Wann, Daniel L. "Preliminary Validation of a Measure for Assessing Identification as a Sport Fan: The Sport Fandom Questionnaire." *International Journal of Sport Management* 3 (2002): 103–115.

Wann, Daniel L., Daniel L., Frederick G. Grieve, Ryan K. Zapalac, and Dale G. Pease. "Motivational Profiles of Sport Fans of Different Sports." *Sport Marketing Quarterly*, 2008, 17 (2008): 6–19.

Wann, Daniel L., and Stephen Weaver, "Understanding the Relationship between Sport Team Identification and Dimensions of Social Well-being." *North American Journal of Psychology*. 11 (2009): 219–30.

CHAPTER 4

Reviewing and Revising Your Purpose Statement

INTRODUCTION

Developing a coherent purpose statement is perhaps the most difficult part of any research project. With an early version of the *purpose statement* and *research questions*, your literature review hopefully has been made much easier. Now the task of reshaping that purpose statement on the basis of the preliminary *literature review* becomes the next step, which can be a hard one since it is often difficult to let the original go and keep revising it.

The process of reviewing and revising your purpose statement can produce a lot of insights and contribute, immensely, to expanding the breadth and depth of your literature review, the quality of your research design, the effectiveness of the research itself, and the pleasure you derive from the process.

This chapter explains the reasons for revising your purpose statement, the importance of a clear purpose statement, the process of reviewing and revising a purpose statement, criteria to evaluate a purpose statement, and the importance of flexibility. The chapter ends with examples of purpose statements and research questions as well as a few comments about refocusing your reading of the literature surrounding your topic.

REASONS FOR REVISING PURPOSE STATEMENTS

During your reading and taking notes for the literature review, you probably noticed studies that were done directly in the area or related areas of your interest that sound more interesting to pursue. Or you may have come up with other ways of looking at the general topic you were pursuing. For example, if you were interested in determining customer satisfaction with boutique hotels and you discovered a strain of research on customer satisfaction with new and small restaurants, you might want to alter your focus and examine restaurant customer satisfaction. They are both in the field of hospitality and your original interest might have been more focused on customers than boutique hotels. Or you might have been reading widely in niche tourism since you wanted to determine what factors led tourists to take adventure trips, especially exotic ones. But as you read, you discovered the literature on volun-tourism and the categories of tourists interested in that form of travel, so you might decide to shift your focus slightly to examine this newer niche. Or you might have been examining images of female athletes in professional sports and found literature on discrimination in professional sports and decided to shift your purpose statement to that area, an interest that originally spawned your interest in images of female athletes in the first place. Now you have a broader and more engaging purpose statement and some new research questions.

In each of these cases, your original interest remains strong but you found slightly different areas of focus. In these situations, you will need to review and revise your purpose statement and your research questions. Sometimes, the change will be fairly significant, but often it is only minor. However, making the revisions recognizes the new information that you have gathered and provides more clarity to what you want to investigate. Finding scholarly articles on your topic—or the lack of them—and related literature can suggest that shift.

Alternatively, you may realize that there is not much literature directly focused on your purpose statement and little that you can borrow from other areas of research. In fact, the more that you read, the more you recognize the difficulty in focusing on your purpose statement and research questions as well as the challenge in determining a method to answer your questions.

A third reason for altering your purpose statement and research questions comes from the realization that the studies done in this field indicate how impossible it will be to create a coherent and effective research design unless you refocus your purpose statement and narrow the topic considerably.

As you read more literature, you will also start to notice some of the patterns of research in the areas you are interested in and some of them in other areas. Some of it will include research methods with expanding populations or different demographics. Sometimes, you will see a current of research extending into new populations. Considering these new groups may be a fourth reason to alter your purpose statement and research questions since you have come across an exciting line of research that you could not have known about before conducting your literature review.

All these situations provide reasons to alter your purpose statement and research questions. As you review the notes from your literature review, consider the following questions that may help you decide the extent to which you may want to revise and rewrite your purpose statement:

- What did the research tell you about your purpose statement and research questions?

- What has been studied already? To what extent is it valid and useful research?

- What methods have been used, and to what benefit? Are they something you want to replicate? Do they suggest new methods for you?

- What related topics have come up during the process of your literature review, and how do they affect what you want to examine or analyze? Do they suggest that it is useful to alter your original purpose statement and research questions?

- What classical studies have you found that you may want to replicate?

- What important studies have you discovered, and how will they affect what you might like to do?

These questions should remind you of the importance of your purpose statement and research questions.

IMPORTANCE AND SIGNIFICANCE OF A PURPOSE STATEMENT

A good purpose statement and set of research questions can provide a lot of support for a research endeavor. They have already given you suggestions about what to investigate and where you might find critical information about previous studies done on the topic. And they have probably suggested key elements of this area of research as well as side topics—and even some research methods—that might merit some investigation. They can structure the ways in which you think about this research topic and open your mind to possible future research topics. Their power can include inviting you to reflect on other aspects of the topic you are considering researching.

As you read in **Chapter 2, Developing an Interest or Topic**, a good purpose statement and set of research questions are: useful, valid, focused, feasible, and significant. They can help you shape an effective research design or obscure what you really need to do as part of your research.

In cases where you are following a previous line of research, you may already have a pretty clear purpose statement based on the suggestions already made for future research in this area. In situations where you are investigating a new area or opening a new area for research, the initial sense of purpose may be rather vague—sufficient to produce some search terms and identify research that has been conducted on this topic, but not thorough enough to drive the full enterprise.

If you have moved from an initial sense of what you want to investigate, you may find your purpose statement and research questions becoming too unfocused. It may be that you have a sense of what you want to examine, understand, or investigate, but the research questions do not capture these new goals or interests.

In any of these situations, the power and impact of a clear purpose statement and focused research questions cannot be underestimated. As John Creswell, author of many books on qualitative, quantitative, and mixed method research, said, "Whereas introductions focus on the problem leading to the study, the purpose statement establishes the direction for the research" (Creswell 2002, 87). It provides the guidance and direction for continuing and expanding the literature review, a trigger for designing the research, and a framework for interpreting and analyzing the results, regardless of what type of research you conduct.

Revising purpose statements and refocusing research questions can be made easier if you consider a specific structure to these statements and other supporting statements.

PURPOSE STATEMENT AND SUPPORTING DIMENSIONS

There are a number of ways to review and revise a purpose statement and clarify its importance. Focus on the following four central elements—what is the goal, what parts are most important to this research, why is it important, and how will I pursue it—can be a very effective practice. This structure will also help you expand your literature review and compose it because you will be clearer about the significance and impact of your purpose statement. It can serve as a guiding principle to organize the sections of your literature review and to structure the first and last paragraphs of that literature review.

The first challenge is clarifying exactly what you are interested in investigating, analyzing, or examining. Using these verbs and similar ones—such as discover, test, seek, and demonstrate—will help you make a clearer statement or assist you in writing a whole new statement. Focusing on factors, influences, impacts, effects, and relationships will also keep your purpose statement broad enough to help you expand your literature review while narrow enough that you will not read about every aspect of the topic(s) that intrigues you.

The second challenge is formulating or reformulating the research questions that derive from your purpose statement. What specific aspects of the purpose statement do you want to emphasize? What are the questions that you want to ask? What do you really want to know about this topic? What will make a difference in your understanding? What answers will make a contribution to the knowledge in this area?

Although clarifying the purpose and refining the research questions are important, being clear about the reasons for the research can be an important and often overlooked dimension. Since you will spend considerable time and energy on this research design, you should understand and be able to explain to others why it is worth doing. What might be its impact on the industry? Why should you conduct this research? What difference will it make? How come it is important and significant now?

It can be very helpful, to write your purpose statement and its related issues in a four-step format. (For sample outline, see the box **Format for Purpose Statement and Supporting Issues.**) The four issues include:

- Purpose statement

- Research questions

- Significance of the purpose statement

- Possible research methods

Another way to look at these four statements is the famous six questions that reporters always ask in their research—who, what, when, where, why, and how. By writing the answers to these four questions in the suggested format, you will find your thinking gets clearer. If you cannot answer why the topic or the area for investigation is important, then you may want to consider whether it is worth pursuing. You may also realize that it has been done before or in a related way that you can build on as you conduct your own research. For example, there is a lot of research on brand loyalty but not that much on customers' perceptions of brand loyalty and what it really means to them. Or there is a lot of research on coaches and managers as leaders but little about athletes as peer leaders.

FORMAT FOR PURPOSE STATEMENT AND SUPPORTING ISSUES

- My purpose is to_____
  _____ (What do you want to
  learn? What do you want to investigate? What do you want to test? What fascinates
  you?)

- The questions I want to investigate in order to accomplish my purpose
  include_____
  _____
  (What are the research questions? What specifically do you want to examine
  in some detail? What aspects of the purpose statement are most critical and
  important?)

- The reasons it is important include _____
  _____ (Why is it significant? What is the rationale for its importance? What gap in the industry or field does it fill? Why should people care about
  this issue? What does the literature say about its importance? Or its relevance?
  What gap does it fill?)

- Therefore, I will_____
  _____ (What will you do
  to fill in the gap, to discover the information you want to investigate? What research
  method—or methods—will address this purpose statement? What can you do to
  answer your questions and accomplish your goal?)

Writing purpose statements in this suggested format also prompts you to think about aspects of what you want to do that you might not initially consider. It can also be very helpful in organizing your thinking and helping you focus on what you really want to investigate and why. As you record your *purpose statement* and research questions, you need to consider ways that they can be answered. And as you consider ways to answer them, you may alter the exact scope and range of what you want to examine or investigate.

As you begin to ponder these challenges and consider what you want to analyze or examine, it can also be helpful to consider the process of making revisions to your purpose statement and research questions.

PROCESS OF REVIEWING AND REVISING

Once you have revised and clarified your initial purpose statement and the research questions that derive from it, you may feel discouraged. Actually, you should feel encouraged since it shows that you have been reading carefully and comprehensively and are getting a clearer understanding of the area(s) you want to investigate.

To keep this process moving, many researchers keep a dated record of the various versions of their purpose statement and research questions as they write, revise, and change them. It shows the development of the ideas over time and provides a record of their thinking as they have conducted the research. You may find the practice useful as well since in preparing the final revision of your research design, it might be helpful to return to your earlier statements and use them, or a portion of them.

The four statements you wrote and revised above need to be clear and to the point so that you can remember them without having to look them up. After all, what good is it to have a purpose statement and research questions so obscure or so carefully detailed that you cannot remember them? They need to serve as a guiding light as you read in the literature and explore the breadth and depth of research in your area; in this respect, remember KISS—keep it short and sweet, scholar!

Another approach to defining, clarifying, and revising your purpose statement, the research questions, their significance, and possible methods is to give your statements three different tests: the spousal or partner test, the Thanksgiving test, and the public speaking test. If you cannot describe to your roommate, partner, or close friend what you are trying to investigate, chances are you are not very clear yourself what it is all about, much less why it is important to pursue. This spousal or *partner test* is a good first test because your significant other cares what you are doing and wants to listen and understand what this project is all about even if the person is not in the field. However, if your goal is so fuzzy that you cannot explain it clearly given plenty of time and a good listener, you need to do a lot of more reading, writing, and thinking.

The second test—*the Thanksgiving test*—makes your purpose even clearer. If you were to describe the goal of your research—the purpose statement, the research questions, and the significance of your research—to your Aunt Sally and Uncle Joaquin at a Thanksgiving family dinner event, would they understand it? While they may not have the background to appreciate fully what you are trying to do, can you make it clear to them what you want to find out and why it is important? If you cannot do so, it may not be very clear to you, and you may need to revisit and revise your purpose statement.

A third way to ascertain if you have a clear and useful purpose statement is *the public speaking test*. Can you stand up among a group of peers—such as fellow students in a course or colleagues at work—and explain the purpose statement, the research questions, and their significance? Are you proud of them? Can you say them clearly without having to read from notes? If the answer to any of these questions is no, then you may have to continue to work on revising to make the purpose statement and research questions clearer to yourself and to others.

After you try any of these three strategies, stop and reflect on what you have learned and what changes you might want to make in your purpose statement. Sometimes, the change is minor, but often the experience of explaining the purpose statement in public points out some unclear thinking on your part or some aspect of the topic or issue that you did not consider. Take a moment to reflect and record those insights that can improve your purpose statement immensely.

While these tests may sound brutal and unhelpful, remember that are you embarking on a long and thoughtful journey to somewhere. If you don't know where you are going, you will get somewhere, but not likely where you want to get. And if you really want to find out the answers, think about the purpose statement and research questions in terms of what it would be like to really have the answers. What would you know more clearly than you know now? How will this insight help you or the industry?

CRITERIA FOR A GOOD PURPOSE STATEMENT

As you revise your purpose statement and research questions, consider their breadth and depth. Have you asked questions that have a future? Does your purpose statement have enough breadth to investigate? Are there enough research questions associated with it to make a difference? One way to know the answers to these questions is to imagine that the problem was solved or that the research yielded new information about the topic you chose to investigate. Whether it be customer service, revenue models, brand loyalty, hiring and retention, sustainability practices, crisis management, sponsorship models, real estate values, or new segments of tourists, imagine that you actually completed the research—would you be satisfied and pleased with the answers you obtained? If so, then your purpose statement and research questions have the breadth and depth they need to guide significant research. If not, then you may want to broaden your interests a bit more.

You may also want to consider some of the criteria for a clear and well-written purpose statement and research questions. Since their role is so critical to the development of a productive research design, it is often worth comparing them to a set of previous criteria—in this case the five I's:

- **I**—Important—Is the topic or the problem really worth investigating? Will anything important be discovered or tested if you pursue this area of research, or is it a backwater area of little or no interest?

- **I**—Interesting—Is the topic something that professionals in the field—scholars, researchers, managers, or consultants—really want to know? Do they now—or would they really care about the purpose statement and research questions as written?

- **I**—Intriguing—To what extent does this topic and the questions pose an interesting issue or problem? Who would find the topic fascinating, and why?

- **I**—Investigable—Can you realistically conduct the research to find answers to these questions?

- **I**—Impactful—In what ways will this purpose statement make a difference in the industry, the profession, or the field, either conceptually or pragmatically? What kind of impact might it have on companies, events, best practices, or others? What impact would it have on the field?

THE I's FOR A PURPOSE STATEMENT

- I—Important
- I—Interesting
- I—Intriguing
- I—Investigable
- I—Impactful

Comparing these five I's with your purpose statement and research questions may be hard, but the practice will help you refine and improve them so that they can function as the Occam's razor, or guiding principle, to differentiate between a good purpose statement and a bad one, that you can use to decide what other literature to review and what to ignore. This practice will also help you see what gaps you have not noticed in the material you have read and what you have not read or even thought to investigate.

REFOCUSING THE RESEARCH

As you review and revise your purpose statement and research questions, you have opened the possibility of new ideas about what you have read and what you want to learn. Review the literature you have consulted and consider what parts are missing. What areas have you not read about that you now need to consider? How can you see parallel areas of research that were not clear—or even envisionable—before you reviewed and revised the purpose statement and research questions? What new ideas were suggested by reframing your purpose statement and research questions?

One way to focus this process involves reviewing the original key words you used to search the literature the first time. How do those words serve the newly revised purpose statement and research questions? What new words can you consider, or should you consider, that never occurred to you before? What synonyms have you not considered? What words occurred to you when you were explaining your purpose statement and research questions? What other issues came up that prompted you to consider new search terms?

A FLEXIBLE PROCESS

The research process involves a lot of iterative processing. As you develop a purpose statement and research questions and then read some of the literature on the topic and related topics, you have probably found yourself changing the focus of your work or revising the research questions. You might find that what you want to investigate has already been done, but you discover an aspect that has not been fully analyzed and that insight gives you a new direction. Or you might find a new way to test a hypothesis or model. Or you might learn that the answers to the research questions you posed were answered but in a different context and time frame than what interests you.

Alternatively, you might find that the literature you read suggests another dimension to your purpose statement. In those cases, you will find that your purpose statement and research questions need to change as a result of what you have been reading. The very broad purpose statement that seemed useful and appropriate sometimes becomes undoable after some significant reading about the topic. Here are a few examples that illustrate the evolution of purpose statements and research questions.

DOPING IN THE TOUR DE FRANCE—CHANGING IMPOSSIBLE TO ATTAINABLE

One example involves the examination of the Tour de France, a powerful iconic sports event. The initial purpose statement was "Can doping be eradicated from the Tour de France?" However, a close reading of the literature produced the insight that this idea could never be tested nor answered. Additionally, the notion that any form of doping or taking illegal substances could be eliminated from the sport of cycling (a sport plagued by doping since virtually its inception) seemed idealistic and unattainable. Therefore, in order to focus on a valid topic and one that would be useful to the industry, the new purpose statement was radically revised to read "This research study examines the forces and factors that influence doping and performance enhancement drug use in the Tour de France" (Spalten 3). The breadth and scope of this purpose statement led to clearer research questions that could be examined:

- What is the culture and dynamics of a cycling team, peloton, and the Tour de France as a whole? Does this culture have a direct relationship or contribute to doping within the sport? If so, how?

- What is the relationship between the culture of "secrecy" and doping?

- Was the evolution of the team unit (inclusive of doctors, physiologists, psychologists, and nutritionists) a result of increased doping, or did it give birth to the rise in doping?

- What is the individual psychology of a cyclist? Are there certain characteristics that might lead to a propensity to dope? What are the characteristics that Tour de France riders share?

- What is the role of technology in cycling? Is the line between medical technology and equipment or training technology blurred? Is medical enhancement necessary for the sport? What is the future of cycling technology?

- What is the impact of doping and performance enhancing drug use on the Tour de France? What are the perceptions about drug use? Has it increased, decreased, or stayed the same?

- Does the Tour de France have a doping problem?

- What are the current drug-testing strategies and protocol? What problems or issues exist within the current testing system?

- Is the Tour de France too difficult?

- Should the Tour de France take ownership of the doping problem or should the ownership rest with the individual riders?

  These questions led to specific ideas to test with the research design.

> *"I hypothesize that the secretive culture of the sport breeds an environment where doping usage thrives. Additionally, I hypothesize that certain race factors, including the 'spectacle' atmosphere and Tour de France organizer's need to play to sponsors and television contracts, has created a race so difficult that riders and their teams have had to seek help in the forms of technology and medical enhancement. Finally, I hypothesize that the 'team unit' includes active participation from the riders, managers, doctors, physiologists, psychologists and nutritionists, thus resulting in a dynamic that blurs the line between what is human and what is technology"* (Spalten 5).

LOCALLY GROWN FOOD—FROM BEHAVIOR TO MODIFICATION

In the following example, initial questions about customer interest in local food led to a purpose statement of "to determine if/why consumers are willing to pay more for locally grown foods." The research questions associated with this purpose statement were:

- How does the current local food movement mirror the recent organic food movement?

- Is this a regional phenomenon, or one seen widespread across the country?

- Do people feel a sense of local pride? Of social/economic responsibility for local farmers? Of status or keeping up with trends? That "local" and "seasonal" imply better quality?

- What role do media play in consumer decision making? (Food Network, Cooking Channel, Top Chef, etc.; education vs. entertainment)

- How exactly have farmers been affected by this movement?

- What are the implications of the local food movement on restaurants?

  The literature was searched using key words such as "food miles," "seed to plate," "farm to plate," "food co-ops," "organic food," "LOHAS (Lifestyles of Health and Sustainability)," "green restaurants," "farmers' markets," "locavore," "local farms," "Green Restaurant Certification," and "local food movements."

  The result was a lot of literature and studies on the topic, many of which were more observational reports than carefully developed research. All angles appeared to be covered. However, the topic of restaurant customers wanting local food had not been studied from the perspective of the restaurant owners and operators. Therefore, the original purpose statement of "to determine if/why consumers are willing to pay more for locally grown foods" was rewritten to be "The goal of my research is to identify the motivation of U.S. consumers to purchase locally grown and produced food" (Zanker 2).

And the research questions for the exploratory study became:

- To what extent and in what ways do these restaurants support the local food movement?

- What role does the local food movement play in the philosophy of the restaurant?

- What is the process by which these restaurants plan and design their menus?

- How is the restaurant's menu used as a marketing tool by the restaurant, especially as a means of marketing the local food movement?

The final result then became:

> While many restaurants may now source at least some ingredients from local producers, certain ones have the reputation of being true champions of the local food movement. The Zagat New York City Restaurants 2011 survey identifies several of these, including Blue Hill and Craft (Zagat 13). What have these restaurants done to earn their reputations as "Locavore" hotspots (13)? The proposed research seeks to explore how restaurant executives—owners, managers, and executive chefs—of previously identified, reputable "Locavore" restaurants in New York market the local food movement to their customers. Specifically, I would like to find out if restaurant executives deem it important—or even necessary—to market the use of local foods on the menu. This exploratory study will answer the following research questions:
>
> - To what extent and in what ways do these restaurants support the local food movement?
>
> - What role does the local food movement play in the philosophy of the restaurant?
>
> - What is the process by which these restaurants plan and design their menus?
>
> - How is the restaurant's menu used as a marketing tool by the restaurant, especially as a means of marketing the local food movement? (Zanker 4–5).

SERVICESCAPE TO SELF-SERVICE TECHNOLOGY

Another example involves an interest in researching servicescape and ways that unique service delivery methods might impact a guest's behavior, which led to a purpose statement asking if consumer satisfaction was dependent on or connected to unique service encounters. This purpose statement produced a major research question of "Is a guest more satisfied with a unique and memorable service encounter than with a standardized encounter?" However, a lot of research using keywords such as unique, servicescape, and memorable did not produce many significant sources.

In fact, the search led to very few overlapping studies with many that covered a wide range of fields.

A refined focus on self-service and customer satisfaction in hotels produced some interesting articles. The literature review also produced the insight that some studies had already been conducted on customer satisfaction with self-service technology but not many focused on satisfaction as a middleman, linking self-service technology usage and different post-purchase behaviors. The shift to the link between self-service technology usage and satisfaction, as well as between satisfaction and willingness to pay more, gave a new focus, and the purpose of the research became "to understand consumer usage of self-service technology in the hospitality industry, and consumer willingness to pay more."

The final result then became:

> *The purpose of the proposed research, therefore, is to understand consumer usage of self-service technology in the hospitality industry, and consumer willingness to pay more. The study will explore questions such as: What are the benefits of using self-service technology in the hospitality industry? Are people willing to pay more to use self-service technology in the hospitality industry? and What are the antecedents of willingness to pay for self-service technology in the hospitality industry? These questions will be answered through an analysis of an online questionnaire, completed by a sample of hotel guests who have previously used self-service technologies in the hospitality setting. Performing this analysis is necessary because technology is revolutionizing the way in which services are delivered across industries; exploring consumer preferences will shape how hospitality firms design their service delivery methods and practices. The following proposal provides a research foundation, a sample method, expected findings, as well as conclusions and limitations (McDermott 4–5).*

PRODUCT PLACEMENT IN VIDEO GAMES

Another example of a shift in purpose statement from the research is the story of studying video games. An original purpose of the research was to investigate the question of "Does player interactivity have an effect on product placement effectiveness in video games?" That purpose led to several research questions such as:

- What do traditional studies say about branding?

- What is meant by product placement in general and what are the findings for traditional media?

- What research has been conducted on product placement in video games?

- What are the different types of product placement in video games?

And the following discussion:

> *Companies are always searching for new and better ways to place a product or brand in order to grab the consumer's attention. Over the*

years, advertisers have used traditional channels of communication such as television programming and movies. However, companies and advertisers need to keep up with advancements in technology and look for new and innovative ways to place their products. One of these 'new' ways is through product placement in video games. Although highly popular, research on this topic is still in its infancy stage (Kim, Walsh and Ross 44; Lewis and Porter 56), there is a clear need for more studies of product placement in general. The following research will respond to this call and contribute to the current literature. The research would be very significant for marketing practitioners in the current economic climate. Nowadays it is even more important to stay on top of their budget and companies want to know which marketing channel would be the most effective. Furthermore, the research is also significant for future researchers because of the ample research opportunities into this field of research (Hanrath 5).

This analysis and extensive literature review led to a new purpose statement addressing in what ways player interactivity affects product placement effectiveness in video games and the following research questions:

- What variables affect the effectiveness of product placement?
- What does interactivity involve in video games?
- How can "effectiveness" be measured or analyzed?
- What research methods have other studies used, and what were the limitations?

These changes led to new areas of reading, which helped in developing a coherent and feasible research design.

These changes demonstrate the value of developing a clear purpose statement and research questions and then revising them in light of more discussion and additional reading. The result of the revisions was a clearer purpose statement and useful research questions.

FINAL THOUGHTS

As a result of your extra reading or changes in events, the process of writing and rewriting your purpose statement changes as you proceed throughout the research process. It becomes different as you read the literature and shapes what you really want to investigate, and it alters as you develop the research design. Consequently, it takes some willingness to alter it as you go through the process of developing your research proposal.

In fact, your purpose statement often takes on a life of its own and expands to fill the void of knowledge and research results you discover or it shrinks to fill a lacuna in the research conducted so far. Honoring this process will help you enjoy it and learn from it. Trying to stick with one set of statements regardless of what you find will make it much it much harder for you to write as you go forward.

Often, the final version of the purpose statement—and the research questions—show little resemblance to the first versions that prompted the research in the initial phase. In other situations, they remain fairly consistent. It is up to you, so long as you stay honest with what you read and how you think about what you want to do.

SUMMARY

This chapter has reviewed the importance of a purpose statement, the ideal structure of a purpose statement, the process of reviewing and revising purpose statements, and the criteria for a good purpose statement. It has provided you with ways to consider adapting and changing your purpose statement and research questions for the future.

The next chapter addresses the challenges of writing your literature review.

KEY TERMS

Impactful	Investigable	Purpose statement
Important	Literature review	Research questions
Interesting	Partner test	Thanksgiving test
Intriguing	Public speaking test	

WORKS CITED IN THIS CHAPTER

Andrews, Richard. *Research Questions*. London: Continuum, 2003.

Booth, Wayne, Gregory G. Colomb, and Joseph M. Williams. *The Craft of Research*. Chicago: University of Chicago Press, 2003.

Corbin, Juliet, and Anselm Strauss. *Basics of Qualitative Research Techniques and Procedures for Developing Grounded Theory*. Minneapolis: Sage Publications, Inc., 2007.

Creswell, John W. *Research Design Qualitative, Quantitative, and Mixed Methods Approaches* (2nd ed.). Minneapolis: Sage Publications, Inc., 2002.

Hahnraths, Rachel. "Product Placement in Video Games." Unpublished manuscript, 2010.

McDermott, Kate. "Self-Service Technology: Preferences and Impact on Willingness to Pay." Unpublished manuscript, 2010.

Spalten, Shannon Shae. "The Doping Crisis in Cycling: Can The Tour De France Clean Up its Act?" Unpublished manuscript, 2010.

Zenker, Andrew. "Using the Menu to Market the Local Food Movement: A Research Proposal." Unpublished manuscript, 2011.

With thanks to:

- Andrew Zenker

- Kate McDowell

- Shannon Shae Spalten

- Rachel Hahnraths

CHAPTER 5

Writing a Literature Review

INTRODUCTION

As you learned in **Chapter 3, Conducting a Literature Review**, undertaking a literature review is a valuable step in refining your research topic and understanding the range of studies that have been done in your topic area and in surrounding or parallel areas. It also provides you with suggestions and insights about research methods that have been used.

Once you have read widely and broadly and taken copious notes, you are ready to take the insights, information, and references gained and formulate them into a written document called a literature review. A well-written literature review both establishes the foundation for the research design and provides insights to use in interpreting the data that will be collected during the research process. In fact, as Hart, author of two books on literature reviews, indicates:

> The literature review is integral to the success of academic research. A major benefit is that it ensures the researchability of your topic before 'proper' research commences. All too often students new to research equate the breadth of their research with its value. Initial enthusiasm, combined with this misconception, often results in broad, generalized and ambitious proposals. It is the progressive narrowing of the topic, through the literature review, that makes most research a practical consideration (Review 13).

Conducting a literature review can be a lot of fun since you get exposed to a wide range of articles. There is so much fascinating information that can be derived from the studies that have been conducted in your topic area, and in related areas, that offer insights in the topic you are interested in investigating. However, your reading will not help the field, your peers, or anyone around you unless you take the time to prepare a carefully constructed, well organized, and clearly written literature review.

Although a literature review is an unusual type of writing and takes a perspective very different from most papers, it can be fascinating and challenging to compose. The pleasure comes from having a chance to share your perspective and insights and make professional judgments. The challenge comes from converting your notes and comments into a coherent and logical essay, written from a scholarly or professional perspective, which sets the stage for the rest of your research proposal.

This chapter provides information about the purpose of a literature review, the audience, the perspective for writing it, the criteria against which a literature review is assessed, and some tips on preparing it. It also discusses the role of background information, which does not typically draw on research literature but may be essential to your research proposal.

PURPOSES OF A COMPLETED LITERATURE REVIEW

A literature review is an essay that provides information about the scholars, the articles in scholarly journals, and the trade publications that you have consulted. Its purpose is to present the reader with a sense of the range of research that has been conducted in the topic area, and related subjects, of your purpose statement. It should include information about key researchers in your field, insights from a wide range of studies, and background data about the topic of your research. At the same time, a literature review raises questions about issues that have not been examined or limitations of previous research, both of which suggest reasons for conducting your research. Since a literature review focuses on the patterns of past research and identifies gaps in scholarship, it makes a credible and carefully argued case for you to conduct your own research. Well-written literature reviews are a pleasure to read since they supply information in a coherent and well-organized essay.

A literature review also serves a number of critical purposes for your research, the most important of which is providing background, credibility, and depth for your design. It shows the reader that you have read enough of the research literature to place your project in the context of what other people have done and that you can differentiate good from inadequate research.

The background is essential since it gives the reader a scope of the field and a sense of the range of studies that have been conducted in the area of your research and in related topics. It should also demonstrate a command of the key findings, methods, and limitations of these studies in such a way that the reader can trust the depth and breadth of what you have analyzed. The following examples illustrate the ways in which a literature review can indicate the range and breadth of research on the topic:

> Several studies have highlighted the growing purchasing power of Generation Y, suggesting their influence within the tourism industry to be truly significant (Heung et al. 81; Kim et al. 346; Richards & Wilson 15). Sullivan suggests Generation Y consumer expenditures have already bypassed those of the Baby Boomer Generation (285). Though Sullivan primarily examines Generation Y retail shoppers, her findings may be applied universally. Within the sphere of tourism, "young people stay longer [and] spend more than the average tourist" (Richards and Wilson 1). Their role within the industry is of vast importance, as "college students have the opportunity to travel during school recesses. . . it is hoped they will be significant contributors to the total tourism market and develop permanent attachments to individual service providers"

(Field 375). Heung et al. also found student travelers to be an impor-
tant and instrumental market segment, particularly during the summer
and Christmas recesses periods. Based on findings from Heung et al.,
tourism service providers are urged to begin advertising specifically to
student travelers prior to the recess period (94). Findings also stress the
importance of providing individualized, and professional, travel consult-
ing services to student travelers (93) (Ditto 4).

Notice that this paragraph begins with an overview comment, supported by several citations and then proceeds to contrast insights and findings from various sources, documenting each of them in turn. The tone is clear, objective, and straightforward. The next example also points out various perspectives about consumers' expectations and experience. The author provides an overview of several studies and draws a conclusion based on the review of several sources. Notice that some sources are used several times in the same paragraph.

Consumers become satisfied when they compare service performance
with prior expectations about the service and find that their percep-
tions meet or exceed their expectations (Bitner 70; Beatson, Coote, and
Rudd 853; Dabholkar 29; Ekinci, Dawes, and Massey 35; Surprenant
and Solomon 86). Many scholars have investigated the effect of service
encounters on consumer satisfaction (Beatson, Coote, and Rudd; Bigné,
Mattila, and Andreu; Bitner; Bitner, Brown and Meuter; Crotts and Ford;
Ekinci, Dawes, and Massey). Researchers have studied the antecedents
and consequences of customer dis/satisfaction in service encounters
with specific reference to personal service encounters in the hospital-
ity industry and have found a strong, positive relationship between the
two variables. Beatson, Coote, and Rudd examined how personal ser-
vice impacts satisfaction and commitment, finding that both have a sig-
nificant impact on overall satisfaction (853). Crotts and Ford found that
the organizational and employment structure of a firm aids in customer
satisfaction, and that the most effective service designs (mainly, a strong
organizational commitment to exceeding expectations) led to satisfac-
tion (238). Customer satisfaction depends directly and strongly on the
management and monitoring of individual service encounters (Bitner
69; McDermott 7).

In addition, your review should describe the range of studies and indicate the boundaries of what has been investigated and how it has been investigated. Showing the scope of the research that has been conducted builds the credibility of your review and helps to illuminate the patterns of thinking—conceptual and methodological—in the areas you are planning to research (Fink 3).

Since your goal is to demonstrate that you have a command of the material, you also need to illustrate the depth of your understanding of the research. That may mean pointing out relevant research from other areas or parallel research in other fields. It might mean showing how some of the classic models or theories have changed and developed over time. It might also mean showing a chronological understanding of how studies in your area have developed and changed—or how they have not—over the past ten years. The point is to communicate background and depth in such a manner that enhances the credibility of the literature review.

The following example puts the research on sport fan motivation into some perspective:

> From the factors that have been analyzed as influential for sporting venues attendance, a couple of them appear repeatedly in the academic literature: vicarious achievement and team identification (Cialdini et al. 368; Bernthal and Graham 235; Fink and Parker 214; Kim et al. 117; Zhang et al. 50; McDonald, Milne and Hong 106; Kwon, Trail and Lee 215; Kwon, Trail and Anderson 265; Van Leeuwen, Quick and Daniel 114; Andrew et al. 207; Funk, Trail and Anderson 18; Correia and Esteves 586; James and Ross 23; Madrigal 222; Laverie and Arnett 238; Wann et al. 14; Hill and Green 158; Mahony et al. 15; Pilus et al. 56; Santa Cruz 209; Pesce 40; Wann 381; Wakefield and Sloan 165).
>
> Cialdini et al. opened that path of investigation with their 1976 study of students' associations with their university sport teams (367). As a major breakthrough, the concept of BIRGing—"Basking in reflected glory"—was studied in the sport context. Looking at the apparel worn by students of universities, the authors theorized that when their teams won, individuals were more prone to wear clothes that would identify them with the winning team, associating themselves with the victorious endeavor even when they had no participation at all in the conclusion of the objective (370). Moreover, they found that subjects used the "we" expression to associate themselves with positive results more than when negative results occur, in which case individuals tended to use the word "they" to refer to the team (374). Taking into account those two reflections of BIRGing—wearing apparel to relate oneself to a successful venture and usage of the expression "we" when talking about a winning institution—the authors found that personal images define fans. The outcome of a game, be it positive or negative, was reflected as personal success or failure for the spectators (374). Therefore, one of the factors that affected spectators' attendance or interest with a sporting event is their desire to affect their self and social image through BIRGing (375).
>
> The concept of BIRGing has been used by different authors that developed scales to measure factors that influenced sport attendance. It was labeled self-esteem enhancement (Wann 378), achievement (Trail and James 115), achievement-seeking (Zhang et al. 43), vicarious achievement (Funk, Ridinger and Moorman 6), and attachment (Laverie and Arnett 230). The only difference stated between this terms and BIRGing was made by Kwon, Trail and Lee: vicarious achievement is the need of achievement that might be fulfilled through the association with a successful other, while BIRGing refers to an attempt of promotion of the association with a successful other (209).

A strong relationship between BIRGing and team identification was found by Madrigal in his research addressing sporting events' attendance satisfaction conducted in college women's basketball (222). In other words, fans who view association with team as an important factor influencing their attendance to a game, experience more joy and reach for a greater amount of associations with the successful outcome of the game (222).

Following the team identification relationship with "basking in reflected" constructs, Campbell, Aiken and Kent introduce their concepts of BIRFing—basking in reflected failure—and CORSing—cutting off reflected success—in an attempt to address the gap present in literature about those fan behaviors that can't be explained by the BIRGing model (151). According to these authors, fans that embark on BIRFing and CORSing are also trying to get a personal benefit out of the team performances. Those who keep supporting an institution despite its lackluster performance develop a sense of victory because they are truer fans than anybody else; presence, in this case, is highly influenced by loyalty (155). Those who stray away from a team when it starts getting successful are looking to highlight the uniqueness value on their attitude (156). For fans that are involved in a BIRFing attitude, stadium attendance is majorly determined by demonstrating team identification through bad times (156).

Regardless of the differences in nomenclatures, the concepts of Basking in Reflected Glory or Failure seems to be preponderant in explaining sporting event attendance (Kwon, Trail and Anderson 265; Madrigal 222; Laverie and Arnett 239; Mahony et al. 16; Kwon, Trail and Lee 215; Zhang et al. 50) and has to be included a priori in an analysis of stadium attendance factors in Chile.

However, even among the authors that have studied the BIRGing construct, some contest its relative importance: the impact on spectators turnout is only minor, compared to other factors such as the ticket value (Correia and Esteves 586) or the sport itself (Lough and Kim 39; Wann 381; Andrew et al. 207, Kim et al. 116; Ceppi 9–10).

Depending on the areas in which you have conducted research, any or all of these approaches might be useful; the point is to communicate background and depth in a way that enhances the credibility of the review.

AUDIENCE

Since the literature review is a document that provides a context for your research, it needs to be written with a clear perspective about the *audience*. For most research designs, the audience will be professionals in the field; their position may mean that they know something about your topic or have an interest in the topic. However, sometimes they do not know the specific studies that you are reviewing. In either case, the reader needs an orientation to the structure of your literature review.

ELEMENTS FOR THE AUDIENCE OF A LITERATURE REVIEW

- Tone
- Logical flow
- Coherence and focus
- Point of view

Well-written reviews have an introduction, a conclusion, and plenty of sections in between, each of them written from an analytical perspective. The introduction orients the reader to the perspective of the literature review as well as to the structure, tone, and style of the essay. Therefore, writing the introduction needs to be done carefully.

The four important elements of considering the audience include: *tone, logical flow, coherence* and *focus*, and *point of view*. Since a literature review is aimed at the audience interested in your topic, or related subjects, consider the tone that you bring to your writing. It should be an objective, clearly focused point of view about the topic or field, and it should carry that particular perspective consistently throughout what you write (Booth 263). The tone of a literature review should be matter of fact and dispassionate. Although you may care a great deal about the topic you are writing about, that passion should show through a carefully reasoned overview of what has been discovered and published about the topic at hand. There is no place for an emotional tone or biased language; in fact, the voice you use in a literature review is very important.

VOICE AND TONE

One of the hardest parts of constructing a literature review involves finding the right *voice* to use in the document. Since a literature review should provide a clear and objective assessment of the range and quality of the scholarship about a particular topic—in this case, the area of your potential research—you want to ensure that you maintain an objective and dispassionate voice in your writing. Therefore, consider carefully the voice that you want to establish in writing your literature review.

There are several voices you want to avoid—condescension, familiarity, and lack of enthusiasm. While you want to indicate your command of the material and show that you understand where there are common studies and where there are real gaps, taking a point of view that shows you are the wise one and know-it-all will not add to the credibility of your literature review. Explaining terms that any reader will know or overdefining terms indicates that you have not considered your audience carefully. Explaining terms when they are first introduced, especially well-known abbreviations or acronyms, should be enough. Reviewing basic material too often or in a careless manner also often comes across as condescending, even if you do not mean to indicate that you think the reader will not know the material. It also mars your credibility, a key aspect of writing your literature review. (For more information on credibility, see **Chapter 9, Validity, Reliability, and Credibility in Research**.)

Familiarity will not contribute to the quality of your literature review, either. Referring to authors by their first name or explaining ideas in slang indicates a lack of objectivity and awareness that the literature review is designed to show your mastery of the material and indicate your interest in and command of the material. The goal is to establish a good relationship with your reader.

One way to find the right voice for your literature review is to consider the reader and what he or she wants to know. Most readers—whether faculty members, other students, or industry professionals—do not care how you got to the point you did. They care about what you found, how clearly you can describe your insights, how well you support them with evidence—references to the articles—and how clearly your review contributes to their understanding of the field. Therefore, consider developing an objective, matter-of-fact tone and using a voice that indicates mastery but does not condescend. In addition, there is no place for the words "I," "me," we," or "us" in a literature review.

The voice you want to establish should be an objective, thoughtful, and careful one. Try writing a paragraph or two, focused on just one or two articles with a focus on finding this voice in the way you write. Using the third person point of view and monitoring the logic of your literature review will help you to establish and maintain this voice and help you develop the right perspective.

THE PERSPECTIVE OF A LITERATURE REVIEW

Since a literature review is a particular kind of writing—and very different from research papers and other essays—it is important to understand its scope and *perspective*. A good literature review provides a broad picture of what scholars and researchers have found in the areas of your potential research, and it shows what has not been done as well. That means that the scope needs to include a number of categories of information and relate the categories to each other in a logical and coherent manner.

Some of the categories include: scholars of research methods in the field, classic studies, key findings, considerations, insights from other fields, and areas that need research. The most important aspect of the literature review is the consideration of classics in the area of your research (Collis 294). In writing the literature review, make sure that you highlight the major thinkers or scholars in your field and point out what they have contributed to establishing this area as a field of research. Examples include: Aaker in branding, Kotler in marketing, Zimbalist in stadium financing, or Porter in business strategy. Point out what they have contributed to establishing this area as a field of research (see the **Works Cited in This Chapter** at the end of this chapter for examples of their work). That task means pointing out—and referring to—basic foundational studies and demonstrating how these individuals have established lines of research and improved on them over the years.

Key findings need to be clustered together in ways that show common patterns of insight, common approaches to the topic, similar findings from other fields, insights that build on previous studies, and alternative explanations to similar phenomena. For example, research on customer service can focus on staff training, staff attitudes and backgrounds, hiring processes, customer appreciation, measures of customer perception of service quality, service quality as an aspect of brand identity, or customer service as a marketing difference. Similarly, research on cultural heritage sites can include site designation, definitions of authenticity, types of tourist motivations, destination management, and sustainability.

Sometimes, the common insights can draw on research in similar but different fields such as the staff training literature if you are investigating delivering high quality service, research on dark tourism if you are investigating cultural and heritage tourism, or scholarship on community politics if you are examining stadium financing. Other times, it means identifying and categorizing the range of problems that have been addressed—rather than the insights gained—and how they have been approached (Hart 56).

As you consider the point of view of your literature review, think about the reader and what he or she needs to know about the quality and range of research that surround your topic so that he or she can appreciate the importance and need to undertake your project. That means that the literature review should provide a coherent and persuasive analysis of what has been published around your topic (Sekaran 67). It needs to be cogently organized rather than a description of one study after another *ad seriatim*.

One aspect of convincing your reader is the correct use of scholarly conventions—APA or MLA—that indicate the sources of all the information in your literature review. That means that you need to document your statements and show the sources of the findings, limitations, and methods. The typical way to document involves parenthetical citations, completed in the style requested by the professor or organization. For APA, the format is (Mayo 2005), and for MLA, the format is (Mayo 17) where 2005 is the date of publication and 17 is the page reference (Hacker 129, 166). In either case, the full citation should be listed in the Bibliography or Works Cited section of your proposal. Although the details of the various documentation formats are beyond the scope of this chapter, it is critical to document your statements. (For references about documentation see the list of **Works Cited in This Chapter** at the end of this chapter.) You might use a single source several times to support your comments about findings, methods, areas for future research, or patterns of geographical focus, and each time, you need to provide that documentation.

One way to get a clear perspective about the literature you are analyzing is to imagine yourself one hundred feet off the ground looking at all of the studies as a whole and thinking about the following questions:

- What do you see about what studies have been done?

- What are the common findings?

- What are some of the unusual insights? How well are they explained and supported by the research project within which they were discovered?

- What variables have been studied and what has the research found about them?

- What populations, geographic areas, or aspects of your topic have been examined?

- What related studies have been done and how do they contribute to this topic or arena?

- What methods have been used to investigate the topic of your interest? Are there duplicate or iterative studies in that area? If not, why not? If so, what have they shown?

If you consider these questions and focus on providing a clear and well-organized objective analysis of the commonalities, differences, and gaps of what has been done and what needs to be done, your literature review will be clear and convincing.

CONSTRUCTING THE WRITTEN LITERATURE REVIEW

Crafting a literature review is not a difficult task if you have taken notes of findings, research methods, research design details, limitations, and suggestions for future research.

Organize your thoughts so there is movement from one section to another. Consider carefully what you are trying to say and what evidence you can use to support the statements that you make about the literature. Pay attention to transitions between sections of the literature review—start one section with a few introductory statements and end each section with a few summarizing comments. It also means that the entire literature review should have a paragraph at the beginning—probably something that you want to write last—so that the reader is prepared for and aware of the structure and logic of your review. Pay attention to transitions between sections of the literature review—start one section with a few introductory statements and end each section with a few summarizing comments.

If you have taken notes according to the suggestions in **Chapter 3, Conducting a Literature Review**, then you have plenty of documents that you can use to compose your work. Take the time to organize the notes into categories—findings, limitations, methods of collecting data, size of sample, date of publication, opportunities for further research, implications or applications, and method of analyzing the data—and then start to write paragraphs about the areas that have been identified as future subjects that could be examined or need to be pursued. From those paragraphs, you may see some patterns and gaps that need to be identified and described in a different set of paragraphs. Working with those insights, you can then prepare an overall organization for the review, thinking always about sections that will help structure it.

Next focus on key findings, highlight the central concepts, models, and theories that have been brought to bear on your topic, and then write paragraphs about where there are similar findings and where there are very dissimilar findings. As you do that, make sure to document all of your statements and point out the nuances between various studies. Add insights to what you have found and help the reader notice what has happened or is happening in the field.

A second section might be studies from similar or related fields, and sometimes from fields that do not seem related but offer insights that bear on the topic you want to study. Examples include literature on the psychology of purchasing behavior that might be relevant to a study of fan avidity or work on branding in the retail area that might be relevant to assessing hotel brands.

A third section might focus on research methods—what are the methods that have been used to study adventure tourism or travel with the disabled, or fan purchasing behavior or college athletic recruitment of college athletes, or hotel development, or customer service in luxury hotels? In some cases, the methods have included interviews, questionnaires, statistical analyses of databases, observations, and content analysis. (For more information on different methods, see **Chapter 10, Research Techniques: Interviews**; **Chapter 11, Research Techniques: Questionnaires**; and **Chapter 12, Research Techniques: Observations, Focus Groups, and Content Analysis**.)

Noticing and commenting on the limitations of the methods, the pretesting of instruments, the use of pilot studies, the adaptation or reuse of already validated instruments, or variations of other techniques can illustrate your awareness of the methods used and demonstrate the value and merit of your particular approach.

As you write, remember to keep the third person objective voice and not make editorial comments; they belong at the end of the project and not in the middle of a professional, analytic literature review (O'Leary 82). Also remember to point out patterns and trends in the literature rather than give detailed reports on each particular study. While details count, they should support your comments rather than substitute for them.

Since a literature review is aimed at the audience of persons interested in your topic or related topics, consider the tone that you bring to your writing. It should be an objective, clearly focused point of view about the topic or field, and it should carry that particular perspective consistently throughout what you write (Booth 263).

CRITERIA FOR A GOOD LITERATURE REVIEW

When evaluating a literature review written by others or yourself, consider the following *Criteria to Assess a Literature Review*, the way in which you and others will assess the quality of a literature review.

Besides the basic organization and writing clarity, a literature review is most typically assessed on the comprehensiveness and the quality of the references, particularly their recency and relevancy. Whether you are examining stadium financing, boutique hotels, or hotel development models, if your studies are dated, then your review will be missing key information. You need to be sure that you have current studies as well as classic ones. However, that does not mean that classical studies or basic conceptual information should not be included in your review; in fact, that information may be more critical in establishing the merits of the conceptual structure you want than current studies. Remember that information from basic and foundational studies, current studies, and related studies are all valuable.

CRITERIA TO ASSESS A LITERATURE REVIEW

To what extent is it coherent?

To what extent is it comprehensive?

In what ways does it include a range of quality references?

To what extent does it describe patterns of research?

To what extent does it cover research methods?

To what extent is it clear and well-written?

To what extent does it summarize the research in the field?

In what ways does it address the limitations of current research?

Other criteria used to assess a literature review include the analysis of patterns, the depth and clarity of your explanation of the findings you have discovered, the clarity with which you explain common themes or approaches, and the identification of gaps. If you cannot make clear statements about the research already done—or underway—in your arena, then it is clear that you are not prepared to pursue the research design that you are proposing.

In fact, the power of a good literature review is the way in which it both establishes the foundation for the research design and provides insights to use in interpreting the data that will be collected during the conduct of the research. Indicating that you are aware of the limitations of the research that has been done can be as helpful to your credibility as comments on the merits of the research. Therefore, you need to focus on both the strengths and the missing gaps of current research while also preparing a coherent and well-written review.

SUMMARY

This information about how to organize and draft a literature review has included an explanation of the reasons for a good literature review, ways to increase its credibility, and strategies for creating the review as a coherent and well-organized essay. The focus always should be on providing sufficient background to establish the need for your research design.

The scope and scale of the research design are also important issues, and the next chapter addresses these issues by examining questions of validity, reliability, and credibility in creating a research design.

KEY TERMS

Audience	Focus	Point of view
Coherence	Logical flow	Tone
Criteria for evaluation	Perspective	Voice

WORKS CITED IN THIS CHAPTER

Aaker, David A., and Alexander Biel, eds. *Brand Equity and Advertising: Advertising's Role in Building Strong Brands*. Danbury: Lawrence Erlbaum Associates, Incorporated, 1993.

Aaker, David A., and Erich Joachimsthaler. *Brand Leadership: Building Assets in an Information Economy*. New York: Simon & Schuster, Limited, 2000.

Aaker, David A. *Brand Portfolio Strategy: Creating Relevance, Differentiation, Energy, Leverage, and Clarity*. New York: Free Press, 2004.

Aaker, David A. *Building Strong Brands*. New York: Free Press, 1995.

Booth, Wayne, Gregory G. Colomb, and Joseph M. Williams. *The Craft of Research*. New York: University of Chicago Press, 2003.

Collis, Jill, and Roger Hussey. *Business Research*. New York: Palgrave Macmillan, 2003.

Cooper, Donald R. *Business Research Methods*. Ed. Pamela S. Schindler. Boston: McGraw-Hill Irwin, 2006.

Ceppi, Javier. "Literature Review." unpublished manuscript, 2010.

Ditto, Diana. "The Influence of Advertising as it Pertains to Generation Y Student Traveler's Perception of Escorted Group Travel: A Research Design" unpublished manuscript, 2008.

Fink, Arlene. *Conducting Research Literature Reviews: From the Internet to Paper*. Minneapolis: Sage Publications, 2004.

Hart, Christopher. *Doing a Literature Review: Releasing the Social Science Research Imagination*. Minneapolis: Sage Publications, 1998.

Hart, Christopher. *Doing a Literature Search: A Comprehensive Guide for the Social Sciences*. Minneapolis: Sage Publications, 2001.

Hacker, Diana T. *A Pocket-Style Manual*. Boston: Bedford/Saint Martin's, 2003.

Kotler, Philip, and Gary Armstrong. *Principles of Marketing*. Upper Saddle River: Prentice Hall, 2007.

Kotler, Philip. *Kotler on Marketing: How to Create, Win, and Dominate Markets*. New York: Free Press, 1999.

Kotler, Philip. *Marketing Insights from A to Z: 80 Concepts Every Manager Needs to Know*. New York: John Wiley & Sons Australia, 2003.

Kotler, Philip. *Marketing Places*. New York: Free Press, 2002.

McDermott, Kate. "Self-Service Technology: Preferences and Impact on Willingness to Pay." Unpublished manuscript, 2010.

O'Leary, Zina. The Essential Guide to Doing Research [Electronic Resource]. London: Sage Publications, 2004.

Porter, Michael E. *Competitive Strategy: Techniques for Analyzing Industries and Competitors*. New York: Simon & Schuster, 2004.

Porter, Michael E., Hirotaka Takeuchi, and Mariko Sakakibara. *Can Japan Compete?* New York: Palgrave Macmillan Limited, 2000.

Porter, Michael E. *On Competition*. New York: Harvard Business School Press, 1998.

Porter, Michael E. *The Competitive Advantage of Nations*. New York: Free Press, 1998.

Sekaran, Uma. *Research Methods for Business: A Skill Building Approach*. New York: John Wiley & Sons, 2002.

Zimbalist, Andrew, and Bob Costas. *May the Best Team Win: Baseball Economics and Public Policy*. New York: Brookings Institution Press, 2003.

Zimbalist, Andrew, ed. *The Economics of Sport*. Grand Rapids: Edward Elgar, Incorporated, 2001.

Zimbalist, Andrew. *In the Best Interests of Baseball?: The Revolutionary Reign of Bud Selig*. Hoboken, NJ: John Wiley & Sons, 2007.

Zimbalist, Andrew S. *The Bottom Line: Observations and Arguments on the Sports Business*. New York: Temple University Press, 2006.

CHAPTER 6

Forms of Qualitative Research

INTRODUCTION

Qualitative research is one of three key forms of research—qualitative, quantitative, and mixed methods—being practiced among scholars today. Each approach is valid and has particular strengths and benefits; understanding all three will help you make intelligent decisions about what specific research method you choose and why it is the most appropriate one for your specific situation.

In many ways, qualitative methods make significant research contributions, both as initial studies that serve as a pilot for future work or as important discovery activities. Often, because it is the first part of a process, qualitative research is not taken as seriously as quantitative research. However, in order to develop hypotheses to test and prove using quantitative research, scholars conduct qualitative research to understand what might be the critical factors affecting certain behavior or events. Qualitative research also provides more depth and breadth to quantitative results, which provide numbers and patterns of respondents but not necessarily insights about why. For example, the statistics may provide information about RevPAR, occupancy rate, and length of stay, but unless you talk to hotel guests or managers, you might not know why the occupancy rate is low or high and why the length of stay is different from what it was during this same period last year.

This chapter will provide an explanation of the differences between qualitative and quantitative research, the purposes of qualitative research, the distinctions between primary and secondary data, the various forms of qualitative research, and ways to analyze information in qualitative research.

DIFFERENCES BETWEEN QUALITATIVE AND QUANTITATIVE RESEARCH

There are many elements that distinguish between qualitative and quantitative research. They include: purposes, number of subjects, determinations of significance, and reporting expectations. Qualitative research focuses on investigating something and trying to understand it, while quantitative research emphasizes testing and proving a hypothesis.

Qualitative research typically involves fewer subjects (through interviews, observations, survey research, or focus groups) but gathers lots of information from those subjects in an attempt to explore the reasons and background for their behavior. On the one hand, qualitative research focuses on the process of discovering information and analyzing it. Quantitative research, on the other hand, involves far more subjects but is focused on less information or fewer factors and issues. In a study of tourists, qualitative research would seek to determine what they wanted from their experiences and involve detailed interviews. Quantitative research would testshypotheses about difference in age and gender and reasons for traveling and how that affected the choices that the tourists make.

Another distinction between the two involves the ways in which the results are reported or described. Typically, quantitative research results are written up in terse and highly focused articles that include a literature review, the research design, the data collection methods, and the statistical analysis of results, their interpretation, and conclusion. Qualitative research articles contain a literature review, a research design, and data collection methods, but the analysis of results takes a different approach since the reports are more carefully reasoned and written in carefully constructed prose to explain the range of insights and the nuances that the research has found. Demonstrating the validity of the findings takes more writing and more careful reasoning since there is often no statistical significance to them. (See the **Comparison of Quantitative and Qualitative Research** chart in **Chapter 1, Reading and Analyzing Research.**)

The other type of qualitative research, an extensive literature review or review of the status of research in the field, contains less information about research design and data collection methods because it provides an analysis of the work done in the field— often with the suggestion of a model that explains the field or the area of research, and sometimes with a list of research projects that needs to be undertaken, as Sirgy and Su did in developing propositions and models for traveler self-congruity and travel behavior with destination images (Sirgy and Su 341–49). Likewise, Chathoth developed an overarching conceptual framework for addressing the impact of information technology in hotel operations (406). The framework encompasses diverse aspects of operations, including information technology's impact on costs, efficiency, and guest satisfaction, part or all of which may be utilized in performing future research.

Qualitative research may also seek to develop conceptual frameworks. One prominent example is the work of Pine and Gilmore in *The Experience Economy: Work Is Theatre and Every Business a Stage,* who created a four-quadrant model to understand what they call the experience economy (46). They crossed a scale of guest participation with a scale of connection to form an axis that is divided into four quadrants: entertainment, educational, esthetic, and escapist experiences (Pine and Gilmore 47–56). Wann and James' classic Psychological Continuum Model, which provides a way to analyze sports fans involvement in sports through the stages of awareness, attraction, attachment, and allegiance, is an excellent example of a conceptual contribution that fostered significant future research (Funk and James 122). Current quantitative research has been testing these models on various populations to ascertain their validity and value.

PURPOSES OF QUALITATIVE RESEARCH

The characteristics of qualitative research are several. Primarily, qualitative research is an endeavor to investigate or understand phenomena, activities, company practices, impact of actions, or behavior of consumers. It is an attempt to learn what is really happening, and the goal is to explore, discover, investigate, and learn about something where there is not a lot of previous research. For example, qualitative research on customer loyalty to hotels has provided insights about why and under what conditions customers feel loyal to hotels and how that loyalty affects their purchasing behavior. In tourism, qualitative research investigates what market segments visit specfic cultural and heritage sites. Even when there are many studies in an area, the *qualitative method* encourages scholars to keep an open mind to nuances of information and threads of inquiry that might produce new insights.

By contrast, the *quantitative method* focuses on theories to ascertain their validity in explaining various phenomena. (For more information on quantitative research, see **Chapter 7, Forms of Quantitative Research**.) Therefore, quantitative research uses a large quantity of respondents while testing them for a limited number of variables, while qualitative research remains open to a large number of variables while often only using a small number of respondents. The large number of respondents is essential for quantitative research to ensure that the variables have been well measured and broadly tested against a wide range of respondents.

Both forms of research require careful planning, disciplined implementation, and a focus on valid ways of conducting research. In some ways, qualitative research can be more difficult because it requires a careful and consistent application of observation, interview, or focus group tools to ensure that the findings have some significance. As one of the foremost explicators of qualitative and quantitative research has said,

> *Qualitative research is an inquiry process of understanding based on distinct methodological traditions of inquiry that explore social or human problems. The researcher builds a complex, holistic picture, analyzes words, reports detailed views of informants, and constructs this study in a natural setting (Creswell 15).*

Another role for qualitative research involves preparing for future studies. In some fields, there is limited knowledge and a paucity of published research, which make it extremely difficult to conduct qualitative or quantitative research. In these areas, qualitative research can explore a field in order to develop the theories or hypotheses that can be tested using quantitative research methods. If no one has studied senior citizen independent travel behavior, then conducting a wide range of interviews can help unearth the range of reasons that they prefer independent behavior and what types of independent travel they undertake. From these results, qualitative research can help to develop a series of hypotheses and create a survey instrument to measure the validity of those hypotheses. In another example, studying fan reactions to new ticket pricing patterns might start with a focus group or some interviews in order to develop the hypotheses to test in more systematic survey research.

Qualitative research can also examine the state of the research in a field and make suggestions about gaps that need to be filled and opportunities for further research. This extensive analysis of the state of scholarship in an area makes a significant contribution since it identifies common areas of knowledge, orients scholars to a specific area of research, and encourages new scholars to undertake research where it can clearly make a big difference. Providing a review of the research on fan behavior helps other scholars see opportunities for their research. It also brings together studies from areas that one might not come across and opens new lines of inquiry for researchers to consider.

A third purpose of qualitative research involves assessing the merits of a program or business strategy. Since there is no preconceived theory to test and a real interest in learning about the effectiveness of the program, qualitative research methods focus on evaluating the program, policy, or strategy in terms of its initial goals, its implementation, its effectiveness, and its impact. Evaluating the effectiveness of a new marketing strategy for a hotel or sports team requires openness to discern the differences between what was planned and what really happened. It also focuses on discovery rather than testing. For a way to remember the various purposes of qualitative research, consider the model below.

PURPOSES OF QUALITATIVE RESEARCH

A—Advocate for a cause, situation.

V—Verify information using a variety of sources.

I—Investigate or interpret events and actions.

D—Describe events, decisions, policies, programs, or business strategies.

E—Evaluate programs, actions, organizations.

O—Open a field of inquiry.

Given these purposes, qualitative research focuses very carefully on the collection and interpretation of primary data.

PRIMARY AND SECONDARY DATA

In qualitative research, *primary data* can come from a variety of sources. You can use documents, interviews with appropriate professionals or consumers, statistics acquired from reputable sources, observations of behavior, reports, focus groups, or other sources of information.

The basic issue with primary sources is their accuracy and validity. If you are using databases acquired or developed by another party (*secondary data*), then you need to determine how they acquired that information and how reputable it is.

If you are using databases, it is important that the database utilized is frequently cited and provides data routinely collected and updated through disclosed methods. The form in which they are distributed should also be carefully controlled, as data in open formats such as Excel could be accidentally or purposefully re-edited after being distributed. Commonly used hospitality databases from private firms include Smith Travel Research and PKF. Research firms such as Maritz Research and Mintel Research produce a variety of research reports that are drawn from their own proprietary databases. Mintel reports offer intelligence and trend reports that often include hospitality and travel. (See **Appendix C, Websites in Hospitality, Tourism and Sports**.) Websites of associations and organizations may offer databases, as do the UN World Tourism Organization and the U.S. Travel Association in travel statistics. Magazines and online news publications may offer repeated databases of rankings, as does *Hotel & Motel Management* each year with its *Top U.S. Hotel Companies Survey* ranking hotel companies by size internationally and domestically. Alternatively, *SBJ* (*Sports Business Journal*), *Hotel Interactive*, and *Nation's Restaurant News* provide you with news events, but they do not build or distribute databases consistently over time.

The use of primary data in interviews and questionnaires also raises issues of validity and truthfulness, important aspects to consider when conducting research using qualitative methods. (For more information, see **Chapter 9, Validity, Reliability, and Credibility**.)

TYPES OF QUALITATIVE RESEARCH

There are several common forms of qualitative research: biography or history, case studies, conceptual overviews or reviews of the field, content analysis, ethnographies, grounded theory, phenomenology, program evaluations, and advocacy.

TYPES OF QUALITATIVE RESEARCH

- Biographies
- Case studies
- Conceptual overviews
- Content analyses
- Ethnographies
- Grounded theory papers
- Phenomenologies
- Program evaluations
- Advocacy papers

Some of the most common tools used in qualitative research involve observations, interviews (both structured and semi-structured), focus groups, administration of questionnaires, observation, and content analysis, all of which will be discussed in later chapters.

BIOGRAPHIES AND HISTORIES

A classic and longstanding type of qualitative research is the *biography*, a historical examination of an individual and the impact her or she had on a company, a trend, new products or services, or ways of doing business in hospitality, tourism, and sports. Biographies involve great deal of careful research using documentary sources and interviews wherever possible. Since there are many famous persons who have had significant impacts on the field—J.W. Marriott, Ian Schrager, Fay Vincent, LeBron James, Danny Meyer, Thomas Kelleher, Richard Branson, Ray Kroc, Drew Nieporent, or Bobby Flay, to name a few; studying their background, behavior, and work can contribute a great deal of insight to our industries.

Conducting research for a biography or a history requires using a range of research skills—documentary analysis, bibliographical research, interviewing, observing, textual examination—while also assessing and integrating data from a variety of sources. When writing a biography, having access to an individual or collection of persons as well as original documents can add a great deal of depth to your research. Locating them and arranging permission to meet and interview them takes considerable talent, perseverance, creativity, and, often, luck. It also requires a great deal of background research so that you can draw the most benefit from your interaction with the individuals involved. Writing a biography or a history also takes significant detective work to locate primary documents and to sort out accurate from distorted information.

One example of a collection of biographies is the I-CHRIE (International Council on Hotel, Restaurant, and Institutional Education) publication *Pioneers of the Hospitality Industry: Lessons from Leaders, Innovators, and Visionaries.* The publication provides biographical profiles of several historic and contemporary industry leaders from all over the globe, highlighting their common leadership characteristics. Sandoval's classic work *Hotel: An American History* provides a biographical context for the U.S. hotel industry.

The challenges of conducting historical research derive from the problems in interpreting and analyzing both primary and secondary sources, as well as the difficulties in deciding what the truth and facts are, and how the gaps in sources can be filled. Maintaining an objective point of view and reading the sources with considerable skepticism is a significant aspect of writing a biography or a history.

CASE STUDIES

A *case study* is a form of qualitative research that involves detailed investigation of a particular company, situation, program, project, event, or activity with the goal of drawing lessons for other similar companies, situations, events, or activities. It involves intensive investigations in which the goal is to determine what happened, why it happened, and how others can learn from it. Typically, conducting a case study involves careful study of corporate documents, interviews with key players, observations of operations or employee behavior, and the development of a framework for the analysis.

Undertaking a case study involves selecting a case to examine, collecting all of the information about that case, and analyzing that information in a careful and systematic method. A case study could examining the Hilton HHonors program, the Priority Club program, Hyatt Gold Passport, or SPG, which provides rewards and recognition to loyal and repeat customers of several hotel chains. It could involve analyzing a new hotel concept or plan such as Courtyard by Marriott, Aloft by Starwood, Elite by Marriott, or Indigo by Intercontinental Hotels when they were first introduced.

There are several models for case studies: individual case studies, comparative case studies, and parallel case studies. Individual case studies can be focused on one specific company, such as Hyatt or Hilton, or they can involve the examination of a program such as personal seat licenses for Yankee seats or the Starwood Preferred Guest Program. They can also be comparative case studies examining promotional programs at two different hotels. Parallel case studies involve analyzing the development of two different companies, two different customer reward programs, or two cultural heritage sites and comparing the insights from the two analyses.

CONCEPTUAL OVERVIEWS OR REPORTS OF THE FIELD

One of the rare, but very important, methods of qualitative research involves the careful analysis of the state of a field or the range of studies in a particular topic. *Conceptual overviews* are very careful analyses of the studies already undertaken in a field or topic of study with recommendations for further study or the suggestion of a conceptual model that helps identify and encourage future research to fill in the gaps in current research. They also paint a large picture of the research that has been done in an area that gives readers a sense of what has been done and what remains to be studied and how it could be investigated (Kuenzel and Katsaris 14–20; Sirgy and Su 340–50). McKercher examined past tourism models in the literature and evaluated their strengths and deficiencies. From his analysis, he devised a new tourism model that addresses chaos with the tourism system (425). Other examples include Chen, Cheung, and Law's analysis of the concept of culture and Smith and Stewart's classification of four models of fan motivation (Chen et. al. 53; Smith and Stewart 157).

Although very difficult to prepare, conceptual overviews serve an important function in reviewing the status of current research, showing changes in research topics, identifying questions that need answers, reviewing methods of research being undertaken, and appraising the audience about the quality of the research that has been conducted. One of the key contributions of these studies is the explanation of what has been studied and what questions are left unanswered.

Another common contribution or a conceptual overview is the development of a set of questions that provide suggestions for future research. The value of the suggestions for future research is that it encourages and impels other researchers to address those questions. An illustration can be seen in Wäsche and Woll's work on developing a conceptual framework for Regional Sports Tourism (RST) networks based on a themed adaptation of interorganizational networks:

> *In this paper, a conceptual framework has been developed which aims not only to provide a theoretical explanation of organization in RST, but also to lay a foundation for further empirical research and implications for the management of RST (Wäsche and Woll 211).*

The challenge of this type of research design is ensuring the breadth of the reading and analysis involved. It takes someone who has been involved in research for some time to locate and analyze all of the studies that have been conducted, detail the quality and depth of the studies, and identify threads that have been opened up by persons who have been doing the research in the field.

In addition, authors of these conceptual reviews identify areas of common agreement among a range of scholars, point out different research approaches, explain the gaps in the research, and make suggestions for further research. These groundbreaking studies provide a valuable source of ideas for other researchers and help describe the state of research in a particular area (Funk, "Fan Attitude" 1–26, Lugosi, Lynch, and Morrison 1465–1473). For example, De Bosscher and others analyzed dozens of studies on the factors influencing success in major sporting events. Building on these past studies, they created a framework for analyzing sports policy in international sporting events (De Bosscher et al. 185–215).

CONTENT ANALYSIS

Content analysis is a careful and objective examination of the words and images around a particular topic conducted through an objective and quantitative analysis of the documents, not from the perspective of the original author (Krippendorff 2). It is a type of qualitative research in which images and words play a significant role in understanding something but the images and words are perceived and analyzed in ways different from their more traditional use (Krippendorff xviii).

Since content analysis involves the systematic examination of images or words that depict a specific phenomenon, set of persons, or strategies, the research needs to be conducted in a very carefully structured and systematic method (Berelson 203). A content analysis of the language used on various websites can indicate some of the assumptions about the potential audience for the websites. A content analysis of the images of professional athletes in various publications can provide insights into the ways in which female athletes are portrayed differently from male athletes. Conducting a content analysis of the language used to describe boutique hotels can provide insights about how professionals define boutique hotels and determine if there is some consensus among professionals.

The challenges involved in conducting content analysis include determining the unit of analysis, selecting the range of documents to examine, developing a coding manual, training the individuals doing the coding, developing a consensus about how to code the words, and then analyzing the counts and their significance. It is critical to establish a regular pattern of analysis and maintain objective judgment.

Given the increasing number of content analyses and their importance for understanding what is happening in cultural thinking, symbol making, and experience interpreting, it is not surprising that the field has now developed a wide range of detailed approaches. They include discourse analysis, social constructivist analysis, rhetorical analysis (analysis of delivered speeches), ethnographic content analysis, and conversation analysis (Krippendorff 16).

ETHNOGRAPHICAL STUDIES

An *ethnographic study* involves the examination of a group of people in order to understand the folkways, mores, or activities of that group and the meanings of those activities. It involves capturing the essence of what it is like to be a member of that tribe or group and live in that situation so that it is clear to outsiders. Examining the behaviors and activities of individuals at a luxury resort, describing the patterns of visitors to civil war memorials, and analyzing the rituals among tailgaters at football games could be useful ethnographic studies. To conduct these studies in a careful and valid manner requires significant discipline and consistency in approach.

The challenges of conducting a serious ethnographic study require the ability to observe a range of behaviors, analyze patterns of behavior, and interpret behaviors that might seem strange if you are not involved or belong to that group. It also requires a strong background in understanding rituals, cultural norms, ways they are enforced, and patterns of group behavior. It normally takes great observational skills and the ability to make sense of idiosyncratic events. However, there can be a lot of wonderful insights generated by ethnographical studies.

GROUNDED THEORY

One of the most common—and most commonly misunderstood—types of qualitative research is called *grounded theory*. Basically, grounded theory is a three-step approach to analyzing information, and is especially useful when there is little or no theory available to guide research (Hardy 108). It is the circular approach of trying to understand behavior by observing it and describing it, developing a model or a conceptual understanding that explains the observations, and then testing that model with the original respondents or a similar group. The power of this method is the ability to validate a model or theory against the respondents similar to the ones from whose responses the first analysis was conducted.

For example, sending questionnaires to members of a tour group to ascertain their experience and then developing an understanding of that situation into a conceptual framework that explains who joins expert-led tour groups and why they do so can provide a series of notions of what the tourists look for in groups and how well groups satisfy those needs. Checking that knowledge against the responses of other tour group participants can corroborate those notions or help the researcher develop a better model that explains tourist purchasing behaviors. It provides a greater level of certainly about the insights and a chance to revise the model based on new information. Marketing professionals who have conducted focus groups and then developed a set of products or promotional campaigns that they then test against another focus group have been practicing an informal version of grounded theory research for years.

If you were trying to understand why tourists are increasingly drawn to volunteer tourism, then you might observe some of the trips, read the literature on voluntourism, interview people at Tourism Cares (www.tourismcares.org), and then create a model or set of factors that explains this behavior and why certain groups of people are attracted to it while others are not. Then you would test the concepts with individuals who organize volunteerism trips of people who travel to other countries to help build buildings, distribute food and clothing after a disaster, or help after Hurricane Katrina or Sandy or the BP Oil Spill in New Orleans. If you were concerned about fans' reactions to various sponsorship activities, you would interview fans or hold a focus group to ascertain their responses and their behaviors. Then you would create a model to explain their behavior based on your reading and your interviews. That model would then be tested with another group of fans to see if they thought it explained their behavior. At its best, this practice can become iterative so that you can develop a more accurate, appropriate, and sophisticated but parsimonious model.

PHENOMENOLOGY

A *phenomenological study* involves the attempt to understand and perceive an event or activity as if one was or is a participant in that situation. Phenomenological studies are valuable to understand what it is like for a fan, guest, or consumer so that you can develop ways to approach that fan or consumer. Knowing what it is like to sit in one of the private luxury boxes at a sporting event, wait in line to buy a discounted theater ticket, or arrive in the United States from a foreign country provides powerful insights into the experience of a sports fan or a tourist. From these insights, marketing experts and managers can develop strategies to increase sales and customer satisfaction.

The challenge of a phenomenological study derives from the difficulty of capturing the experience of another person or group of people. Typically, phenomenological research involves observing behavior closely, interviewing individuals about their experience, and often participating in the experience. In observing and interviewing, the researcher must remain open to a variety of words and phrases that individuals use, and that might carry meanings different from what the investigator expected. It is also hard to maintain openness to the situation and not want to classify it or compare it with other experiences. When the previous experiences of the individuals being observed is so very different from those of the researcher, it can be hard to collect data in an objective manner and not react to it in inappropriate ways. Observers of luxury resorts, private luxury tours, or luxury sports boxes can sometimes not understand the behavior of the individuals in those situations or have difficulty recording and understanding what it is like to live in that experience. Researchers of dark tourism and poverty tourism sometimes face the same challenges.

PROGRAM EVALUATIONS

One of the areas where significant research is being conducting outside of hospitality, tourism, and sports but from which our industries could benefit is program evaluations. The process of conducting a *program evaluation* involves a range of steps, all of which are important parts of assessing the operation of a program, business, or activity. One of the most critical aspects of conducting a program evaluation using qualitative methods involves the use of an expert evaluator who uses interviews, observations, and analysis of documents to perform a careful assessment (Yuksel 79). Evaluating a loyalty program, a series of training activities for tour guides, or a sponsorship plan are good examples of program evaluations.

The steps include the following:

- Determine the mission, goals, or objectives of a program—not always an easy task.

- Develop with the company or organization a plan to evaluate the program and obtain agreement and support for the research necessary.

- Acquire a wide array of documents about the program, or programs, to determine the key factors in establishing or modifying it.

- Collect data from participants—consumers, patrons, users—and from the staff involved in the program.

- Consider the opinions and insights of professionals outside the program.

- Develop a coherent analysis that connects the data collected to the established goals for the program.

- Review the report (if appropriate) with key staff leaders, managers, funders, and other stakeholders for errors and omissions (and not for distortions).

- Develop recommendations for changes, improvements, or additions.

- Clarify the limits and focus of the program evaluation.

- Prepare an abstract summary of the full reports.

Since program evaluations are typically done for funding sources or managers considering changes, it is important to establish the parameters of a program evaluation early in the process and establish your objectivity as a researcher. Many times program evaluations are grounded in a particular ideology or political context; identifying and trying to limit that influence will strengthen the objectivity of your study and improve its validity (Greene 531). Maintaining objectivity in collecting and analyzing data in a sound manner can be easier when you are conducting an evaluation not funded by the business or company whose program or strategy is being evaluated. There are many examples of program evaluations:

- A program evaluation of audit of Green Certification Programs in California

- Framework for evaluating hotel loyalty programs (Hasim, Lee, and Murphy)

- Evaluation of academic programs in hospitality and tourism (Hein and Riegel)

- Program evaluation of tourism at national level for IDB loan proposal process (program evaluation of public policy)

- Loyalty program evaluation (Dreze and Nunes)—interesting structure but not a very revealing study on specific programs.

At the opposite end of the scale from an objective evaluation of a program or strategy is research that seeks to make a point or encourage the adoption of a particular policy or program.

ADVOCACY PAPER OR FEASIBILITY STUDY

An uncommon method of qualitative research is the development of proposals for a particular program, event, facility, real estate acquisition, team, or tourism designation. Often the research involves finding information that supports a goal already established or seeks to establish the feasibility of a particular project. Deciding whether or not to purchase a piece of land for a hotel development, to change the brand of your hotel, to start a new sports agency, or to build a stadium requires careful analysis from a variety of sources. Since you are not testing a theory or desiring to prove a theory but are really interested in determining what the right decision is, the quality and breadth of your research is critical.

In this situation, the challenge is to locate and carefully analyze a wide range of data and consider the opposite conclusion during all of the analysis.

Another approach is the development of a proposal to make a case for a significant program. Developing a proposal to host the Olympics, creating a proposal for increased sponsorship, advocating for the construction of a new visitor's center, and writing a grant to support sustainability developments at a cultural heritage site require careful analysis of information and marshaling the evidence to make the case for the decision maker. While these forms of qualitative research are not typically published in scholarly journals, they happen in the hospitality, tourism, and sports industries and play a significant role in new advances. While the notion of *advocacy* entails the intentional construction of a persuasive argument, the challenge is to present the information fairly, marshal the relevant evidence, and consider all of the arguments and data against the proposal you are making.

In these situations, as in all types of qualitative research, the critical task involves collecting and analyzing data in a careful and consistent manner.

ANALYZING INFORMATION IN QUALITATIVE RESEARCH

When conducting qualitative research, the task of analyzing data is very complex. Since often the data are not a collection of numbers that one can analyze using statistical techniques that measure statistical significance, assessing the relative importance of various facts, statements, and behaviors becomes a difficult challenge. One of the ways to address that challenge involves pattern analysis.

Pattern analysis is the process of examining a host of inchoate data in order to determine if there are common themes or threads that can be found in the data.

Normally, that process involves the reading and interpretation of information by several people. It starts with several individuals reviewing material and sifting through it to find what is important and what is minor. It involves trying to determine any patterns in the data. (Often, this process is conducted with interview transcripts.) Then the patterns or themes are given to others who test those patterns on the same data, only this time empirically, using the deductive as opposed to the inductive approach. When the results are compared, then there is a chance for discussion and debate in order to develop inter-rater reliability about the interpretation of the data.

Analytical software such as NVivo or Atlas.ti can greatly assist in the coding and triangulation process of pattern analysis. Such software can link key words and phrases within transcripts or observation notes and assist with building themes and connections.

The most challenging aspect of qualitative analysis is preserving the objectivity of the research and ensuring that the information collected is truthful. Individuals who are interviewed often color their statements to please the interviewer or because they do not really remember. (For more information on these challenges, see **Chapter 10, Research Techniques: Interviews**.) Information from records and observations may not tell the entire story as well. Consequently, it is important to use *triangulation*—the collection and analysis of information from at least three or more sources—to determine what really happened. Triangulation is an important way to ensure that you are not overwhelmed by one set of data or influenced by a series of interviewees. It requires comparing data from several perspectives and using them to corroborate what you have discovered from other sources. Examples of triangulation include using questionnaire results, interview transcripts, and observation to determine why fans act the way they do at certain sporting events, or using guest diaries, research studies, direct observation, and interviews of hotel staff to ascertain what guests like about a particular hotel.

Another technique used in qualitative research involves the process of collecting and reviewing data several times. Called the *data spiral*—denoting a process of reviewing information, establishing categories to sort it, drawing insights and then reviewing the categories and information again from a new perspective to ensure a careful and objective analysis—it provides a careful and objective way to interpret often confusing and unsorted information and establish some objectivity to the process of analysis (Creswell 142–46). Synthesizing the information into a more objective analysis remains the most critical aspect of qualitative methods of research. (For more information about analyzing data, see **Chapter 13, Analyzing Data and Other Information**.)

SUMMARY

This chapter has explained the purposes and challenges of qualitative research methods, the differences between qualitative and quantitative research, and the types of research methods—biography or history, case studies, conceptual overviews or reviews of the field, content analysis, ethnographies, grounded theory, phenomenology, program evaluations, and advocacy and feasibility. It has also described the difficulties in conducting each type of research and concluded with a discussion of pattern analysis.

The next chapter will explain quantitative methods in more detail.

KEY TERMS

Advocacy
Biography
Case study
Conceptual overviews
Content analysis
Data spiral

Ethnographical studies
Grounded theory
Pattern analysis
Phenomenological study
Primary data
Program evaluation

Qualitative method
Quantitative method
Secondary data
Triangulation

WORKS CITED IN THIS CHAPTER

Berelson, Bernard. "Content Analysis in Communication Research" *Media Studies: A Reader*. Eds. Paul Marns and Sue Thornham. New York: New York University Press, 2000.

Chen, Rose X. Y., Catherine Cheung, and Rob Law. "A Review of the Literature on Culture in Hotel Management Research: What Is the Future?" *International Journal of Hospitality Management* 31 (2012): 52–65.

Corbin, Juliet, and Anselm Strauss. *Basics of Qualitative Research: Techniques and Procedures for Developing Grounded Theory*. 3rd edition. Los Angeles: Sage Publications, 2008.

Creswell, John W. *Qualitative Inquiry and Research Design: Choosing Among the Five Traditions*. Thousand Oaks: Sage Publications, 1988.

DeBosscher, Veerle, Paul DeKnop, Maarten Van Bottenburg, and Simon Shibli. "A Conceptual Framework for Analyzing Sports Policy Factors Leading to International Sporting Success" *European Sport Management Quarterly* 6 (2006): 185–215.

Dreeze, Xavier and Joseph C. Nunes, "Feeling Superior: The Impact of Loyalty Program Struucure on Consumers' Perception of Status" Journal of Consumer Research (2008): 1–32.

Duncan, Margaret Carlisle, and Cynthia A. Hasbrook. "Denial of Power in Televised Women's Sports." *Sociology of Sport Journal* 5.1 (1988): 1–21.

Funk, Daniel C. "The Fan Attitude Network (FAN) Model: Exploring Attitude Formation and Change among Sport Consumers" *Sport Management Review* 7 (2004): 1–26.

Funk, Daniel, Lynn Ridinger, and Anita Moorman. "Understanding Consumer Support: Extending the Sport Interest Inventory (SII) to Examine Individual Differences among Women's Professional Sport Consumers." *Sport Management Review* 6 (2003): 1–32.

Funk, Daniel C., and Jeff James. "The Psychological Continuum Model: A Conceptual Framework for Understanding an Individual's Psychological Connection to Sport." *Sport Management Review* 4 (2001): 119–50.

Greene, Jennifer, C., "Qualitative Program Evaluation: Practice and Promise." The *Art of Interpretation, Evaluation, and Presentation*. In N. K. Denizn and Y.S. Lincoln, eds. Thousand Oaks: Sage Publications, 1994.

Hardy, Anne. "Using Grounded Theory to Explore Stakeholder Perceptions of Tourism," *Journal of Tourism and Cultural Change* 3.2 (2005): 108–33.

Hassim, Noor Hazarina, Richard Lee, and Jamie Murphy. "A Framework for Investing the Components of Hotel's Loyalty Programs" International Conference on Business and Information. July 2006, Singapore.

Hein, Stephanie, and Carl Riegel. "A Systematic Model for Program Evaluation and Curricular Transformation: A Tale from the Trenches." 2011 CHRIE Conference. July 29, 2011, Denver, CO.

Krippendorff, Klaus. *Content Analysis: An Introduction to Its Methodology.* 2nd ed. Thousand Oaks: Sage Publications, 2004.

Lindeman, Neil. "Creating Knowledge for Advocacy: The Discourse of Research at a Conservation Organization" *Technical Communication Quarterly* 16 (2007): 431–451.

Kuenzel, Sven, and Nektarios Katsaris. "A Critical Analysis of Service Recovery Processes in the Hotel Industry." *TMC Academic Journal* 4 (2009): 14–241.

Lugosi, Peter, Paul Lynch, and Alison Morrison, "Critical Hospitality Management Research." *The Service Industries Journal* 29 (2009): 1465–1478.

McKercher, Bob. "A Chaos Approach to Tourism." *Tourism Management* 20 (1999): 425–34.

Metheny, Eleanor. *Connotations of Movement in Sport and Dance.* Dubuque: WC Brown, 1965.

Pine, B. Joseph II, and James H. Gilmore. *The Experience Economy: Work Is Theatre & Every Business a Stage.* Updated Edition. Boston: Harvard Business School Press, 2011.

Poon Tip, Bruce. Sustainable Tourism. http://www.tradeforum.org/news/fullstory.php/aid/1402/ Sustainable_Tourism.html.

Sandoval-Strausz, Andrew K. *Hotel: An American History.* New Haven, CT: Yale University Press, 2007.

Shea, Linda, Christ Roberts, and the Council on Hotel, Restaurant, and Institutional Education (US). *Pioneers of the Hospitality Industry: Lessons from Leaders, Innovators, and Visionaries.* Washington, DC: International CHRIE, 2009.

Sirgy, Joseph, and Chenting Su. "Destination Image, Self-Congruity, and Travel Behavior: Toward an Integrative Model." *Journal of Travel Research* 38 (2000): 340–52.

Smith, Aaron C.T., and Bob Stewart. "The Travelling Fan: Understanding the Mechanisms of Sport Fan Consumption in a Sport Tourism Setting." *Journal of Sport & Tourism* 12 (2007): 155–81.

Wäsche, Hagen, and Alexander Woll. "Regional Sports Tourism Networks: A Conceptual Framework." *Journal of Sport and Tourism* 15.3 (2010): 191–214.

Xiao, Honggen, and Stephen L. J. Smith, "Case Studies in Tourism Research: A State-of-the-Art Analysis." *Tourism Management* 27 (2006): 738–49.

Yuksel, Ismail. "How to Conduct a Qualitative Program Evaluation in the Light of Eisner's Educational Connoisseurship and Criticism Model." *Turkish Online Journal of Qualitative Inquiry* 1.2 (October 2010): 78–83.

REFERENCES FOR FURTHER RESEARCH

Hotel & Motel Management, Top U.S. Hotel Companies Survey

Maritz Research

Mintel

PKF Hospitality Research

Smith Travel Research

U.S. Travel Association, U.S. Travel Outlook

United Nations World Tourism Organization

CHAPTER 7

Forms of Quantitative Research

INTRODUCTION

Quantitative research is perhaps the most common form of published research. Even people not interested in research follow voter polls or consumer research, both of which are forms of quantitative research. Finding numbers or hearing that researchers found information about fan behavior, ticket sales, travel patterns, or restaurant preferences can be reassuring to some people and suggest idea for new practices for others. Since quantitative research involves establishing as much control as possible over the process of data gathering and data analysis in order to assure the validity of findings, it is a form of research that provides valuable insights.

In addition, quantitative research involves a desire to understand and establish a basic knowledge of how one thing affects another. Quantitative research focuses on proving the three Cs—connections definitely, correlation whenever possible, and causation if at all possible. *Connection* involves proving that one thing is connected to another. In what ways is the economic situation related to lower room rates? It does not mean that the economic recession caused the lower room rates— in fact, there are many intervening variables that may explain the lower rates, but clearly the two elements are associated in some way. (For a discussion of intervening variables see the section on **Overcoming Confounding Variables** below.) Decreased sales of season tickets may be connected to the practice of charging for personal seat licenses as well, but it does not mean that one once caused the other, but the two are related.

THE THREE Cs OF QUANTITATIVE RESEARCH

C—Connection

C—Correlation

C—Causation

What researchers want to establish goes beyond establishing a connection since that relationship can be easily recognized and does not provide any new information or a more useful understanding. Researchers want to establish *correlation*—the ways in which one variable changes in relationship to the movement of another variable. For example, what effect does the economic situation have on hotel occupancy rates? Other questions include: How does salary affect performance of professional baseball players? or What have been the effects of visa policies on inbound tourists? How that correlation can be determined is the type of challenge for which quantitative research methods are excellent. Correlation can be proven, and there are several statistical techniques to ensure that an actual correlation exists with some certainty. Connection is the easiest to prove, but it may not contribute much insight and often does not provide sufficient proof to validate a particular hypothesis.

The most difficult element to prove is *causation*. While causation is the hardest to prove beyond a reasonable doubt since there are so many potential influences on a guest's decision to stay at a hotel, buy a ticket to a sporting event, or undertake a journey, it is hard, if not impossible to ascertain what led to the decision and the action that followed it. To what extent does one thing make another thing happen? Does lowering room rates cause occupancy rates to increase, or are they correlated but one does not cause another? The difficulty in proving causation is the strong possibility that other factors—such as seasonality, other options, political influences, business cycles, and convention or meeting plans—might affect occupancy rates as much as lower rates. Understanding more about quantitative research methods is the focus of this chapter.

This chapter will explain the purposes of quantitative research, the role of hypotheses in quantitative research, types of quantitative research, issues of significance, confounding variables, experimental research, pre-experimental research, quasi-experimental research, survey research, developmental research, forecasting, and mixed methods.

PURPOSES OF QUANTITATIVE RESEARCH

One of the several distinctions between qualitative and quantitative forms of research derives from the focus of quantitative research on testing theories or hypotheses, while qualitative research emphasizes discovering and understanding. Often qualitative research is used to develop the hypotheses that quantitative research validates or tests. In assessing the validity of a *hypothesis*, quantitative research uses a large number of responses to a questionnaire or survey or a large quantity of data in order to ensure the validity of the testing process. Although a large quantity of respondents is involved, the research does not test a large number of variables in validating or proving a hypotheses; in fact, it focuses on a few hypotheses and a few variables to ensure that the research is valid and fair and that the influence of outside forces can be limited.

Quantitative research also uses standard data collection techniques and a range of statistical tests to ensure that the results are not due to chance. It is important to prove that the results are statistically significant; otherwise, the research does not have much merit. Because the tests of significance are critical to ensure that the results mean something, quantitative research demands a sophisticated use of regression analysis, analysis of variance, tests of independence, and other statistical tools to determine the validity of the findings.

The purposes of conducting quantitative research are many, but mostly they cluster around proving a hypothesis or retesting the validity of a hypothesis or set of hypotheses by testing them in different situations, contexts, or time periods. For example, Wann's early research on team identification and fan behavior (Wann, Schrader, and Wilson 117) led to a string of studies on different competitive conditions (Wann 98–102), other dimensions of social and psychological health (Wann and Weaver 221–22), and discussions of gender issues (Wann and Waddill 488–89). Each study expanded the area of study and further tested the usefulness of the hypotheses that social well-being was connected to identification with a sport team.

There are other purposes of quantitative research methods that distinguish them from qualitative research methods. Although the primary purpose of most quantitative research involves verifying a hypothesis (as opposed to opposed to qualitative research which is primarily about discovering and understanding), quantitative research also aims to validate a model or conceptual framework that explains human behavior and corporate operations. It can be used to confirm the value of financial models, loyalty programs, marketing strategies, and promotional techniques.

Quantitative research is often confused with qualitative research when there are numbers involved. Unfortunately, the inclusion and analysis of numbers does not distinguish quantitative research from qualitative research. In quantitative research, numbers are required to prove a hypothesis or hypotheses. Careful quantitative designs ensure that numbers are valid and indicate what they purport to explain. In qualitative research, numbers are also used, but they provide support and details of the findings; they are not normally used to prove a hypothesis.

PURPOSES OF QUANTITATIVE RESEARCH

P—Prove a hypothesis or hypotheses

A—Assess or test a hypothesis or hypotheses

V—Validate

E—Examine a phenomenon

D—Demonstrate the accuracy of a model or a conceptual knowledge base

Quantitative research uses numbers and careful analysis of data to test out hypotheses about business. Therefore, the process of collecting accurate numbers and ensuring that other influences did not affect the numbers becomes an important part of any quantitative research endeavor. If the administrators of a survey do not collect all the responses, they risk altering the accuracy of their results and the value of their research. If they let questionnaire administrators affect who gets a survey and who doesn't, that lack of control can affect the responses and the validity of the results (for more information on questionnaire administration and bias, see **Chapter 11, Forms of Research: Questionnaires**). Therefore, careful and systematic procedures are essential in quantitative research.

TYPES OF QUANTITATIVE RESEARCH

There are many types of quantitative research, the most common one being survey research, which is used to determine individual perceptions, understanding, knowledge, awareness, intentions, or reasons for behavior. Perhaps the most common form of survey research is the opinion poll used regularly in political situations and elections. Other forms include experimental methods, post-hoc research, developmental research, and forecasting. Classically, the clearest to understand and the most difficult to conduct is an experimental design; the most commonly used is survey research.

SURVEY RESEARCH

The most prevalent form of quantitative research is *survey research*, which involves the administration and collection of questionnaires to determine opinions and attitudes, whether they are voters' opinions and intentions to vote for one candidate over another, customer reactions to new facilities and services, tourists' interest in adventure tourism, or fan reactions to promotional strategies, giveaways, and other forms of sponsorship activation. Acquiring this information involves establishing hypotheses to test with actual respondents, selecting a sampling strategy that enables the research to be representative of the entire population, conducting careful administration of the survey instrument, and analyzing the results. (For more information about sampling, see **Chapter 8, Sampling Issues in Research**.) All of the steps are essential to ensure that the results will be valid and that the findings can be generalized to the population at large. To accomplish these tasks takes careful planning and scrupulous implementation before even analyzing the numbers.

The process starts with clarifying the hypothesis or hypotheses that you want to test and ensuring that you have been able to incorporate it or them into the questions that you ask. This task should be easy if you have a clear purpose statement and focused set of research questions from your literature review. That step will have helped you to develop clear hypotheses as well. If not, you will find as you develop a survey instrument that the process will encourage you to improve the specificity of your research questions and refine your hypotheses.

Developing a clear questionnaire, or survey instrument, is not easy. There are many elements to consider, such as the format of the instrument (pen and paper, online, electronic pad, or telephone), the forms of the questions (category, rating, ranking, list, or open ended), their sequence, the number of questions, the amount of time that it will take a respondent to complete the survey, the way in which it will be administered, and your plan for analyzing the results. Since the order of the questions and the words used will affect the respondent's answers, it is critical to proceed carefully and deliberately through this process. One way to help yourself during the development process is to develop a pilot questionnaire and try it out to see if the questions are clear, if the potential respondents understand them the way you do, if the responses make sense to you, and if the questions flow well (Brace 164–65). (For more information on questionnaire development, see **Chapter 11, Forms of Research: Questionnaires**.) While developing questionnaires, you need to pay attention to the format and professionalism of its presentation. In fact, the quality of the design and the layout of the questionnaire will dramatically affect the value of the results and their applicability and usefulness (Brace 141).

The value of survey research is the amount of information that you can acquire relatively easily and the ways in which you can analyze the data to provide a lot of information about the respondents and their answers. It is also possible to obtain a large quantity of responses. For example, learning about how and why tourists use mobile phones provided a great opportunity to use survey research and capture information from 283 respondents (Oh, Lehto, and Park 774–78).

Although survey research is the most common form of applied quantitative research, the most powerful—and the most difficult to carry out in hospitality, tourism, and sports—is pure experimental research.

EXPERIMENTAL RESEARCH

There are several forms of *experimental research*, including pure experiments, quasi-experimental research, and pre-experimental research.

A *pure experiment* involves creating a design that measures the influence of one variable on another and prevents outside factors from influencing the results. Although experimental research can be the most difficult to conduct since the control of outside factors is so essential to proving correlation or causation, it can provide very powerful and useful insights about what is happening. There are five key elements involved in an actual experiment:

1. A contrived situation designed to measure the influence of one thing on another

2. A testing situation to assess participants' experience before and after the experiment

3. The selection of participants for the experiment and control over who receives the experimental treatment and who does not

4. A carefully designed experimental treatment that the participants receive so that there is a difference between the treatment received by the experimental and control groups

5. Data that can be analyzed in a statistically valid manner

Although these elements sound easy, conducting research on human subjects makes it extraordinarily difficult to design experiments that work and make sense. Since the issue of protecting the privacy and well-being of human subjects influences all research on human subjects, it can be difficult to obtain agreement from individuals to participate in an experiment in which you do not want them to know what you are trying to test since that knowledge might affect their responses. As opposed to survey research in which the purpose of the questionnaire is clearly stated and individuals who participate know they are being asked for their honest opinion, some experiments are designed to see what various strategies might affect their decisions or behavior. Therefore, if you tell them that they are participating in an experiment to determine the influence of thread count of sheets on their sleep or structure of a tour on their experience, they will notice the thread count or tour structure more carefully than they might otherwise. That attention will most likely alter the results. One of the ways around this paradox involves not explaining clearly and fully the reason for a certain experiment since if the participants really understood the goals, they might act in a way that created a false situation and that would corrupt the data.

Another problem is finding the participants for an experiment. Most adults do not have the time or inclination to volunteer as guinea pigs in experiments. How many persons want to read sponsorship materials and demonstrate their support or lack of it, for the sponsor? How many adults want to experience various levels of service and indicate how they affect future behavior? One common way that some scholars have addressed this challenge of finding adults is by using college students as respondents, whether it is about restaurant visits, fan identity, or customer loyalty College students are available and often willing—sometimes in return for an incentive such as payment or extra credit—to participate in an experiment (Matilla 76; Wann and Weaver 221; Melnyk, van Osselaer, and Bijmolt 84).

The critical aspect of a pure experiment involves measuring respondents' opinions or patterns of behavior before and after conducting the experiment to ensure that the variable that was part of the experiment actually made a change in the respondents' behavior. Developing the *pretest* and *posttest* instruments becomes, therefore, a critical aspect of experimental research. However, one of the difficulties in these designs is the potential influence of the pretest on the outcome of the experiment even though a pretest remains essential to ensure that the change in behavior of the respondents—from the pretest to the posttest—was due to the treatment or intervention that was part of the experiment.

Another aspect of this form of research involves carefully designing the treatment or strategy—the variable—whose impact or effect you are testing. If you are trying to prove that a particular way of treating customers leads to their return to the stadium or the hotel, then it is critical to develop carefully what that treatment is and how it differs from the service that the nonexperimental group will receive. The *pure experiment* entails the administration of a pretest and posttest, the selection of participants into two groups, and the differential treatment that they receive. Other forms of quantitative research involve less influence on your part. One of them is quasi-experimental research.

Quasi-experimental research is very similar to experimental research in that it provides control over selection of respondents, treatment and pretesting and post testing. However, in quasi-experimental research, there is less chance to prove cause and effect and only the chance to prove correlation since there is less control over who becomes a subject of the experiment. In addition, you can select the respondents carefully, but you cannot control the randomization of respondents into a *control group* and a *treatment group*, which limits your ability to generalize your findings to other situations.

If you are trying to assess the validity of your hypothesis that season ticket holders have a higher recall of sponsors' advertisements than non–season ticket holders, then you need two fairly large groups of ticket holders, approximately, half season ticket holders and half not. However, you cannot control how much of the sponsorship advertisements they may have seen. If the season ticket holders do not attend games very regularly but the non–season ticket holders are there more often, then you have two groups but you do not have the ability to use a randomizing schedule—a mechanism to ensure random selection of possible respondents—to select the individuals that you will interview or ask to complete your questionnaire asking their impressions and attitude toward the sponsor's material or products that you give them. Since you have some control or influence over the experiment, however, you can often draw significant insights and make useful and applicable generalizations.

In *pre-experimental research*, you do not have control over the two most important aspects of an experiment—balancing the control groups and the treatment group or ensuring that the treatment happens in a certain way. Because of these limited controls, this form of research design does not carry much validity or reliability and often produces results that need to be further tested or developed. If there is no influence over the treatment—or the changes in the independent variable being tested—it is hard to show with any certainty what happened in the experiment. For example, if it is not clear who got the extra bobbleheads or baseball caps at a game or how they were chosen, it is hard to determine the influence of those actions on subsequent fan behavior such as rooting for the team, buying more paraphernalia or purchasing tickets in the future. Did they like the game because of the score, the winning team, the quality of the play, the length of the game, the gifts, the weather, or the people they were with? It is hard to conclude what influenced what, when there is no conscious choice or even clear record about what happened to whom.

Since you cannot influence or control the treatment, or the variation in the independent variable, it is hard to measure its effect on dependent variables. Therefore, the level of validity is very low. The same situation is true for the lack of ability to influence the selection of the persons who fit into the treatment group or the control group (that does not receive treatment). The result is that one cannot say if there are variables influencing the results other than the ones being measured. For more information on this dilemma, see the section on **Overcoming Confounding Variables**.)

POST-HOC RESEARCH

Another form of quantitative research is *post-hoc research*, which is conducted after an event, treatment, or program. It differs from a program evaluation in that it is an assessment of the impact or effect of something that was not planned but made a real difference. Examples include an analysis of the effect of 9/11 and the opening of the memorial on tourist demand, the effect of hurricane and tsunami disasters on hotel occupancy and tourist bookings, the influence of the AIG effect on luxury hotel bookings, and the impact of personal seat licenses on season ticket sales. None of these events were scheduled and planned. Program evaluations would include an assessment of a new loyalty program on return bookings, or the evaluation of the effectiveness of new services on customer satisfaction.

In post-hoc research—a common one in hospitality, tourism, and sports—you are asking individuals for their opinions or reactions after they have been part of an experience such as attending a basketball game, staying in a resort hotel, or visiting a prison. Although you are interested in their perceptions of the experience and want to find out what led to their satisfaction, you have had no control over who attended the game, stayed in the hotel, or visited the famous dark tourism site. Doing a demographic analysis of the individuals who complete your questionnaire can provide you with some factors with which to conduct a cohort analysis, and you can find out some interesting factors that might have influenced their satisfaction. You can even prove that elements of the experience actually led to satisfaction—whether it was the food and beverage at the game, the amenities at the hotel, or the tour guide at the prison. However, you cannot prove cause and effect with any certainly.

Another problem with this form of research is the limitations of and influences on memory. It is hard enough to ask sports fans why they did something in the past or whether they might do something in the future since those questions measure memory and recall—something more fallible than most of want to admit—and intention to act in the future. It is even more difficult to prove that they did actually participate or will in fact do in the future what they say. Research that relies on self-reports confronts this difficulty a lot. However, there is often no way to measure whether the intent actually leads to action. (For more information about these problems, see **Chapter 10, Forms of Research: Interviews,** and **Chapter 11, Forms of Research: Questionnaires**.) However, this research is conducted all the time, and there are valuable insights that can come from carefully acquiring and analyzing the options of sports fans, hotel guests, restaurant patrons, voters, and tourists. (For more information on how to assess the information acquired, see **Chapter 13, Analyzing Data**.)

DEVELOPMENTAL RESEARCH

Another form of quantitative research is *developmental research*, an investigation conducted over a time period to measure the effects of some activity, event, or program. It can involve examining the purchase patterns of season ticket holders after they were forced to purchase personal seat licenses, the repurchase behavior of hotel guests who experienced poor service but excellent service recovery, or the performance of employees after a particular training program. In these situations, the goal is to measure the influence of these strategies over a period of time. To conduct this research well, it is important to use a pretest early in the time frame being examined so that you can compare the scores on the early instrument with the scores on the later instrument. If it is not possible to conduct the pretest, then you are working on post-hoc research, which is explained above.

Although the pretest is important, it does not have to be completed by the same people that complete the posttest. If you are measuring the influence of a sponsorship program on sports fans and you can ensure, with a reasonable sense of accuracy, that the population was fairly sampled at the beginning of the period and at the end, then you can still draw useful conclusions.

Often developmental research focuses on longitudinal studies that monitor the development of a cohort of specific individuals. In this situation, you need to build relationships with the individuals and continue to obtain information from them periodically so that you can draw conclusions about their maturation or change over time. This form of research has proven very successful in analyzing the growth patterns of children and adults, in particular female and male adult development. The challenge of conducting this research requires a careful design that is consistently followed over time even though the original researchers may no longer be involved in the project. It is a way to determine the influence of cultural factors and other influences on human behavior. Cohort analysis, on the other hand, examines the behavior of various cohorts at different stages during a process. Following visitors to Disney World from their youth to their later years would be a form of developmental research. Surveying Disney World visitors and analyzing them in age groups would be a form of cohort analysis.

Unlike post-hoc or developmental research, which examines past events or actions, a very different form of quantitative research involves forecasting or determining what might happen in the future.

FORECASTING

Forecasting, the attempt to use logic to predict future behavior or events, is another important form of quantitative research and critical for many businesses. Forecasting typically involves approaches ranging from the use of expert opinions to statistical analyses of data. Most commonly, forecasting incorporates the use of mathematical formulas and tests of perceptions or assumptions about the future; therefore, forecasting is included in this chapter on quantitative research. Since most of these mathematical or quantitative models use data from the past to predict what might happen in the future, they rest on the assumption that most current conditions will continue into the future, an expectation necessary to develop hypotheses about the future.

In cases, where there are no data or when conditions do not seem to have any stability, qualitative forms of forecasting are more effective. Expert panels, including unaided judgment groups, structured judgment groups, and structured analogies have been used to predict future situations especially when there is no reliable data upon which to base a trend analysis. The most common form of expert panels involves the Delphi technique. (For more information on the use of expert panels, see **Chapter 12, Research Techniques: Observations, Focus Groups, and Other Techniques.**)

One of the most popular areas for forecasting has been in revenue management for hotels, airlines (where it is called yield management), and cruise lines, since these industries all share the difficulty of perishable products and limited inventory with high capital costs (Sun, Gauri, and Webster 307). The desire to see the right room at the right price in order to increase or maximize revenue has led to the importance of these forecasting models (Rajopahdhye et al. 2).

Forecasting has also been a powerful tool in the world of finance and hotel development for years because deciding about various projects or expanding into new markets requires careful thought about future possibilities. The level of significant investment demands careful planning, and forecasting is often part of that planning.

The range of forecasting methods available is extensive. A *time series analysis* involves the use of several data points taken at common intervals of time and examined to determine any changes in the series, new developments, or possible trends. It is most useful for predicting short-term developments when you have a significant amount of accurate data and little knowledge about what affects those data points. Time series analyses have been used to predict hotel room demand, restaurant visitation patterns, and sales of airline seats.

Smoothing is a technique that typically gives differential treatment to various data from the past; typically, more recent data are given more weight in analyzing trends than data that are considerably older since the expectation is that current data are more reliable in predicting the future. Sometimes a moving average is used to reduce the aberrations or extreme outliers in the data; other times, greater emphasis is placed on more recent numbers or numbers that are associated with greater quantities of behavior.

Regression analysis is another model used to create a trend line based on a number of discrete points. It involves the use of statistical formulas to measure the impact of one variable on another over a period of time. Using the appropriate method, you will be able to determine what is the most likely behavior pattern of that variable in the future. Regressing hotel rack rate on occupancy rate or weeks left before a cruise departure on number of bookings are common ways to use regression analysis (Sun, Gauri, and Webster 310).

Trend analysis is the examination of current trends and the extrapolation into the future of the same trend line or pattern of actions and behavior using whatever method is most appropriate. Sometimes a time series analysis or a regression analysis is performed to identify a trend; other times, other methods are used. Expected numbers of visits to historic sites or visitor centers by international tourists are often predicated on past counts of those visitors with some percentage increase. Often hotels plan for the future based on the same kind of expectation that current trends will continue, and they often do. Restaurants develop their staffing patterns on the same basis. Unexpected events—such as a restaurant week promotion or snowstorms—change that pattern, but the assumption that some trends will continue is often necessary for the continuing conduct of business.

Forecasting typically involves the use of sophisticated statistical techniques to manage these numbers and to assure that the results have some validity. Sometimes, the forecast provides an actual number for a specific point and other times, it shows an interval of possible numbers with the recognition that there is some variability in the prediction.

Decisions about what method of forecasting to use often depends on a number of criteria including the value of the forecast or the amount of time, money, and staff expertise that you want to spend on creating a valid and useful forecast. Other considerations include the availability of useful and relevant historical data, the presence of appropriate statistical software, the degree of accuracy that you want to obtain in the forecast, and the time available to develop the forecast in a valid manner (Chambers, Mullick and Smith 45). In any case, all of these methods are used to test assumptions or hypotheses about the future.

In any form of quantitative research, developing clear and testable hypotheses is a critical task that dramatically affects the quality of the research.

ROLE OF HYPOTHESES

One of the most critical and challenging aspects of quantitative research involves the development of hypotheses to test. Often, investigators conduct qualitative research to increase their understanding of an area or a topic. From the analysis of that research and considerable reading in the literature of a field, they develop several hypotheses to test in some form of quantitative research, whether in a survey or a real experiment. Examples might be that U.S. citizens between the ages of 60 and 70 traveling abroad prefer independent travel, while U.S. citizens ages 70 to 80 traveling abroad prefer organized tours. Or U.S. citizens with a higher level of formal education are more interested in sustainable hotel practices and more willing to pay extra for them. Developing these hypotheses came after some open-ended interviews with tourists and hotel guests who seemed to exhibit a pattern of preferences; quantitative research was used to test the extent and validity of the pattern.

Creating hypotheses can be a significant challenge because it involves isolating possible factors that explain consumer behavior, business decisions, consequences of events, or results of programs. Often, the process requires refining the possible factors that explain behavior and isolating the key ones. For instance, do guests return to hotels due to the quality of the service, the location of the hotel, the actual brand, the price, their loyalty to the brand, their sense of identity that is connected to that hotel, their membership in a rewards program, or some other factor? Isolating the actual reasons takes a lot of analysis and examination of previous studies in order to develop clear hypotheses and an acceptable manner of assessing their predictive qualities.

Another element of testing hypotheses involves determining the critical variables in a situation and deciding the relationship between the independent variables and the dependent variables. The *independent variable* does the influencing; the *dependent variable* is the one affected by the movement of another variable, the one upon which it depends. Clarifying which variable might affect the other one takes some careful analysis and awareness of the effect of explanatory variables and confounding variables. An *explanatory variable* is one that provides an explanation for what happened; a confounding variable or moderating variable is a factor that intervenes or causes effects in place of the independent variable. (See the section on **Overcoming Confounding Variables**.)

For example, in the previous situation, which variables are dependent and which are independent? Some might say that the brand of the hotel and the membership in a rewards program are independent and returning to the hotel is dependent. A person with a different perspective would argue that the quality of the service is the dependent variable and returning to the hotel is the independent variable. It all depends on what you want to investigate and how that investigation can best be conducted.

TYPES OF VARIABLES

Independent—a variable or factor whose behavior influences the changes in another variable

Dependent—a variable or factor that changes with the movement of another one

Explanatory—a variable that explicates a phenomenon or behavior of individuals, groups, or a company

Confounding or moderating variables—factors that may intervene or cause the effects instead of the independent variable

Besides determining the independent and the dependent variables, the challenge becomes making the variables measurable in some way. For example, in the previous situation, if the dependent variable is returning to a hotel and the independent variable is membership in the rewards program for that hotel, it is fairly easy to establish membership in the rewards program—but how does one measure returning to the hotel? Is there a timeline or a pattern? Returning within a month? Or returning several times within a year? Or does it matter if the return is for a shorter stay and the guest spends less money? Operationalizing variables—defining them in terms that can be measured and counted—becomes a critical part of any research design, more importantly with quantitative research.

Once you have established the dependent and independent variables carefully, understanding the influence of one on another becomes the goal of quantitative research. Often, the difficulty in ensuring that the independent variable caused or influenced the behavior of the dependent variable derives from not accounting for a confounding variable. Also called a *moderating variable*, the *confounding variable* often may influence the behavior of the dependent variable in ways that are not often obvious. Research on tourist behavior at cultural and heritage sites might determine that the designation of a UNESCO World Heritage site influenced tourists to visit a certain location, even though it might instead be a stop on a regular tour and the site happened to be in the region. Then the research must determine if the tourists took the trip because of the World Heritage site designation or the travel company. There are often so many factors to consider that it becomes essential to determine what the critical ones are and how they can be isolated to analyze the real influences on the decision to visit that World Heritage site. The name of the company that is running the tour or their previous experience may be the confounding variables; they may explain the behavior better than the designation of the location as a World Heritage site.

One way to test a hypothesis, whether in an experiment or a survey, involves isolating the possible other factors that can explain the behavior, a difficult task. Investigators and researchers often develop a hypothesis and a *null hypothesis*, the opposite of the hypothesis that they want to prove. However, the null hypothesis can be easier to disprove and if the conditions have been set up such that only one of the two hypotheses can explain the customer's behavior. Then disproving the null hypothesis can lead to acceptance of the original hypothesis. For example, if the main hypothesis states that personal seat licenses will increase revenue from certain groups of season ticket holders, the null hypothesis would be that there will be no increased revenue from personal seat licenses. If the hypothesis and the null hypothesis match each other, disproving the null hypothesis is one way to prove the other hypothesis. However, increasingly, this matching strategy is being challenged as too limited (Schwab et al. 1106). Often, actual situations are not so easily limited to a null hypothesis and another hypothesis as if only the two of them can explain behavior or the situation being examined. In addition, the influence of moderating variables can change the situation dramatically and limit the validity of assuming that just because the null hypothesis is rejected, the other hypothesis is valid.

OVERCOMING CONFOUNDING VARIABLES

There are several strategies to use in designing research to overcome the effect of confounding variables: keeping things constant, using a control group, selecting people using a randomizing technique, ensuring equivalence where possible, treating all participants the same way, and using statistics carefully and intelligently.

Keeping things constant works when the experiment can control all the forces or influences on an individual or a group; in other situations, limiting the influence of outside factors—such as external influences—can be arranged by carefully structuring who receives a questionnaire or who does not. Using a control group that does not get a treatment and making sure that the regular group of participants who get a treatment are relatively similar to the control group is one way to reduce outside factors on whether the treatment triggered or influenced the behavior being examined. Another way is to construct the questionnaire or instrument so that respondents explain what treatment they experienced. Then that influence can be factored into the analysis of the responses.

A proper sampling strategy, or the selection of persons to participate in an experiment or complete a survey, is one way to limit the influence of outside factors. A group of participants that does not match the larger population or is selected through one or more biasing factors—such as friendly look, eagerness to participate, old age, or color of hair—may introduce other explanatory variables that explain the responses to the question. It is, therefore, essential to use a *randomizing technique* to ensure that participants in any research project have an equal chance of being involved in the research and that there are not arbitrary or willful decisions involved in selecting potential participants or respondents (Bryman and Ball 96). Asking persons to reflect on their experiences at a particular World Heritage site by posting a notice on a cultural tourism website may yield a number of positive responses, but it raises the question of whether those website visitors reflect the population at large. You may be getting a limited perspective from people who already know and are excited about World Heritage sites. That would limit the insights that you can draw from their survey responses.

Ensuring equivalence of participants wherever possible can be fraught with difficulty, but it is one strategy to limit the influence of confounding variables. Deciding what participants are equivalent to others can be a daunting task. What does *equivalence* mean in various settings? Does it mean equivalence in age? Ethnicity? Professional background? Educational experience? Reason for traveling? And how does one determine this equivalency? To make matching groups of equivalent participants, one must consider what factors might lead individuals to answer question in one way or another, and that involves making a lot of assumptions that could distort the findings even further.

Interpreting respondent statements and scores is a critical task in quantitative research because the goal is often to test a hypothesis and draw useful insights. The process involves determining significance of the findings.

DETERMINATIONS OF SIGNIFICANCE

One of the most critical aspects of any quantitative research which uses large quantities of responses to test hypotheses is validity and generalizability from the sample that you have employed. (For more information on sampling, see **Chapter 8, Sampling Issues in Research.**) That process typically involves the application of a range of statistical techniques to prove, beyond a reasonable doubt, that the hypothesis does explain behavior or that the hypothesis is not supported. To ensure that the numbers, in fact, prove what you think they prove, there are a number of useful statistical packages. Among the common ones, you may find the following useful:

- SBSS–Statistical Package for the Social Sciences (one of the first)
- PSPP–Public Social Private Partnership—an open-source and free version of SPSS
- Minitab–software for analyzing, reporting, and presenting data
- EasySample–a tool for statistical sampling
- Statgraphics–a general statistical package

The primary goal of the statistical tests is to prove that the results could not happen by chance alone. Tests of *significance* are also used to indicate the value of the research and its replicability (Killeen 350). For example, if you wanted to test whether the use of audio guides increased satisfaction of museum experience, research data might show that visitors who used audio guides reported high satisfaction. To show significance and eliminate the possibility of chance, however, data would also need to show that those who did not use audio guides had a less satisfying experience. You need to prove that there is a high positive correlation and that the response is statistically valid in order to draw a useful conclusion. In this situation, significance does not refer to the meaningfulness or importance of the findings but that it is very unlikely that they have occurred by chance and that the numbers show something worth noticing.

Statistical packages are also used to determine the correlation between dependent and independent variables. (For more information, see the previous section on **The Role of Hypotheses**.) Did one variable actually correlate with the other variable? And is the level of that correlation significant? Regression analysis is conducted to examine the influence of one variable on another and to chart their relationship in statistically valid ways. Other statistical tests of data include the analysis of variance, a comparison of the means of a set of data; analysis of covariance, an alternative method when the data require this technique; and multiple analysis of variance, a comparison of data when there are two or more dependent variables.

Another dimension of quantitative research is the growing use of mixed methods in research.

MIXED METHODS

Although this chapter and the previous one addressed qualitative and quantitative research methods as if they were totally separate and distinct, they are often combined in mixed method research. Many researchers use qualitative research methods to investigate a topic and then develop a set of hypotheses that they test with some form of an experiment or survey research. It also happens that researchers test their hypotheses, acquire statistically significant findings, but cannot explain those findings so they conduct focus groups or interviews to understand the behavior. In many cases, both approaches are needed to acquire a more complete set of information and to enable more useful findings (Creswell and Plano Clark 31–35). Although these activities have happened in different research designs, more recently, professional researchers have started to create mixed research designs that incorporate quantitative and qualitative research designs into one coherent research project. They are undertaking carefully developed and coherent mixed method designs that integrate the best of both approaches. In these mixed method designs, the purpose statement is not simply a combination of a quantitative purpose statement and a qualitative purpose statement, but a coherent mixed method purpose statement (Creswell and Plano Clark 98-99). Although there have been a wide range of mixed methods and many lists of their uses in a wide range of fields, the four most useful to hospitality, tourism, and sports are the triangulation design, embedded design, explanatory design, and the exploratory design, as described by Creswell and Plano Clark (59).

A *triangulation design* involves simultaneously using both quantitative and qualitative data collection methods to compare results in order to obtain clearer and more comprehensive answers to your research questions. A triangulation design, like the triangulation method of analysis, uses several data sources, but the triangulation design operates several research models at the same time. The information can be analyzed using separate methods or can be combined by translating one set of data to the other format in order to analyze the data in one step (Creswell and Plano Clark 64–65). Collecting survey information from a large quantity of resort hotel guests while at the same time conducting interviews or a focus group on a small group at the same time provide two very different sets of data that will expand the usefulness of the study. It also assures that time and seasonal factors do not influence the results.

Although a useful model, a triangulation design is very complicated to operate with two simultaneous designs happening at the same time; if you do not have the staff or the resources to develop a triangulation design, an embedded design might make more sense.

An *embedded design* involves complementing a quantitative design with a small qualitative design to enrich understanding. In an embedded design, one model—either the quantitative or qualitative—takes precedence and drives the design (Creswell and Plano Clark 69). For example, in an experiment about fan reactions to various sales promotion strategies, some interviews might be used to obtain a clearer picture or to enable the development of suggestions for sales promotion strategies. This model can be easier to operate than a triangulation design; however, the challenge is to operate one design within the context of another and to ensure that the timing of one does not affect the operation of the other. Conducting the interviews before administering the survey to fans may introduce other variables into the responses to the questionnaire and holding the interviews after the survey may change respondent's answers. (For more information about the influences on respondents, see **Chapter 10, Research Techniques: Interviews,** and **Chapter 11, Research Techniques: Questionnaires**.) Combining the insights from two data sources can also be challenging (Creswell and Plano Clark 70–71). A simpler model is the explanatory design.

The *explanatory design* provides you with the opportunity to help explain or interpret quantitative data with qualitative data. It requires developing a quantitative design, and after collecting the data and analyzing it, using a qualitative method to help interpret and understand the information from the first part of the research. Surveying cruise ship passengers about their experiences and future plans might provide some information, but not enough to draw detailed insights. The survey results might provide clues for interviews and focus groups that will provide much better insights on what passengers like about this type of vacation, ship size, certain itineraries, and specific activities, but it may not provide sufficient information about why and what changes they might like. A set of interviews or focus groups can produce that detailed data that can be analyzed and incorporated into the findings. While easier to design and implement than a triangulation or embedded design, in part because of the priority of the quantitative design, an explanatory design requires a long time period since you must analyze the quantitative data first and then develop the details to implement the qualitative design (Creswell and Plano Clark 74–75).

The *exploratory design*—often used to develop a new instrument—reverses the sequence of the explanatory model since its two phases begin with qualitative research, which explores a situation in order to gather data for a the elements that might be included in quantitative research using a questionnaire. It can be very useful when there is no commonly accepted instrument to use or adapt or when the situation is new and requires the investigation of possible factors that can explain behavior (Crewell and Plano Clark 78–79). For example, an exploratory design could be used to investigate the growing interest in dark tourism, the fascination with visiting prisons, incarceration camps, and other locations of human suffering and tragedy. Several observations, interviews, and tours might help you develop ideas about what motivates these tourists; from this information, you can then design a questionnaire to test these ideas, even if only in a preliminary form. This approach lends itself to a series of research designs, each building on the previous one, but it can be difficult to explain to outsiders and it can be challenging to find the same individuals for the first and second aspects of the design (Creswell and Plano Clark 78–79).

This combination of methods has produced a wide range of useful studies and insights that would not have been possible alone. When you want to know more about why people answer questions on a survey in a certain way, using a mixed method design can help you. Or if you want to conduct a design that provides both insights and even recommendations to implement, using a mixed method design can be the best choice. However, mixed methods are more complicated to design and to implement; therefore, consider whether they are the best way to proceed (Creswell "Research Design" 209).

Both qualitative and quantitative research methods are productive and effective. The growth of mixed research methods has increased their visibility and usefulness. Although more complex to implement, they can produce more powerful insights at the same time. Whether you use qualitative, quantitative, or mixed method research, you will need to create a research design that builds from your purpose statement and uses the insights from your literature review. One way to understand that process is to consider an hourglass.

THE RESEARCH HOURGLASS

The process of any research project proceeds from a broad sense of a topic to the details of a careful research design; the best image of that process is an hourglass— wide on the top and wide at the bottom with a very narrow middle.

Creating a research design starts with a wide sense of possibilities and questions, typically refined into a purpose statement and a series of research questions, or research objectives, that elucidate the purpose statement behind the research investigation. (This part was explained in **Chapter 2, Developing an Interest or Topic,** and **Chapter 4, Reviewing and Revising Your Purpose Statement.**) After reading widely and analyzing the quality of the research that bears, either closely or distantly, on the purpose statement, you are ready to consider the elements of your research design. (See **Chapter 3, Conducting a Literature Review,** and **Chapter 5, Writing a Literature Review.**)

The decisions about what form of research method—qualitative, quantitative, or mixed methods—are most appropriate for your research design must also be considered. The research design decisions also involve questions of what data will be collected, from whom it will be collected, how it will be collected, how it will be analyzed and interpreted, and how the insights can be generalized. (For more information, see **Chapter 8, Sampling Issues in Research,** and **Chapter 13, Analyzing Data and Other Information**. Those questions raise issues of validity and reliability as well as sampling strategy, subjects of future chapters. See **Chapter 8, Sampling Issues in Research,** and **Chapter 9, Validity, Reliability, and Credibility in Research.**)

The image for understanding this process is the hourglass that has a wide top and a wide base. In the middle sits the research design since it needs to be very carefully focused and developed in order to assure that you can answer the research questions that you have posed and draw useful and significant insights from your analysis of the data.

RESEARCH HOURGLASS

Topic

Purpose statement

Research questions

Research design

Sampling

Data collection

Data analysis

Generalizations

The wide reading you undertook for your literature review and the careful analysis of your findings enable you both to identify limitations of the design and indicate future areas of research, some of which are suggested by the conduct of your research project and some by the findings and how they can be interpreted. This prior work also helps you apply the insights from your study to other situations and draw implications for practice. Generalizing your insights makes your research more significant and helps contribute to the hospitality, tourism, and sports industries.

SUMMARY

This chapter has focused on the forms of quantitative research—survey research, experimental research, development research, forecasting—as well as mixed methods. It has also provided explanations of the power of hypotheses, the challenge so overcoming confounding or moderating variables, and the importance of determining significance. It has ended with a discussion of the research hourglass and information about how all the parts of the research process fit together.

The next chapter will provide a discussion of a critical aspect of any design—sampling. Who will be the subjects of your research design? Who will you survey? Who will you interview? What documents will you review? What parameters do you need to consider in deciding how to gather data? How can you prevent, or at least limit, bias in the sampling process so that you can draw reasonable insights from your research?

These questions and others will be addressed in **Chapter 8, Sampling Issues in Research.**

KEY TERMS

Causation	Forecasting	Randomizing technique
Confounding variable	Hypothesis or hypotheses	Regression analysis
Connection	Independent variable	Significance
Control group	Moderating variable	Smoothing
Correlation	Null hypothesis	Survey research
Dependent variable	Pre-experimental research	Time series analysis
Developmental research	Pretest	Treatment group
Embedded design	Post-hoc research	Trend analysis
Experimental research	Posttest	Triangulation design
method	Pure experiment	
Explanatory variable	Quasi-experimental research	

WORKS CITED IN THIS CHAPTER

Alreck, Pamela L., and Robert Settle. *The Survey Research Handbook*. Homewood: Irwin, 1985.

Brace, Ian. *Questionnaire Design: How to Plan, Structure, and Write Survey Material for Effective Market Research*. London and Sterling: Kogan Page, 2004.

Creswell, John W. *Research Design: Qualitative, Quantitative, and Mixed Methods Approaches*. 2nd ed. Thousand Oaks; Sage, 2003.

Creswell, John W. *Qualitative Inquiry and Research Design: Choosing Among Five Approaches*. 2nd ed. Thousand Oaks: Sage, 2007.

Creswell, John W., and Vicki L. Plano Clark. *Designing and Conducting Mixed Methods Research*. Thousand Oaks: Sage, 2007.

Corbin, Juliet, and Anselm Strauss. *Basics of Qualitative Research: Techniques and Procedures for Developing Grounded Theory*. 3rd ed. Los Angeles: Sage, 2008.

Imai, Kosuke, Luke Keele, Dustin Tingley, and Teppei Yamamoto. "Unpacking the Black Box of Causality: Learning about Causal Mechanisms from Experimental and Observational Studies." *American Political Science Review 105* (2011): 765–90.

Iarossi, Giuseppe. *The Power of Survey Design: A User's Guide for Managing Surveys, Interpreting Results, and Influencing Respondents*. Washington DC: World Bank, 2006.

Killeen, Peter R. "An Alternative to Null-Hypothesis Significance Tests." *Psychological Science* 16 (2005): 345–53.

Lawrence, Michael J., Robert H. Edmundson, and Marcus J. O'Connor. "An Examination of the Accuracy of Judgmental Exploration of Time Series." *International Journal of Forecasting* 1 (1985): 25–35.

Leedy, Paul D., and Jeanne Ellis Ormrod. *Practical Research: Planning and Design*. 9th ed. Boston: Pearson, 2010.

Matilla, Anna S. "Emotional Bonding and Restaurant Loyalty." *Cornell Hotel and Restaurant Administration Quarterly* 42 (2001): 73–79.

Melnyk, Valentyna, Stijn M.J. van Osselaer, and Tammo H.A. Bijmolt. "Are Women More Loyal Customers Than Men? Gender Differences in Loyalty to Firms and Individual Service Providers." *Journal of Marketing* 73 (2009): 82–96.

Oh, Sujin, Xinran Y. Lehto, and Jungkun Park. "Travelers' Intent to Use Mobile Technologies as a Function of Effort and Performance Expectancy." *Journal of Hospitality Marketing & Management* 18 (2009): 765–81.

Rajopahdhye, Mihir, Mounir Ben Ghalia, Paul P. Wang, Timothy Baker, and Craig V. Eister. "Forecasting Uncertain Hotel Room Demand." *Information Sciences* 132 (2001): 1–11.

Schwab, Andreas, Eric Abrahamson, William H. Starbuck, and Fiona Fidler. "Researchers Should Make Thoughtful Assessments Instead of Null-Hypothesis Significance Tests." *Organization Science* 22 (2011): 1–11.

Sun, Xiadong, Dinesh K. Gauri, and Scott Webster. "Forecasting for Cruise Line Revenue Management." *Journal of Revenue and Pricing Management* 10 (2011): 306–24.

Wann, Daniel, Michael Schrader, and Anthony Wilson. "Sport Fan Motivation: Questionnaire Validation, Comparisons by Sport, and Relationship to Athletic Motivation." *Journal of Sport Behaviour* 22.1 (1999): 114–39.

Wann, Daniel L, "Motivational Profiles of Sports Fans of Different Sports." *Sport Marketing Quarterly* 17 (2008): 6–19.

Wann, Daniel L., Jodi Martin, Frederick G. Grieve, and Lisa Gardner. "Social Connections at Sporting Events: Attendance and its Positive Relationship with State Social Psychological Well-being." *North American Journal of Psychology* 10 (2008): 229–38.

Wann, Daniel, and Stephen Weaver, "Understanding the Relationship between Sport Team Identification and Dimensions of Social Well-being." *North American Journal of Psychology* 11 (2009): 219–30.

Wann, Daniel, and Paula J. Waddill. "Predicting Sport Fan Motivation Using Anatomical Sex and Gender Role Orientation." *North American Journal of Psychology* 5 (2003): 485–98.

Wann, Daniel L., and Stephen Weaver. "Understanding the Relationship between Sport Team Identification and Dimensions of Social Well-being." *North American Journal of Psychology* 11 (2009): 219–30.

Werhan, Patricia H., Laura P. Hartman, Dennis Moberg, Elaine Englehardt, Michael Pritchard, and Bidhan Parmar. "Social Constructivism, Mental Models, and Problems of Obedience." *Journal of Business Ethics* 100 (2011): 103–18.

CHAPTER 8

Sampling Issues in Research

INTRODUCTION

Sampling is one of the most critical aspects of planning research since it is impossible to survey a complete population all at the same time. It involves selecting a small number of respondents from a total population in a carefully planned manner so that you can generalize findings from the smaller number of respondents to the larger population. The sample is the smaller group and the population refers to all persons that might be surveyed if you had unlimited resources. Surveying an entire population is referred to as a *census*.

In conducting qualitative, quantitative or mixed method research, there are a number of sampling issues to consider: rationale for sampling, selecting a sample, types of sampling, sampling bias, and sample size. The size of the sample, the scope of the research, the nature of the people (or data) you consult makes a tremendous impact on the quality of your findings. Therefore, it is critical to consider the range of sampling issues in designing any research project.

Sampling is a challenge for most researchers; in both qualitative and quantitative research, you must consider how to sample observations as well as select individuals to interview or question, documents to analyze, or participants for focus groups. In all of these situations, making careful and intentional decisions will affect the quality and rigor of your research. Although some think sampling is a simple issue of selecting individuals to interview or complete questionnaires, thinking and planning carefully can make a huge difference in the validity and reliability of your research. (For more information on validity and reliability, see **Chapter 9, Validity, Reliability, and Credibility in Research**.)

In fact, when you hear polling results, you often hear about the sampling issues when the report includes an error factor of plus or minus a few points and information about confidence level.

Accordingly, this chapter will examine the reasons for sampling, strategies for selecting samples, types of research, and their impact on sampling, sampling bias, and sample size, both in creating a design and in actually implementing the design. It is one thing to develop a plan and another to actually put that design into practice.

REASONS FOR SAMPLING

Sampling can become one of the most complex processes in conducting research and one of the most critical if you want to ensure the validity and usefulness of your findings. In most cases, it is impossible—if not improbable or unnecessary—to test a complete population (the entire group of units, individuals, or programs from which a sample will be drawn). It takes too much time, energy, money, and other resources and often does not produce better insights than a carefully chosen sample (Sekaran 267). In fact, selecting a careful sample (a subset of the whole population) by using a structured sampling strategy can produce good insights and save considerable time and money (Sekaran 265). Some research indicates that for a general population, the level of precision will not increase after a sample size reaches 380, and most research does not need to exceed this level of precision (Krejcie and Morgan 670).

There are many reasons for sampling a group of people or respondents rather than an entire population. They include issues of staff, time, efficiency, accuracy, and money. (See the box **Reasons for Sampling**.)

REASONS FOR SAMPLING

S Staff

T Time

E Efficiency

A Accuracy

M Money

One of the critical problems in conducting any research is the use of resources and the amount of time and energy you have to devote to collecting and analyzing information. In the case of sampling, it takes *staff* to interview a number of individuals, transcribe the results, and then analyze them for patterns. In addition, you need to train each of the interviewers to conduct the interviews in an objective and professional manner. When conducting observations, the training can be even more complex, and many people need to be involved to be able to develop a comprehensive picture of what is being observed. (For more information about preventing interviewer bias and what is involved in conducting good interviews, see **Chapter 10, Research Techniques: Interviews**.)

If you decide to do the interviews or observations yourself, then they will absorb a great deal of your time. Distributing questionnaires in person—using any form of contacting potential respondents—takes staff time as well. Even mailed questionnaires take time to create copies, address envelopes, stamp the envelopes, and then place the envelopes in the mail. Electronic questionnaires also involve energy because developing the instrument and reviewing it as well as locating and collecting email addresses can be complicated tasks.

A second concern is the *time* involved in conducting the research. Picking a smaller sample size typically means less people to interview, fewer questionnaires to analyze, and less data to collect. Along with less time comes more *efficiency*. The decisions you make about sampling a part of the population can affect the level of efficiency that you can bring to the task.

The fourth issue involves resources—*money*, software, and energy that you have to spend on the sampling process to ensure that you get results that are worth your effort. Sometimes, the lack of unlimited resources can yield a better research design since you are forced to be very thoughtful about the sampling process and the results that you want to find. Other times, the purpose statement and research questions require considerable financial resources to gather the data and analyze them carefully even if you have the staff. If you are analyzing the reasons that visitors come to a tourism site, you need to question enough of them and in a systematic manner to be able to draw reasonable and valid conclusions.

The key question relates to the *accuracy* that you need with the results, relative to your potential findings and the credibility of your research. If you need perfect accuracy, then the care you put into sampling and the size of your sample will increase exponentially. However, most research can be adequately conducted at the 95% confidence level (Sekaran 288).

The issue of confidence level is your degree of certainty that the result you have obtained from your sample is within x percentage of the answer for the total population that your sample represents. If you have unlimited resources or a fund to support the data gathering and analysis aspects of your work, then you can think more broadly about how many people you want to contact or how many data sources will be important to consult. However, it is very easy to get fooled into thinking that more information is better. Sometimes, less information is better since you think more carefully about what data you want to collect and how you will analyze it. In addition, more respondents do not automatically mean the answers change or are more valid. Therefore, a smaller sample may yield as much, if not more, information.

STRATEGIES FOR SELECTING A SAMPLE

The process of selecting a sample depends on a variety of factors, chiefly the purpose statement and the research questions you want to answer, your knowledge about the population, the type of research you are conducting, and the resources available to you in conducting the research.

When you are conducting quantitative research, you need to select a sample size and selection process that enables you to assess the validity of your hypotheses with a level of significance that you can support. The collection of all the elements of a sample is called the *sample frame*. All the possible persons in a group who might be selected as members of a sample is called the *population frame*.

Your resources will affect what kind of sampling that you can do. If you want a national or regional sample, for example, you need access to databases, email lists, or other ways of contacting that population as well as a mechanism or strategy for organizing that data into a sample.

SAMPLE SELECTION PROCESS

There are many factors to consider in selecting a sample. They range from the issues already mentioned above—staff available, time to spend, efficiency that you can achieve, accuracy needed, and money to spend on collecting and analyzing data—as well as the nature of your purpose statement and research questions. The key issue comes back to your purpose statement and the research questions.

Your purpose statement and research questions should determine what your population is and then assist you in organizing your sampling strategy. If you are trying to explore an issue, then it might not be important to obtain a certain type of respondent or ensure that he or she is representative of the entire population. For example, if you are investigating baby boomers taking volunteer work vacations or determining the reasons travelers stay in boutique hotels, it might be worth conducting a pilot study to determine what factors should be part of a more comprehensive study. If you are trying to determine why customers patronize certain restaurants, then the population could be all restaurant patrons, but it would be impossible and inefficient to survey all possible restaurant patrons. Therefore, you need to select a subset of the population—called a sample—to survey.

In certain types of qualitative research in which the research is trying to establish the parameters for a future investigation, the quantity of responses and their representativeness might not be so important. The depth or range of the answers to questions on a questionnaire or in an interview might be sufficient for your purposes.

If, on the other hand, you are trying to prove a hypothesis or several of them, then the way in which you select a sample becomes critical. You want to make sure that your sample represents the larger population from which it was drawn. You may also need to make sure that your sample reflects certain categories or groups of respondents that mirror the composition of those groups in the population at large (see cluster and quota sampling in the following section).

SAMPLING STRATEGIES

There are many forms of sampling, and all of them have their value and usefulness. Deciding which method is most appropriate depends on knowing the advantages and challenges of each method and selecting the form that meets your needs as defined by the problem you are trying to solve or the purposes of your research.

Sampling strategies are normally divided into probability sampling (also called representative sampling) and non-probability sampling (Robson 261). *Probability sampling* works best when you need to ensure that your sample reflects, in certain important ways, the larger population from which it is drawn. It also requires randomization—or some specific and systematic process of selecting respondents so that their choice is not based on arbitrariness or criteria that would distort their responses.

For *non-probability sampling*, however, the issue of randomization is not critical since there is no need to guarantee that the sampling units reflect the larger population. In fact, in some non-probability sampling methods, you choose the respondents specifically for a reason such as their job, experience, position, or insight. (For more information, see the section on **purposive sampling** below.)

Recently, there has been an increase in *Internet sampling*, which involves using the World Wide Web to locate persons to complete survey instruments. Some of the strategies that have been used include inviting visitors to websites or blogs to complete questionnaires, providing Internet users with URLs to online surveys, or recruiting *ad hoc* groups with various software packages such as meetup.com. More sophisticated strategies involve creating panels of persons who agree to become survey recipients on a range of topics (similar to a focus group), and the use of opt-in groups whereby persons can join a group that is being established for the sole purpose of responding to questionnaires or other documents.

One of the challenges of Internet sampling is the inherent limitation of a group of respondents who stumble across your website, blog, or opt-in group while they are surfing the Internet. Their common backgrounds and behavior in surveying the Internet may distinguish them as different and distinct from the general population. They may also not fit the profile of the persons you want to complete your survey.

There is also no way to measure the seriousness with which these individuals respond to your survey instrument, which raises questions about the usefulness and relevance of their responses. For example, if you are hoping to survey guests who have recently eaten at a restaurant with a tasting menu, your respondents might complete the questionnaire but not have really participated in that experience. There is also an inherent distinction between those people spending time surfing the web and the general population at large. Internet sampling is neither probability sampling nor non-probability sampling, which limits its usefulness.

PROBABILITY SAMPLING STRATEGIES

The most common type of probability sampling is *simple random sampling*. Simple random sampling is the process of selecting respondents for a sample on the basis of a systematic method that ensures all members of a population have an equal chance of being selected to become a participant or respondent in your research. It is critical to provide that system to ensure that you as the researcher knows what chances each participant or respondent has. The procedures enable you to make careful statements about the sample and the extent to which it represents the full population from which it is taken.

In either case, the principle of establishing a process and method for randomizing becomes really critical. In fact, the word *random* as used in research means something very special and is very different than random in everyday life. In research, random means randomized—i.e., a process of choosing subjects or participants has been implemented to make sure that there are no arbitrary or capricious factors affecting the choice or respondents or participants.

Stratified random sampling is the process of ensuring that the randomized process of selecting members of the sample is arranged so that particular aspects of the total population are reflected in the sample. Stratified random sampling brings the same method to a section of a population to make sure that all critical subsets or groups of a population are likely to be chosen as participants or respondents. For example, while a simple random sampling process might work for hotel guests, you might want to stratify the sample for reasons of traveling—such as leisure, business, or friends and family—or by gender or category of hotel guest—single traveler, couple, or family. In this way, you will get sample results from each of these groups that reflect the proportion of those sections of the larger population.

In effect, you stratify the population into sections and sample according to those sections. Most researchers do it for efficiency and ease in applying various statistical methods. If you are interested in comparing the responses of regular restaurant customers to first-time visitors to a restaurant, then you will want to stratify the sample so that you randomize among those who are regular patrons and those who arrive for the first time or come casually but not regularly. Maintaining the randomizing process helps prevent adding bias to the results and ensures that each person—with their stratification group—has an equal chance of being selected as a respondent in the survey.

Proportional stratified random sampling, like stratified random sampling, uses a random process for each stratification group but also ensures that the balance among the stratification groups matches the proportion of those stratifications in the population at large. It makes the statistical analysis easier, but it requires knowledge of the stratifications in the total population and the ability to ensure that the sample stratification groups match the total population. In the restaurant example previously described, if you want to stratify by education, occupation, and visitor type (regular versus casual visitor), you would need to know the ratios among those groups in the total population in order to design the sampling strategy. However, once you have collected the data, the analysis of it will be easier since you have already replicated the ratios in the sample to match the ratios in the population at large, and making generalizations is easier, too.

Area sampling involves selecting participants for your research that come from certain areas or regions such as a neighborhood, city, or local district. Typically, area sampling involves defining a geographic area and requires the application of randomizing the population who live or work in that area. For example, you might identify and survey persons who lived near a stadium or arena to understand their impressions of having a new stadium in their neighborhood. Or you might want to interview persons regarding the building of a new hotel and sample residents in the area closest to the hotel, as well as residents in more distant areas to determine if differences in opinions about the hotel vary with distance from the hotel or other neighborhood idiosyncrasies.

Cluster sampling involves picking a subset of the population by common characteristics such as age, ethnic background, commitment to travel, economic situation, pattern of hotel stays, sports avidity, or other key characteristic (Sekaran 274). Conducting tourism research by surveying people according to their common demographic or ethnographic background would be cluster sampling.

An unusual form of probability sampling involves double sampling. *Double sampling* is a form of acquiring information from a group of participants and then resampling the original population to test out ideas or interpretations of activities, events, or situations. It does not necessarily mean that an individual will be surveyed twice, but it does mean that the members of the population will be sampled and surveyed a second time. Double sampling involves sampling twice by returning to the original population and employing another random sampling model for the same population base from which the original sample was taken. By using probability sampling techniques again, you can test information from the first survey or corroborate and expand insights by asking questions different from the first sampling activity. Some individuals may get a second survey and others may not. In some cases, double sampling is used in a mixed model when the persons chosen to be respondents the first time were selected through a randomized method, but their contact information was kept and the second sampling was directed, intentionally, to the same individuals who responded to the first survey.

Besides probability sampling strategies, there are significant reasons to organize a sampling strategy in which you intentionally select your respondents. In these situations, you are not interested in making sure that your respondents reflect the large population. You select them using a range of strategies different from probability sampling.

NON-PROBABILITY SAMPLING STRATEGIES

In qualitative research when you are not trying to prove or test a hypothesis or other perspective on industry practice or consumer behavior, you are more likely to use non-probability sampling since your respondents do not need to represent the larger population from which they are drawn. In fact, you may want to select your respondents carefully and intentionally because of their background or their situation. The types of non-probability sampling include purposive sampling, quota sampling, convenience sampling, intercept sampling, snowball sampling, and destructive sampling.

Purposive sampling, often called *judgmental sampling*, involves carefully selecting the individuals that you want to interview or survey based on their expertise or position. It is a form of intentional sampling that requires finding persons with insight, expertise, or experience so that they provide you with the level and detail of information that you need. For example, if you are interested in the training practices for front desk staff, then it makes sense to interview training staff about front desk staff training rather than front desk managers since the training directors are the most knowledgable about their training experience and practices. A second example would be interviewing trainers and coaches about athlete's concussions since these individuals would know from their professional experience and training about concussions. Athletes would not. Another example would be surveying museum directors and their directors of development about the success of their philanthropic efforts; they are the only ones who know what they are doing and how well the strategies are working. It is easier, quicker, and more valid to survey them than others. Surveying large donors might also be helpful but the donors might not know the range of philanthropic efforts and their history; they would only know what affected them. It does not matter that you have not sampled the population at large; in fact, that experience would not be useful.

Interviewing front desk staff and front desk managers about their experience would be using a *target sample*, surveying the persons involved in the experience or who are the subjects of a program or activity or *relevant sample*. They know what the training was like from a participant's perspective but do not have the expertise about training. Using a relevant sample becomes important since it would not make sense to do a random sampling of hotel employees who do not have the expertise to answer the questions you want to pose.

When using judgmental sampling, so long as you select the individuals carefully, depending on your purpose statement and research questions, and explain the criteria that you use to choose them, you contribute to the validity of your research. If you cannot—or do not—explain why you chose the individuals you did, then your sampling method becomes a form of convenience sampling. Remember that in purposive sampling, you choose the respondents based on their position or expertise, not just because of their experience although their experience can be a factor. Choosing people who attend a basketball game, a Broadway show, or an art gallery opening is not a form of purposive sampling; these examples are forms of target sampling. Rather, purposive sampling would involve selecting trainers to interview because of their positions. In purposive sampling, it is critical to find the persons with the expertise to contribute to the situation. Interviewing players about their salaries is very different from interviewing experts in player compensation.

Another version of judgmental sampling is *quota sampling*, the process of selecting possible participants so that their characteristics mirror the large population from which the sample is being drawn. Often, quota sampling is done to make sure that the sample reflects the gender balance or ethnic background or ratio of business travelers to tourists in the population at large. It may be used to ensure that research on sports fans reflects the balance of season ticket holders to individual ticket purchasers or the members of a repeat guest rewards program to those who do not belong to one. It does not, however, randomize possible respondents within that group so the sampling does not represent the population at large. To make quota sampling work, you need to know the proportions in the general population of the issues upon which you will build the quota for the sampling process. If you do not know, or cannot find out, the gender balance of sports fans among all fans of a team or the balance of business and tourist hotel patrons among all hotel guests, then you cannot establish the criteria for a quota system. Instead, you will be employing a target sampling strategy.

A third form of non-probability sampling is *convenience sampling*, the use of respondents who are easy to locate and use. As the word implies, finding accessible respondents who are easy to interview or survey makes the data gathering process easy but raises other questions about the extent to which the group is representative of the large population that you want to make statements about. However, convenience sampling can be used effectively in a pilot study when you are testing an instrument before using it on a large scale or when you are not concerned that your sample reflects the population at large. This sampling method is very convenient for the researcher or the team. Sometimes faculty members use college students as subjects for research since they are easy to locate and will often participate in a survey for extra credit, to assist their faculty member, or for the fun of doing it. However, generalizing the results of a survey of college students to hotel general managers or museum directors is a big stretch.

Convenience sampling will not determine what specific groups of persons think because it is a non-probability form of sampling and does not represent a larger population; therefore, the results are not easily applied to other situations.

Intercept sampling is a form of sampling that involves finding and interviewing or surveying individuals based on their location or the time that that are in a particular location. It is often used to survey persons when they are arriving at or leaving a particular venue, such as surveying fans leaving a stadium, the audience leaving a game, or the tourists in Times Square. Handing out questionnaires about audience expectations and experience as people leave a theater is also a good example of intercept sampling. Other examples of intercept sampling include interviewing persons in airports about their experience in the country or their future plans. Since they are waiting to board flights, they typically have plenty of free time and are often amenable to answer questions.

One of the problems with intercept sampling involves the many factors that can influence the results. Persons who stop to answer your questions may not be representative of the group in several ways. Those who are willing to talk tend to be better educated and more thoughtful about their responses. Those that stop often do not have to catch public transportation, or are not in a rush. Unfortunately, many individuals are increasingly concerned about being approached by strangers in an unfamiliar location and are afraid to give them any information or answer questions.

Snowball sampling, similar to intercept sampling, is a method of sampling respondents by asking current respondents to suggest other respondents. In effect, you snowball from one person to another. The use of social media and websites has made snowball sampling an increasingly popular method of sampling respondents since the process encourages referral and self-selection. Only people really interested or involved in your area will complete your survey or be interested in being interviewed. Snowball sampling happens at racetracks and sporting activities when one fan completes a questionnaire or an interview and is encouraged to suggest other persons to come and get interviewed or complete a questionnaire. It yields useful information from people who know or care about a topic.

In some situations, it is necessary to eliminate the sample that you are testing. *Destructive sampling* is a form of sampling in which the sample members are eliminated or altered in a way that they cannot be measured or analyzed again. Typically, destructive sampling is used with objects that may need to be taken apart or otherwise damaged in order to be analyzed. Tasting beverages or food in order to assess the temperature, texture, color, and flavor is a form of destructive sampling. After the food has been tasted, it is no longer available to be examined again. Destructive sampling often happens with products such as badges, tickets, football helmets, or library records when the material is damaged or the object is deconstructed in some way by the process of analyzing it. Other examples include chemical tests of body fluids, physical examination and dismemberment of stadium chairs, museum benches, lobby rugs, or hotel bedding.

Normally, destructive sampling is not used with people, although an application of the process would be a situation where a small group of people have been interviewed and questioned in such a way that going back to them will not yield any more information, especially since they may now be fully aware of the purpose of the research and may not be able to respond freshly to the questions you may want to ask. Examples include participants at a business meeting that is now over or audience members after a concert when you can no longer sample their expectations of that concert. Often, the process of examining images in newspapers and magazines or in movies and films can involve destructive sampling if it is necessary to take apart or fundamentally alter the nature of the materials that you are analyzing.

All of these methods of sampling—probability sampling and non-probability sampling—have their place in a research design. Each can contribute to the process of advancing knowledge, and each has its own strengths and challenges. Whichever strategy you select, you will face another challenge if you are interviewing or questioning human subjects: overcoming the presence of bias in the data collecting and data analysis phases of your research.

SOURCES OF SAMPLING BIAS: SYSTEMIC BIAS

One of the problems in sampling is that bias can creep into the process of selecting a sample. There are three major types of bias—systemic bias, respondent bias, and interviewer bias. The most common and prevalent form of bias is systemic bias.

Systemic bias refers to the way in which you have structured the process of selecting a sample. Systemic bias is a form of distortion introduced by the processes and strategies used to select and process that sample. Most often it comes from inadequate planning of all the aspects of a research design or not accounting for what might happen in conducting the research. *Systemic bias errors* or *sample selection process errors* can occur in the design decision or the implementation process. They include errors in determining the population from which the sample will be drawn, a lack of clarity about the sample frame (the list of members that constitute the sample), inadequate attention to randomizing the sample, or a lack of access to the respondents.

A second source of systemic bias can occur from faulty implementation of the research design. If you, or your team, do not follow the design as planned, or if you do not collect the right information or record it correctly, or if you make arbitrary decisions during the process, then the research may produce distorted results. Sometimes faulty instruments—such as an interview protocol that does not really encourage individuals to share the information that the researcher needs or a poorly designed questionnaire that does not test the hypotheses—can be part of systemic bias. Bias can also occur in the data analysis. Called *analytic process errors*, these mistakes made during collecting or analyzing data can be due to coding errors, lack of interpreting statistical results carefully, use of incorrect statistical methods, and poor inter-rater reliability. (For more information about validity and reliability, see

Chapter 9, Validity, Reliability, and Credibility in Research.) More commonly, these process errors come from errors in interpretation, inference, and lack of a careful and appropriately sophisticated pattern analysis.

And, of course, there is the influence of moderating variables. *Moderating variables* are factors that influence the results but were not the dependent or independent variables that you were testing for. Sometimes there are just things that happen that you did not plan for. Some of them include seasonality, or changes in access to certain members of the population, or sample, due to changes in business or movement among companies. Uncontrollable events such as weather, seasonality, and economic changes can also distort the results. Individuals are not likely to spend time completing a questionnaire when it is raining; respondents who have recently lost their job do not often have patience for certain interview questions, and people on vacation respond differently to those same questions than persons at home.

The last element of systemic bias can arise from a faulty conceptual framework for the research; using a limited model when a more complex model would be appropriate or borrowing a model from a different field without altering it carefully can distort what you find since the model may cause you to look at factors other than the important and significant ones. For example, Porter's classic "diamond model" for measuring a nation's competitive advantage has been considered insufficient to use in measuring the competitiveness of tourism destinations since several factors unique to tourism had not been included in the model (specifically cultural and historic resources and tourism superstructure). Therefore, the model had to be adapted to make it valid for tourism research (Crouch and Richie 145–49). Another example would be discussing loyalty without recognizing the cognitive, affective, conative, and behavioral aspects of loyalty (Back and Parks 429–32).

SOURCES OF SAMPLING BIAS: RESPONDENT BIAS

Biases can come from respondents as well. *Respondent bias* can take many forms, and it arises from the respondent not giving you true answers. The forms of respondent bias are discussed below.

Acquiescence bias occurs when a respondent answers questions because he or she likes the person or feels that it is his or her obligation to help the person with the survey or interview. The respondent may answer even if he or she has little knowledge of the subject; the respondent just wants to be helpful. The answers may be inaccurate or have no basis in fact. Often, senior citizens want to help out graduate students and will complete questionnaires even if they have no knowledge of the topic. To avoid this form of bias, you need to make sure that respondents have information and do not feel pressured to respond. The quality and details of the permission letter help with this bias. Avoiding leading questions also helps to diminish acquiescence bias.

Auspices bias is typically created by the position or status of the organization sponsoring the research. Often people will respond to the questionnaire or the request for an interview or observation because they are impressed with the organization conducting the research. Their answers may be inaccurate or accurate; in fact, respondents may alter responses due to the prestige of the institution or organization. For example, hotel guests answering a questionnaire from a luxury hotel manager may answer differently than if a graduate student asked them. Sometimes, auspices bias occurs because the respondent has an association with the organization; season ticket holders or college alumni often succumb to auspices bias and do not answer honestly because they are proud of their team or university. They may also answer questions differently if asked by a senior director than by a graduate student.

Nonresponse bias derives from persons who do not complete a questionnaire or an interview leaving you with partial information that will distort the results when you analyze them. That means that you may need to eliminate their responses in your analysis.

Extremity bias explains the behavior of persons who feel very strongly about a certain situation or event. Sometimes, persons who have had poor restaurant service and are angered by it do not answer questions in an honest way; they use the questionnaire to get rid of their frustration, which distorts the situation. They can often not remember the actual situation since their emotional state has taken over their perceptions. Extremity bias can also be very positive; people who loved the play may not notice some of the dialogue errors, fans of a winning team do not complain about their stadium seats, and people who love the river cruise are not critical of the long waits or poor entertainment in their evaluations of the experience.

Social desirability bias involves the respondent wanting to give you the appropriate or socially acceptable answer—in his or her eyes—rather than what the individual really feels. It differs slightly from acquiescence bias in which a respondent wants to answer to help out the administrator of the interview or questionnaire but the content of the answers are not affected. In social desirability bias, respondents answer in what they think is the "right answer" or the socially acceptable answer rather than with the truth or their own knowledge of the question. Examples include hotel guests answering that they liked the hotel ambience and lobby appearance when they really did not like it or praising customer service because they thought it was the right thing to say. Often, restaurant patrons answer a server's question about their enjoyment of the evening with, "It was wonderful," when it was often far from special. To counteract this form of bias and extremity bias, you need to ask a number of questions around the topic and see if the answers are consistent.

SOURCES OF SAMPLING BIAS: INTERVIEWER BIAS

Other forms of bias come from the behavior of the interviewer or questionnaire administrator during the process of collecting information.

Interviewer interaction bias involves the way in which the interviewer responds to the person that he or she is interviewing. If the interviewer likes or feels drawn to the person, or is intimidated by his or her position or presence, then the interviewer may not conduct the interview in the most effective manner or may make changes in the format, questions, order, or recording that affect the results of the interview. For example, graduate students interviewing hotel general managers may fear that they will look stupid asking for more information about a statement that the hotel general manager makes when they should really probe for more information. Sports students interviewing key executives in the National College Athletic Association, or the offices of the National Football League or Major League Baseball may find the presence of the executive intimidating enough that they forget the questions or do not ask them carefully enough to collect useful information, especially in parallel structured interviews. Relinquishing control over the interview situation is another side effect of interviewer interaction bias.

Sometimes interviewer interaction bias arises from positive or negative feelings about the person being interviewed or the process of conducting the interview. Interviewing is a carefully structured conversation, and it is important to monitor the feelings that arise when hearing someone talk about important issues or having strong opinions that may support or differ from yours as the interviewer. The best strategy for this possible situation is to recognize your own bias and discuss it with colleagues before or after the interview by answering the same questions that the interviewee will (if appropriate); listening carefully to what is being said, asking good questions, and recording answers accurately is the most critical way to avoid interviewer interaction bias (Rubin and Rubin 82–83). One way to avoid interviewer interaction bias is to keep checking on the accuracy of your notes by asking the interviewee if what you wrote down is accurate. (For more information on Interviewing, see **Chapter 10, Research Techniques: Interviewing.**)

Interviewers who do not have the ability or the commitment to listen carefully and to record accurately what the individual is saying also produce other errors. *Interpretation errors*—mistakes made by the person conducting the interview due to not listening carefully to what the interviewee is saying or analyzing the statements instead of just recording them—can produce any number of problems. One of them is the loss of the original statements if the interpretation is recorded in the notes and not the actual statements. There is no way to recover what the respondent actually said unless there is a recording of the interview. A second difficulty is the shorthand used in some interviewers' notes, which may be necessary to take the notes but leads to misinterpretation if the handwriting is not clear and the abbreviations or other writing shortcuts are misunderstood. One of the reasons to make sure to record actual statements and not interpret during an interview is that the role of interpretation comes later, often in the form of thoughts in a memo file that can be reviewed in its own right (Rubin and Rubin 203).

Inference errors are mistakes made by assuming something about what the interviewee said. Sometimes, the error comes from word choices that differ between the interviewer and the interviewee. Other times, it comes from the interviewer wanting the interviewee to say a certain thing or to make statements that help the research process. While that inclination is understandable, it distorts the results. Encouraging honest responses from interviewees and recording their statements carefully will help diminish the tendency to make inferences and keep you focused on the interview and asking the right questions to discover what the person can tell you honestly.

Recording errors, another mistake, refers to the behavior of an interviewer and his or her perspective to the answer. It comes from not recording carefully and accurately the words that an interviewee uses or taking poor notes that are later made more complete by the interviewer so that the interview notes look good. They may be inaccurate, but they are complete.

SAMPLE SIZE

One of the most common concerns is the *sample size* necessary for quality research. The answer can vary a lot, depending on the purpose of your research and the level of precision and confidence that you need in your research. In qualitative research when you are trying to understand guest behavior or sport fan activities, you may not need to be able to state that the behavior you have analyzed is statistically valid. If, however, you are testing some hypotheses, you may want to be able to state your conclusions with a certain level of precision and a specific level of confidence. *Precision* refers to the exactness of the numbers that you want to obtain; often it takes great effort in collecting data to find absolutely accurate numbers. For example, the time and staff needed to count the actual persons in a stadium is probably not worth expending; an approximate count, complemented with information about tickets sold, is typically sufficient for most purposes.

Confidence level refers to the extent to which you can claim that the numbers you report are accurate within a certain range. In making an approximation, you will give up some confidence that the number is exact since it may be necessary to have too high an assurance about the numbers. In fact, often the demand of conducting research requires assessing the balance between the demands of precision and confidence that you need for your research. You can have good numbers with a lower level of assurance, which is often what happens in conducting research using samples. Determining exact numbers for a population with a high level of confidence would take extraordinary efforts, which may be unnecessary for the quality of the research (Sekaran 288–95).

In thinking about the size and structure of your sample, there are lots of issues to address; they include the precision of the results you need. Do you need absolutely accurate answers or approximately accurate answers? What if your numbers are off by a few percentage points?

Primarily, the size of a sample will depend on the realities of the time and budget you have to conduct research, but it is also affected by the size, variability, and other characteristics of the population that you are sampling (Cooper and Schindler 413). In addition, the level of precision, or accuracy, that you need for your numbers and the confidence with which you want to be able to use the numbers affects sample size as well (Sekaran 292).

In fact, sample size can affect the validity or accuracy of the sample, depending on the situation. Random sampling error decreases as the size of the sample increases, which is why larger samples tend to have higher likelihood of reflecting the population from which they are drawn and which they purport to represent (Zikmund 423–30).

In practical terms, the maximum size for most probability samples is about one thousand (1,000) respondents (Alreck and Steele 89). The actual size of a sample will, however, be affected by a number of factors, one of which is the size and nature of the actual population from which your sample has been drawn. If you are trying to work with a large heterogeneous population, the variability in the population and the sample may require a larger sample. In the case where you are surveying college students attending a college football or basketball game, the match between the entire population of persons who attend that game and the sample that you survey may be so clear that a smaller sample is possible. When you have a large population, you need a larger sample or a more sophisticated model for selecting the size of your sample.

Sample sizes between 30 and 500 are good for most populations in which you want a representative sample. Another way to consider sample size is to ensure that you have a minimum number of 30 responses for each category of population or demographic that you want to sample. The third rule of thumb is to ensure that the sample size is ten times as large as the number of variables being examined, especially if you are using complex multiple regression analysis (Roscoe quoted in Sekaran 295). If you are measuring guest satisfaction on six dimensions, then you will need a sample size of at least 1800 respondents (6 variables times 30 respondents times 10).

When sampling a population with wide variability, you may need a larger sample as well. There are statistical formulas to determine the actual size, and these formulas take into account the sample means of the basic population, the standard deviation, and other factors.

SUMMARY

Selecting a sampling strategy and considering the range of formats to use are critical aspects of any research design. This chapter has explored those issues, reviewed the range of forms of bias that can interfere with the accuracy and validity of the findings that you hope to acquire from your research, and pointed out the dynamics of sample size. With this information, you can now consider issues of validity and reliability in the next chapter—**Chapter 9, Validity, Reliability, and Credibility in Research**.

KEY TERMS

Accuracy	Efficiency	Nonresponse bias
Acquiescence bias	Extremity bias	Population frame
Ad hoc	Inference errors	Precision
Analytic process errors	Intercept sampling	Probability sampling
Area sampling	Internet sampling	Proportional stratified
Auspices bias	Interpretation errors	sampling
Census	Interviewer interaction bias	Purposive sampling
Cluster sampling	Judgmental sampling	Quota sampling
Confidence level	Moderating variables	Recording error
Convenience sampling	Money	Relevant sample
Destructive sampling	Non-probability	Respondent bias
Double sampling	sampling	Sample frame

Sample selection process errors	Snowball sampling	Systemic bias
	Social desirability bias	Systemic bias errors
Sample size	Staff	Target sample
Simple random sampling	Stratified random sampling	Time

WORKS CITED IN THIS CHAPTER

Alreck, Pamela L., and Robert B. Steele. *The Survey Research Handbook*. Homewood: Irwin, 1985.

Back, Ki-Joon, and Sara C. Parks. "A Brand Loyalty Model Involving Cognitive, Affective and Conative Brand Loyalty and Customer Satisfaction." *Journal of Hospitality and Tourism Research 27* (2003): 419–35.

Cooper, Donald R., and Patricia S. Schindler. *Business Research Methods*. 9th ed. Boston: McGraw Hill Irwin 2006.

Crouch, Geoffrey I., and J.R. Brent Ritchie. "Tourism, Competitiveness, and Societal Prosperity." *Journal of Business Research* 44 (1999): 137–52.

Iarossi, Guiseppe. *The Power of Survey Design: A User's Guide for Managing Surveys, Interpreting Results, and Influencing Respondents*. Washington DC: World Bank, 2006.

Krejcie, R., and D. Morgan. "Determining Sample Size for Research Activities." *Educational and Psychological Measurement* 30 (2010): 607–10.

Roscoe, J. T. *Fundamental Research Statistics for the Behavioral Sciences*. New York; Holt, Rinehart and Winston, 1975.

Robson, Colin. *Real World Research*. 2nd ed. Oxford: Blackwell, 2002.

Rubin, Herbert J., and Irene S. Rubin. *Qualitative Interviewing: the Arts of Hearing Data*. 2nd ed. Thousand Oaks, CA: Sage Publications, 2005.

Sekaran, Uma. *Research Methods for Business: A Skill Building Approach*. 4th ed. Hoboken, NJ: John Wiley & Sons, 2003.

Roscoe, John T. *Fundamental Research Statistics for the Behavioral Sciences*. 2nd ed. New York: Holt, Rinehart and Winston, 1975.

Velicer, Wayne F., and Joseph L. Fava. "Effects of Variable and Subject Sampling on Factor Pattern Recovery." *Psychological Methods* 3 (1998): 231–51.

Zikmund, William G. *Business Research Methods*. 7th ed. Cincinnati, OH: Thomson South-Western, 2003.

Validity, Reliability, and Credibility in Research

Roses are red, validity is blue,
Reliability is important, and so are you;
The roses have wilted, the validity is lost,
Reliability is gone, and the design needs to be tossed;
The roses now stink, and the design is askew
Cause without either part, the proposal is poo;
But submit it anyway because you got some of it done
But remember that trying to do it now will be no fun.
Since you will have no validity or reliability to show
You'll have no findings that anyone wants to know.

(Anonymous)

INTRODUCTION

The last chapter focused on the challenges of carefully selecting an appropriate sampling strategy and protecting your design from forms of bias that could affect the results of your research. This chapter will show you how to protect your research design in ways that makes sense in light of the research that you have done and what the industry needs. Some of the most critical aspects of ensuring the quality of your research involve the validity, or accuracy, of what you plan to do, and reliability, the consistency of your design.

This chapter will discuss credibility, validity, internal validity, external validity, threats to validity, independent and dependent variables, reliability, and feasibility, all of which are important aspects of creating a good research design.

CREDIBILITY

Credibility is a measure of the depth of trust in what you have done. To what extent does your reader believe what you say and can depend on your honesty and integrity? One part of your credibility comes from the clarity of the way that you say things. Do you write clearly? Does the logic of your argument make sense? Do you provide evidence or sources to support the statements that you make in your proposal? Since

these questions are important ones, it is critical when you write that you make qualified statements and develop a clear and thoughtful voice that conveys integrity. This
aspect of your research proposal can make a strong initial impression on your readers
and potential supporters.

A second aspect of credibility that builds trust with readers is the focus and logic
of your proposal. A coherent focus and logical structure in your paper indicate that
you have mastered—to a significant extent—the subject of your research and you can
explain it clearly. Fuzzy thinking and writing will not convince your readers; in fact,
they can obfuscate ideas that have merit. The lack of a logical structure that a reader
can follow also discourages the reader who wants to trust what you are explaining.
However, if readers cannot follow your focus, they will assume you do not know
what you are saying, and they will discredit your proposal. Therefore, try to keep
your focus clear and your logical structure explicit. In this way, you build your credibility. (For more information about preparing a proposal, see **Chapter 14, Writing
a Research Proposal**.)

Another part of your credibility comes from the quality of your literature review.
If you have carefully sampled the research surrounding your topic, you have a sense
of what others have done and how well they have done it. You also have an understanding of the research methods used and their efficacy in producing useful results.
(For more information about the contributions of articles and the way that they state
their limitations, see **Chapter 3, Conducting a Literature Review, and Chapter 5,
Writing a Literature Review**.)

Credibility is hard to determine since it is not clear at the start that your readers
can answer questions about your credibility. However, that situation does not mean
that you should not try to establish your credibility with clear and accurate writing.
By being clear in your writing, you reduce the possibility of being misunderstood
or considered not credible, and you ensure that you have done the best job of going
where you want to go (Saunders, Lewis, and Thornhill 100).

Although credibility is only one of several criteria used to evaluate the merits,
primarily of qualitative, and also of quantitative, research (the others include transferability, dependability, confirmability, and authenticity), it is perhaps the most important one from the point of view of the reader and reviewer of your proposal (Bryman
and Bell 288–92). Another approach to assess a research design is the concept of
trustworthiness that includes credibility, transferability, dependability, and conform-
ability (Schwandt 258). The debate about how one conceptualizes quality research,
however, is mostly about validity, one of the most misunderstood concepts.

VALIDITY

There are many dimensions to validity; some of them include construct validity,
congruent validity, content validity, discriminant validity, face validity, predictive
validity, and statistical validity (Brinberg and McGrath 5). The basic concept behind
validity is the notion of accuracy and honesty—does the research design do what
it says it does? In everyday terms, validity refers to the honesty and accuracy of a
statement and its author. It denotes that something can be trusted to be true. A valid

problem is a real problem; a valid statement is an honest one that can be supported and backed up. For example, the statement "Customer loyalty is an important issue for hotel general managers" is a valid statement, but the statement "Customer loyalty is the only important issue for hotel general managers" is not. Or "Cultural heritage tourism draws a large number of tourists to New York City" is valid, but "Cultural heritage tourism is the major reason that visitors come to New York City" is not. "Many New York city residents attend Yankee games to cheer their team" is valid, but "New York City residents are fanatical about the New York Yankees" is not. The first statements are broad and general, but the second statements make assertions about customer loyalty, tourism motivation, and sports fans that cannot be supported by data and are, therefore, not valid.

In discussions of validity, many investigators have adopted a range of synonyms and related terms to describe validity. Some of them include quality, rigor, and trustworthiness (Golaafshani 602). The central issue, however, remains determining the extent to which a statement is or must be true (Schwandt 267).

Validity has been commonly divided into internal validity and external validity. As an aspect of research, *internal validity* refers to the clarity, focus, and integrity of the research design. Does it actually do what it says it does? Did it actually follow the steps described? *External validity*, on the other hand, derives from the context within which research is conducted. Does the research make sense in terms of other work done on the same topics or on the general area? To expand these ideas, it is first helpful to consider the key issues in any research design—the variables you are trying to examine.

DEPENDENT AND INDEPENDENT VARIABLES

One of the fascinating aspects of validity and reliability involves determining, clearly, the variables that you are examining. When working with variables that you are trying to analyze, there are four major concerns: defining the variables accurately, determining the independent variable, selecting the dependent variables, and clarifying the relationships you expect or are trying to discover. *Independent variables* are the ones that operate separately from other factors; *dependent variables* are the ones that are influenced in some way by other variables, and they are the ones you want to examine if and how they change as a result of alterations or movements in the independent variable. For example, if you are interested in examining the effect of marketing programs on tourists who go to a particular destination, the independent variable will be the marketing programs and the dependent variable will be the amount of traffic to the destination, the measure that you think will change because of the marketing programs.

The first challenge in working with variables involves defining them clearly and accurately. That task typically means developing a functional or *operational definition* of a variable or factor that you are examining. It is easy to want to analyze the effect of brand equity or reward programs on customer loyalty; it is harder to specify what you mean by brand equity and how you will measure it. The same is true for reward programs and customer loyalty. When you are testing for customer loyalty, what specific behaviors will you examine to determine if a customer is loyal or not?

Will it be recommending the hotel or will it be number of stays at the hotel over a specific period? Will it be the amount of money spent at the hotel? Deciding what will be measured or used as a proxy for customer loyalty becomes the first challenge.

The second challenge involves determining the independent variable. In discovering the relationship between various parts of a complex situation, it is often difficult to consider what factor might be the primary influence on another factor. Does brand identity and equity drive customer loyalty and repurchasing decisions or does customer loyalty contribute to the brand identity and equity? Does the quality of service produce consistent patterns of returning customers or does the patterns of returning customers contribute to the quality of the service? Sometimes it is not clear which factor influences the other. In developing a valid research design, however, it is important to specify which variables will be the independent ones and which ones the dependent variables they will influence.

TYPES OF VARIABLES

Dependent variables

Independent variables

Intervening variables

Moderating variables (confounding variables)

Selecting the dependent variable can be as complex as determining the independent variable. In many situations, the independent variable can influence a number of things and affect a range of behaviors. However, based on your research purpose, you will want to focus on just one element and determine what dependent variables you want to examine. Will service quality affect customer length of stay? Will service quality affect customer satisfaction? Will service quality affect customer repurchase decisions? Will service quality affect amount of money spent in the hotel? All of these variables, and more, might be affected by service quality; it is critical to focus on which ones you want to measure. Of course, the challenge will also be defining service quality in such a way that it can be measured.

Clarifying what factors influence events and actions is the last challenge. In most research, you will be interested in what factors influence decision making or actions, but determining what factors may have led to those events takes careful analysis and consideration of what is a dependent and what is an independent variable.

One of the problems in determining relationships involves the influence of moderating or intervening variables, factors that might explain the behavior or actions but that are not the dependent and independent variables. Since your research goal requires you to determine what factors influence behaviors or actions, developing a way to measure and test the correlation is a critical task. In analyzing correlations, you need to determine the extent to which you want to prove a significant correlation and select the correct statistical packages to determine if there is a valid correlation. Sensing the influence of one variable on another is not sufficient; you need to prove the correlation to be statistically significant. However, in developing the design, you also need to be aware of other influences that may explain the observed behavior.

Moderating, or confounding, variables are the forces that influence the behavior of the independent or dependent variable in such a way that affects the relationship. They are factors that surround the interaction of an independent variable on a dependent variable. Often weather is a confounding or moderating variable on attendance at historic sites, art openings, or outdoor concerts. If you are analyzing the patterns of fan loyalty and various promotional efforts of a baseball team, you might forget to consider the moderating effect of the economy, the weather, celebrity players, the history of wins and losses, or the prices and availability of personal seat licenses, that may affect baseball fan's patterns of purchasing tickets.

Intervening variables, by contrast, often also impact the influence of the independent variable on the dependent variable by getting in the way of the direct connection between two variables. The discount on tickets, the affinity group, the availability of tickets on StubHub, or the presence of giveaways like bobble heads may explain the fan's purchase and not just the depth of the fan's loyalty to the team.

Considering and accounting for the effect of independent variables on dependent variables and the influence of moderating and intervening variables is an essential aspect of good research design. Another key element of good research design involves internal validity, the subject of the next section.

INTERNAL VALIDITY

Internal validity has long been an important concept in applied research. The industry needs research findings that it can trust, and internal validity refers to the clarity of the design and often its match with the purpose statement and research questions being investigated.

There are two types of internal validity—general validity and instrument validity. *General validity* refers to the overall research design and its appropriateness for what you are examining. *Instrument validity*, often referred to as measurement validity or construct validity, denotes the accuracy and appropriateness of the questionnaires, surveys, content analysis, and observational tools being used in the research project (Bryman and Bell 41). Internal validity is often used to denote measurement validity or instrument validity, but more particularly, it refers to the overall focus and structure of the research design; it really sets the parameters for good research. (For more information, see the section on **Forms of Instrument Validity**.)

Some of the questions about general validity in terms of a research design include:

- To what extent is the research design really focused on the purpose statement as presented?

- Did the design really collect data relevant to the purpose statement?

- Were the data collected carefully and analyzed correctly?

- To what extent were the data collected accurate and useful in terms of the goals of the design?

- In what ways does the research design provide insights relevant to your research purpose?

- Does the research design really answer the questions posed?

Therefore, researchers look for a wide range of forms of internal validity.

Questions of general validity often concern the clarity of the research design, the conceptual framework behind the design, or the focus of the design. Does the research design actually have a systematic structure and are the data gathering and data analysis methods appropriate to produce the answers to the research questions being posed? Is the logic behind the research design clear and well developed? Is the research design consistent? Asking questions of hotel managers about customer loyalty does not indicate a clear research design when the questions should be asked of hotel guests who know why they continue to return to the hotel or the brand.

The validity and credibility of your findings will be directly related to the clarity of your design and the focus and logic of the data collection methods. The appropriateness of the conceptual framework behind the design and the consistency with which it is integrated into your design will also ensure internal validity.

Besides general validity, the other form of validity, and one about which there is considerably more literature, is instrument validity.

FORMS OF INSTRUMENT VALIDITY

When you think about measurement validity in your research, there are several types to consider: content validity, face validity, construct validity, criterion validity, predictive validity, and discriminant validity. They all address the question of the quality and accuracy of the instruments used to conduct the research.

Content validity refers to the extent to which the information in an instrument actually contains the correct content (Sekaran 206). From another perspective, content validity also emphasizes the information in a research design or in an instrument, whether it is an interview protocol or a questionnaire. To what extent do the questions being asked actually measure what is being investigated? Do the questions cover all of the areas that you need to ask about so that you can be sure that you have examined what is important? One way to check on content validity is to review the questions in your questionnaire or interview protocol and categorize them into sections. This process may aid in the task of analyzing the data as well as structuring your review of the questions. Then you can ask whether you have designed the instrument to collect all the relevant data that you might need or want. Often, the challenge of creating a useful questionnaire can be so complex that you may be reluctant to assess its content validity. (For information on designing questionnaires, see **Chapter 11, Research Techniques: Questionnaires**.)

Content validity is very similar to *face validity*, the test of whether something looks like what it is from a cursory or visual examination. Face validity refers to the possible or potentially obvious match between what the instrument is supposed to investigate and what it really does analyze (Zikmund 301). In other words, does it seem to be valid and accurately aimed? When you review the interview questions, do they seem to uncover or at least address the issues that you have mentioned in your research questions? If a design does not have face validity, it will not focus on the research questions that you have established, and you will spend a lot of time working on an instrument that will not produce the information you want.

Construct validity denotes the extent to which you define terms, and whether the questions you ask in an instrument match the conceptual framework behind your research. It is a measure of the ways in which you operationalize ideas. (Robson 102–104). For example, if you are investigating fan behavior, how do you measure fan avidity? Amount of money spent? Number of visits? Extra purchases of shirts and hats? The emotional connection to the team? How you define avidity should be reflected in the questions in your survey instrument that properly measure that behavior. Construct validity connects the concepts used to create the research design to the elements in the questionnaire. Investigators often use standard questionnaires or ones that have been already developed and tested in order to ensure construct validity since they have been already been assessed as good measures of a series of concepts. The use of standard instruments, such as SERVQUAL, the Gallup Poll, or ESPN's Annual Sports Poll, makes establishing construct validity easier, but it is not necessary. Connecting the constructs or concepts behind the development of the instrument to the actual instrument being used is the key challenge (Parasuraman, Seithaml, and Berry 12; Home 185–202).

Construct validity can be convergent or discriminant. *Convergent validity* measures the extent to which the scores on your questionnaire match scores on other questionnaires designed to measure the same or similar concepts. If you are measuring fan avidity and your scores seem to measure that behavior in a way similar to questionnaires developed by Wann and Pierce, then you have convergent validity (Wann and Pierce 122–23). In a situation where your instrument does not distinguish one form of fan avidity from another, you do not have *discriminant validity*— the measure to which your research separates specific ideas and behavior into their respective parts. In other words, your instrument does not significantly separate two different activities or two different behaviors.

Criterion validity has two forms—concurrent validity and predictive validity. They both involve being clear about the criteria used to assess the validity of an instrument. *Concurrent validity* measures the extent to which an instrument identifies certain responses that can be correlated with other observable behavior or measurable responses (Bryan and Bell 165). For example, if you are thinking that decisions to visit World Heritage sites are made on different grounds depending on the education or background of the visitors, then your instrument will need to ask the questions about decision making and the level of educational background, age, and occupations of the tourists who visit World Heritage sites.

Predictive validity operates on the same principle as concurrent validity except that you determine validity by matching the results of the instrument with future behavior or future responses (Sekaran 207). If you are testing a hypothesis about customer service, does it predict that business guests will have different responses to certain features of a hotel compared to leisure guests? If it does predict that difference, then it has predictive validity. If you ask ticket holders to respond to certain questions and the pattern or response matches later behavior, then the specific questions have predictive validity.

Discussions of measurement or instrument validity focus on the tools used in conducting research. Has the questionnaire been developed carefully enough and is it focused on the variable that it is intended to examine? Does the questionnaire that was used actually measure what it says it does? What proof can you offer that it actually uncovers the information it intended, or are there other explanations for the results of the research? For example, a questionnaire to restaurant patrons about what they ordered and why they order those items might not measure their attitudes about organic food unless the questions were carefully tailored to ask about that issue. Or, a survey of restaurant patrons might not uncover why they chose that particular restaurant if there were not a lot of specific questions about how they heard about the restaurant, what encouraged them to come to this particular restaurant, and what factors influenced their choice.

To overcome the challenges of instrument validity, a number of researchers use instruments that have been previously created and normed on a particular population or tested for validity of design. Tests of validity involve statistical analysis of specific questions to determine if the answers really measure what they are supposed to measure. (For more information, see **Forms of Validity**.) The selection of test items for personality tests or for the GMAT and GRE is based on this kind of assessment of the individual questions. If you choose to use a standardized questionnaire or one that has been used in other research, such as SERVQUAL instrument to measure customer satisfaction, or Wann's measure of Team Identification and Social Psychological Health, or the Traveler Sentiment Index used by the U.S. Travel Association, you can be fairly certain that the instrument has validity. (Parasuraman, Seithaml, and Berry 15; Wann 220; and U.S. Travel Association). However, you need to be careful to use the entire instrument and not just parts of it since it has been normed as a complete and coherent document over certain populations and analyzed in terms of validity. In this way, you can use a tool that has already been developed and focus on collecting the data and analyzing them, rather than having to prove the accuracy of the instrument chosen.

Although these aspects of validity basically refer to the conception of the research design and the instruments (questionnaires, interview schedules) used to measure responses to questions, there is another form of validity that is just as important—external validity.

Types of Internal Validity

Validity	Description
Content validity	Does the measure adequately measure the concept?
Face validity	Do "experts" validate that the instrument measures what the item suggests it measures?
Criterion—related validity	Does the measure differentiate in a manner that helps to predict a criterion variable?
Concurrent validity	Does the measure differentiate in a manner that helps to product a criterion variable currently?
Predictive validity	Does the measure differentiate individuals in a manner as to help predict a future criterion?
Construct validity	Does the instrument tap the concept as theorized?
Convergent validity	Do two instruments measuring the concept correlate highly?
Discriminant validity	Does the measure have a low correlation with a variable that is supposed to be unrelated to this variable?

(Adapted from Sekaran 208)

EXTERNAL VALIDITY

External validity refers to the notion of the credibility of findings due to the context within which the research was conducted. As internal validity derives from the focus and conduct of the research design, external validity derives from outside factors involved in the research. For example, external validity asks the following questions:

- To what extent does the literature review place your expected findings within a broader context?

- Will you be able to generalize from what you find?

- What limitations or qualifications will you have to make about your results?

- How can you extend your findings and suggest opportunities for further research so that you protect its validity?

- How does previous research help you interpret your results?

- Does previous research provide a rationale for your research design and suggestions about the applicability of your findings?

One way to ensure external validity—which relates to the question of generalizability—is to conduct a thorough literature search that enables you to determine if any similar or related research was conducted on the topic and what that research found. If you find similar research, you can benefit from that design and consider replicating the study under difference circumstances. You may even be able to use a questionnaire that the other investigators created and/or adapted to their research. Your work will then be confirmatory of the other study, and you know that you will have a valid instrument to use. If you do not find anything similar to what you want to do, then you have solid grounds to show the importance of doing what you want to do and a reason to make it happen.

THREATS TO VALIDITY

With so much attention focused on validity, you need to consider possible threats to validity as part of your plan to ensure that your research is successful and effective.

Some of the threats include seasonality and timing. During the actual data-gathering phase, seasonal factors may intervene and alter the audience you want to survey or change the factors that might influence respondents' decisions about hotels and food in some ways. A second time factor that occurs in research is that an individual can plan a research project during one year but not get to execute it until a later period when there may be changes in the industry that will affect the design. Research on demand and valuation in the hotel industry that was planned before the 2008 recession would not be useful or even work given the drop in demand, the slow-down in construction, and the rack rate trends of the last few years. The structure and dynamics of stadium and arena financing have changed dramatically over this same period, and research about how to fund new facilities has become irrelevant when the concern is paying for the operation of new and already built ones.

Other threats to validity include: history, mortality, maturation, testing, instrumentation, and ambiguity about causal direction (Robson as quoted in Saunders, Lewis, and Thornhill 102–103). History refers to the timing of the research that you conduct. Certain events that happen at the same time or just before you conduct your research may affect the results that you obtain. Mortality refers to persons leaving programs, checking out of hotels early, or dropping out of longitudinal studies that require several responses over time. Maturation involves research conducted over time. Events—such as bans on travel, economic disruptions, natural disasters, and wars—may happen during your research that could affect the responses from hotel guests in one location differently than in another location.

Testing refers to problems created by the testing situation. In an experiment, the nature of the pre-test and post-test may produce uneven numbers of responses. Alternatively, *instrumentation* is very similar; it refers to problems created by the nature of the instruments that you develop. A long questionnaire may mean that fewer people are willing to complete it or they may only complete part of it, creating a problem with discarded responses. This situation occurs primarily in intercept surveys or situations where the respondents do not have a vested interest in helping you with your research.

Ambiguity about causal direction can occur when it is not clear what factors are dependent variables and which ones are independent. Since it is necessary to determine the influence of one factor on another, you need to be clear about what you are trying to measure and which factors are independent and which dependent, which means that you have an implicit model of causality, often referred to as the classical chicken or egg problem of which comes first. For example, guest opinions of satisfaction may be influenced by staff behavior, or staff behavior may be influenced by guest behavior that results in positive customer satisfaction. In terms of sporting events, purchasing tickets to a game may make people into more avid fans than they were before, but not because of the game or anything about the team, just due to the fact of purchasing the ticket and the satisfaction or increase in self-concept caused by the purchase. That situation raises the question of what led to the purchase of the tickets.

Sometimes, questionnaires that were pilot tested on college students or professional colleagues trigger different responses from the ones from the intended and actual respondents, which means that you need to be careful about drawing conclusions from pilot tests. The way in which the information is gathered may also affect the information and the validity of the entire research design. Using previously accepted questionnaires can be one way of reducing, if not eliminating, this dynamic.

Two other factors—the positive halo of the Pygmalion effect or the negative halo of the Golem effect—may also raise challenges to validity. The *Pygmalion effect* is the notion that a person will respond positively as they are taught or expected to respond, which means that the responses in an experiment or on a questionnaire may not be truthful or accurate. They may be more positive because of the way that the respondents were treated. The Pygmalion effect distorts the real information (Rowe and O'Brien 618). The *Golem effect* operates in the opposite direction. People respond more negatively because they are treated in that manner, and it also distorts the information that they provide during an interview, an observation, or on a questionnaire (Rowe and O'Brien 614–15). Therefore, if you think and treat respondents as if they will not know something, could not know something, or will bring a negative approach to the situation, then the likelihood increases that they will not know or will answer negatively.

RELIABILITY

The concept of *reliability* refers to consistency in the research. To what extent is the design so clear and well organized that you could conduct the research at another time and come up with similar results? To what extent would the findings be the same with a different researcher? To what extent does the time frame affect what you will find? In what ways do the measurement instruments alter the possibilities of replicating the work? To what extent will the key findings last over time and be applicable to other situations?

Types of Reliability

Type	Description
Internal consistency	Examining the contents of an interview schedule or questionnaire, or other instrument, to assess that the ideas are all similar and the questions solicit comparable information
Equivalent form	Matching the content of one instrument with the content of another instrument
Inter-rater	Comparing the judgments or observations of one group of reviewers with those of another group of similar reviewers
Test-retest	Providing a second test or administration of an instrument to determine if the answers are similar to the ones received at the first administration

There are several types of reliability: internal consistency reliability, equivalent form reliability, inter-rater reliability, and test-retest reliability. *Internal consistency reliability* involves the analysis of a survey or questionnaire to make sure that the language used and the concepts applied are consistent (Sekaran 205). A questionnaire that is written in both the second and third person shows inconsistency. Using language about customer loyalty differently in various parts of a questionnaire indicates a lack of internal consistency. One way to encourage internal consistency is to ask colleagues to read any questionnaire. They can often see inconsistencies in language, concepts, and types of questions that you might miss since you created the instrument. Alternatively, reading a questionnaire or an interview protocol out loud can often help you hear the inconsistencies although it does not always work. Sometimes you need a professional to read the questionnaire. *Equivalent form reliability* indicates the extent to which two forms of the test measure the same information and will, most likely, produce similar results. Often, that involves trying out two forms of the questionnaire in a pilot situation, but it needs to be done in a carefully structured manner to determine if the same or similar results come from the different instruments or other moderating or intervening variables, such as setting, time frame, season, and so on. Equivalent form reliability means always considering if the results would be consistent or different if you used Survey A or Survey B.

Inter-rater reliability refers to the measure of similar insights or themes produced by different individuals reading the same information. If two people analyze a number of interview transcripts and come up with similar themes and insights, there is inter-rater reliability. If their insights are radically different, then you have a problem with inter-rater reliability. If their lack of agreement is a problem, then you need to help them work together until they come up with a common understanding of what to look for in the interviews so that their ratings and comments will be consistent. Inter-rater reliability is involved in any sporting event when referees need to make the same call in the same objective manner.

Test-retest reliability refers to the notion that the instrument should produce similar—not identical—results if it was administered a second time to an approximately similar group of respondents. Although you can plan to establish this form of reliability, it is not often used because of the costs and difficulties of conducting the research a second time with approximately the same possible respondents. It is also not always necessary to establish the reliability of what you have done using the method. There are other ways to determine that reliability.

SELECTING A RESEARCH DESIGN

Given this background information on validity and reliability, you should be prepared to make better decisions about your research design. Remembering the purpose of your research should help you decide what should be the elements of your design and how it can be shaped. Research designs need to be oriented to the original purpose statement and research questions that led to the desire to conduct the research in the first place. In fact, once you have an overall research design, reviewing it in light of your original research questions can be a very productive endeavor.

Other elements to consider in developing your research design include the time available for collecting and analyzing the data, the level of significance you want from your research, and your skill in doing the type of research you plan. It can be easy to consider what data you want to collect, but it is harder to determine how to evaluate the data and come to some coherent conclusions that relate to your overall purpose statement. (For more information on how to process data, see **Chapter 13, Analyzing Data and Other Information**.)

If you are interested in the millennial generation and their hedonistic pleasures, a design that focused only on nightclub behaviors might be too narrow in its definition of hedonism and pleasure. It might also be very difficult to collect any information from observations or interviews since persons at clubs are not typically interested in being interviewed for a research project. A better approach might involve interviewing millennials about the range of their pleasure activities. If you want to determine what factors influence fan loyalty to a particular team, asking about why they like sports and why they attend games might not indicate the elements that drive their loyalty to that specific team. Your questions should instead focus on why they feel loyal to that team, that sport, or that stadium.

The other element involved in developing a valid design involves your skills in doing the type of research that you propose. If you want to conduct interviews of a range of professional hotel managers, then you need to be sure that you have the skills to conduct the interviews, the resources to transcribe them, and the staff to conduct the analysis of the transcripts to determine if there are common themes and patterns of answers.

SUGGESTIONS TO ENSURE VALIDITY AND RELIABILITY

There are many ways to ensure validity and reliability in your research. The first one involves planning your research design to improve its validity. Think about the issues raised in this chapter and make sure you are investigating what you think you are, and in a manner that will provide answers to your research questions. Be careful to consider all the elements of the design so that you actually can and will follow through on the design you create. It is essential to ensure that your work has validity, that it can be trusted as true. Second, make sure that one section of your literature review addresses the methods used by other researchers. Third, use survey instruments and interview schedules developed by others—through replicating their study or by adapting their instrument to your own purposes. Fourth, make sure that you address, explicitly, the limitations of your design. The clearer you are about the limitations of your design, the higher your credibility and the better your validity.

Another way to ensure validity and reliability is to explain the specific tools you plan to use in your design. Include the survey instrument or interview schedule in an appendix to your research design, provide sample tables of data that are self-explanatory, and include information about how you will analyze data and draw your conclusions. The more explicit and detailed that you are in explaining your design, the more you will meet the tests of validity and reliability and the better your overall design.

SUMMARY

This chapter has explained the issues of credibility, validity, and reliability; examined both internal and external validity; discussed the relationships between independent and dependent variables; and indicated the threats in any research project to validity and reliability. Since the issues of validity, reliability, and credibility are essential in first-class research, it is critical to understand them and prepare to ensure validity and reliability. The validity and reliability of your design can mark the difference between credible research and irrelevant or invalid investigations. If you cannot be sure that your design is accurate and appropriate to your purpose statement and your research questions and if you cannot provide some guarantee for the reader that your results are consistent with those of other researchers and make sense within the context of other studies, you findings carry little or no weight. Therefore, the chapter also discussed issues of research design.

The next chapters—**Chapter 10, Research Techniques: Interviews; Chapter 11, Research Techniques: Questionnaires**; and **Chapter 12, Research Techniques: Observations, Focus Groups, and Other Techniques**—wil explain some of the research techniques to use in your research design.

KEY TERMS

Ambiguity	External validity	Internal validity
Concurrent validity	Face validity	Intervening variable
Construct validity	General validity	Moderating variable
Content validity	Golem effect	Operational definition
Convergent validity	Independent variable	Predictive validity
Credibility	Instrument validity	Pygmalion effect
Criterion validity	Instrumentation	Reliability
Dependent variable	Inter-rater reliability	Test-retest reliability
Discriminant validity	Internal consistency	Testing
Equivalent form reliability	reliability	

WORKS CITED IN THIS CHAPTER

Bryman, Alan, and Emma Bell. *Business Research Methods*. Oxford: Oxford University Press, 2003.

Cooper, Donald R., and Patricia S. Schindler. *Business Research Methods*. 9th ed. Boston: McGraw Hill Irwin, 2006.

David Brinberg, and Joseph E. McGrath, "A Network of Validity Concepts Within the Research Process" in David Brinberg and Kidder, eds., *New Directions for Methodology of Social and Behavioral Sciences: Forms of Validity in Research* 12 (1982): 5–21.

Golaafshani, Nahid. "Understanding Reliability and Validity in Qualitative Research." *The Qualitative Report* 8.4 (December 2003).

Home, Robert A. "A New Tune from an Old Instrument: The Application of SERVQUAL to a Tourism Service Business." *Innovation in Hospitality and Tourism*. Eds. Mike Peters and Birgit Pikkemaat 6 (2005): 185–202.

Parasuraman, A., Valarie A. Seithaml, and Leonard L. Berry. "SERVQUAL: A Multiple–Item Scale for Measuring Customer Perceptions of Service Quality." *Journal of Retailing* 64 (1988): 12–40.

Robson, Colin. *Real World Research*. 2nd ed. Oxford: Blackwell, 2002.

Rowe, W. Glenn and James O'Brien, "The Role of Golem, Pygmalion, and Galatea Effects on Opportunistic Behavior in the Classroom." *Journal of Management Education* 26 (2002): 612–28.

Saunders, Mark, Philip Lewis, and Adrian Thornhill. *Research Methods for Business Students*. 3rd ed. Essex: Pearson Education, 2003.

Schwandt, Thomas A. *Dictionary of Qualitative Inquiry*. 2nd ed. Thousand Oaks: Sage 2001.

Sekaran, Uma. *Research Methods for Business: A Skill Building Approach*. 4th ed. Hoboken, NJ: John Wiley & Sons, 2003.

Selltiz, Claire, Lawrence S. Wrightsman, and Stuart Wellford Cook. *Research Methods in Social Relations*. New York: Holt, Rinehart and Winston, 1976.

U.S. Travel Association. "Traveler Sentiment Index July 2011." U.S. Travel Association, New York. July 2011. Web. 22 October 2011.

Wann, Daniel L., and Stephanie Pierce. "The Relationship Between Sport Team Identification and Social Well-Being: Additional Evidence Supporting the Team Identification—Social Psychological Health Model." *North American Journal of Psychology* 7 (2005): 117–24.

Wann, Daniel L, and Stephen Weaver. "Understanding the Relationship Between Sport Team Identification and Dimensions of Social Well-Being." *North American Journal of Psychology* 11.2 (2009): 219–30.

Wann, Daniel L., M. J. Melnick, G. W. Russell, and D. G. Pease. *Sport Fans: The Psychology and Social Impact of Spectators*. New York: Routledge Press, 2001.

Zikmund, William G. *Business Research Methods*. 7th ed. Cincinnati, OH: Thomson South-Western, 2003.

Research Techniques—
Interviews

CHAPTER 10

INTRODUCTION

An interview can be a very powerful tool for acquiring first-hand information from experts on the subjects you are researching. Interviews work best when well-planned and focused; however, they are not easy to create, coordinate, or conduct. Since they can provide a great deal of rich information that either corroborates insights you've already acquired or provide new and unexpected insights, they are well worth using as part of any carefully developed research design.

This chapter reviews the key principles of using interviews, the tasks involved in preparing for an interview, the process of interviewing, the stages involved in the process, and the use of the information gathered. It also will discuss special interview situations, such as telephone interviews, group interviews, and door-to-door interviews. The next chapter will focus on questionnaires.

USING INTERVIEWS

Interviews are one of the most common and most useful ways of gathering information, but they are also widely misunderstood. They provide a depth of information and a chance to ask more detailed questions that is not possible in a structured questionnaire. Interviewing someone face to face enables you to read their body language and gain deeper insights into their thoughts and responses to questions. It also allows for follow-up on comments that the interviewee makes, so you can develop a real dialogue on a particular issue or set of issues. People generally seem more willing to talk substantively when sitting down with another person, partly because they are not compelled to write it all down in a questionnaire and partly because the interviewer's expression of interest often encourages individuals to talk.

In an interview setting—barring a legal or criminal investigation—people are usually delighted to talk about subjects that interest them and in which they have experience. In fact, interviews provide a rich source of data that makes them appealing to researchers since there is more time to visit and talk in face-to-face interviews; telephone interviews typically last less than 15 minutes, and 81 percent less than 30 minutes (Metzler 112), but the average in-person research interview ranges from 45 minutes to two hours, with two- to three-hour interviews not unusual (Bernard 258). Typically, in-person and longer interviews provide much more information relevant to your purpose statement.

owever, there are some disadvantages as well. While the answers in an interview may be more creative than the responses to a standardized questionnaire, they
are harder to analyze. The disadvantage of interviews is the time that they take to
conduct, the extent of the skills required to conduct an interview, and the challenges
in recording accurate and full answers to the questions asked. They are best conducted in a quiet space where there will be no interruptions, and they require two
people with the time to commit to the interview.

Advantages of Interviewing	Disadvantages of Interviewing
Provides detailed information	Requires interviewing skills
Encourages more conversation and follow-up	Takes preparation to write good questions for an interview
Enables follow-up questions when information is not clear	Creates challenges in taking notes that can interfere with the process of interviewing and getting all the information
Expands the interviewer's understanding of the situation, action or event	Poses challenges in gathering the right infor-mation when the interactions get in the way
Allows checking on information that is not clear	Requires analyzing the information from inter-view conversations
Allows the interviewer to observe nonverbal behavior, which can provide additional information	Invites distortion from misinterpreting or over-analyzing nonverbal behavior
	Sometimes uses recording devices, which can discourage some interviewees from talking due to discomfort or fear of being recorded
	Requires typing transcripts and coding to conduct thorough analysis

Although many people think they have what it takes to conduct a good interview,
there is a level of expertise required that they often lack, and they do not consider the
importance of designing an interview (Trochim 86). Planning carefully can prevent
two difficult situations from developing—one, gathering data that has no significance
or value, and two, finding out fascinating information that people do not trust you
have collected carefully and that might, therefore, not be true or important (Rubin 78).

Before conducting an interview, an interviewer must address background gaps
and plan to structure the interview carefully. Adequate preparation can spell the difference between success and failure in gathering the information you are seeking.
Generally, you will have only one opportunity to conduct the interview, so it's important to make the most of it. Focusing on the audience, the information, the process,
and the results will help you organize and plan the process of designing and conducting interviews so that they serve as a productive and effective tool for you to use in
your research adventure.

Focusing on the audience means doing some significant research about the
person, or persons, you want to interview. Each interview situation is different.

For example, you may not know or even know about the people you will be interviewing, so you will have to conduct research to find out who these individuals are and how you might identify them. Sometimes that means doing research on the Internet, calling individuals and networking with them, combing recent conference programs, or skimming news stories and industry notes to see which key players you might want to interview. In this case, make sure you capture as much information about the person—or the position—as you can so that vetting the list can be done quickly and effectively. You should cast your net as wide as you can to ensure that you do not neglect to contact anyone important or useful to your research. In other situations, you may know the person or persons that you want to interview, and it will be easy to find detailed information about them as well as how to contact them.

In either case, you will also need to conduct some background research regarding the topic or topics about which you are going to ask questions. There is nothing more frustrating to a person being interviewed than being asked questions that the interviewer could have, and should have, known the answers to before the interview. As you think about whom you want to meet and interview, consider the following questions about the process:

- What information do you want to discover?

- Are you looking for their interpretation of an action or event?

- Are you using these interviews as a part of the literature review process?

- Will these interviews supplement questionnaires or other sources of data?

- Are you trying to measure or test your own hypotheses about how things have happened?

- How will this information be used in connection with other information?

- What parts of an event, business strategy, or situation do you want to understand more thoroughly?

From these questions, you can develop an interview protocol that will list all of the questions that you want to ask—or are prepared to ask—along with the beginning and ending script in an interview situation.

One other dimension to plan for in conducting interviews is *interview fatigue*, the exhaustion or tiredness that comes from being in an interview situation. Fatigue can affect the interviewee or the interviewer. Interviewee fatigue comes from being asked a number of questions that require considerable reflection and analysis, which can be tiring. If the interviewee is asked about painful memories or difficult situations, he or she is more likely to be prone to tire and limit the depth of the responses.

Interviewer fatigue, a common practice in human resource interviews, especially screening interviews for potential employers, can also take a toll on the interviewer. Being open to the person in front of you, showing kindness and consideration, taking good notes, listening carefully, and observing nonverbal reactions is not an easy task. Doing it all day long or for extended periods of time can produce tiredness as well (Presser and Zhao 237).

While planning for these interview challenges, you should focus on research interviews, only one of many types of interview structures.

FORMATS OF INTERVIEWS

When considering interviewing as a technique for gathering data, one should bear in mind that there are many types of interviews. In the human resource management aspect of business, there are screening interviews, hiring interviews, training interviews, disciplinary interviews, and exit interviews. There also are sales and marketing interviews, partnership and alliance interviews, negotiating interviews, and any number of management interviews; all of them are very different from research interviews.

Research interviews are structured interactions between two individuals, an interviewer and an interviewee, organized around the collection, examination, or analysis of information relative to a defined research purpose or problem. They function primarily as a one-way form of communication in which the interviewer is asking the interviewee lots of questions, both general and specific, in order to discover or validate something. The interview is often more like a conversation, but the goal is to collect information from the person being interviewed. The interviewer's goal is encouraging the interviewee to talk.

Research interviews are structured, unstructured, and semistructured. *Structured interviews*—sometimes called standard interviews—are often easier to conduct, more productive in generating a range of information within a limited interview time, and far easier for note taking and analytical purposes. The structured format can also be helpful when you are trying to compare the information gathered in the interview process since each person answers the same questions. Often, structured interviews are easier to arrange, since a potential interview subject may be comfortable knowing that there is a standard set of questions and that several people are being interviewed.

At the same time, the structure may get in the way of allowing the person to talk and share his or her impressions, memories, or analytical comments on the topic of your research. Unfortunately, structured interviews do not allow the interviewee the opportunity to digress or provide additional information, which limits the richness and depth of the data being gathered. However, given the desire to compare information gathered from several individuals and the importance of analyzing patterns emerging from the responses, structured interviews are the most prevalent, and often the most productive, form of interviews in research situations.

Totally *unstructured interviews*, sometimes called open-ended interviews, encourage individuals to talk at length about a program, policy, action, or event, which can provide a level of detail and insight that you might not be able to obtain any other way. Although taking notes can be difficult in an unstructured interview, it can provide extraordinarily useful information (Fontana and Frey 374; Strauss and Corbin 205). Open-ended interviews are often used in the early stages of research when conducting a literature review or a scan of the research field. The downside of an unstructured interview is that the data you gather are more difficult to use for comparing results across a wide range of interviewees. Collecting the data can also become a waste of time since the conversation may be fascinating, but might not provide information that is useful to you in your research.

Semi-structured interviewing is often used when the interviewer wants to collect certain information but feels that a more open-ended approach would provide insights that might not be prompted by structured questions alone. It can be a very useful type of interview, especially in the early stages of research when you are still uncovering the key issues or when you are trying out a set of interview questions. The open-ended questions or unstructured part of the interview may produce suggestions for future interview questions.

Semi-structured interviews start with a clearly defined and prescribed set of questions and then move on to more open-ended questions once the key information has been collected.

Sometimes a structured interview may turn into more of a semi-structured interview when it becomes apparent that the interviewee enjoys talking and expressing points of view that go beyond the structured questions. That free-flowing conversation can provide additional useful information that could not have been planned. Other times, a semistructured interview can turn into an open-ended or unstructured interview unintentionally when the interviewer has not planned well for what might happen during the interview or when the circumstances change.

THE INTERVIEW PROTOCOL

Designing an *interview protocol*, or *interview schedule*—the list of questions including the introduction and concluding comments of an interview—is a difficult challenge; it takes some real thought about what information you want to acquire and how best to obtain it. However, since you will be asking your interview subjects to give you their valuable time and attention, you must carefully develop and refine the questions that you want to ask (Seidman 71). It is also important to prepare your welcoming script and your ending thank-you speech. Even though length of the interview time rarely has an influence on respondents' willingness to participate, you want to use their and your time productively (Iarossi 151).

The first step involves writing down the range of questions that you want to ask. Don't worry about the structure or order at this point. Write down all of the possible questions and also the demographic information you want to obtain. The demographic data will be critical if you are comparing information from a variety of people since you may want to determine the extent to which answers differ based on their current (or past) position, gender, education, age, experience, geographic location, history in the industry, previous work experience, and company affiliation. Consider also the range of questions that you need to ask and write them all down (Metzler 19). Then review them carefully for language and structure so that you are asking questions in a manner that encourages individuals to provide you with the information that you want, rather than the information that they think you want. This phenomenon is referred to as *courtesy bias*—the desire to provide you with information they think you want or that they think would be useful (Bessinger and Bertrand 64). There are other factors you need to consider in conducting the interview as well. (See the section on **Conducting the Interview**.) One of the most powerful limitations in interviewing—called *order bias*—occurs when the sequence of questions affects the way in which the interviewee answers the questions. Another consideration is *status bias*—the impact of differences in position, status, title, or race between the interviewer and interviewee—which may influence the willingness of the interviewee to speak honestly (Katz 248–68). These factors can also dramatically affect the way that interviewers ask initial and follow up questions (Sekaran 228–29).

PRACTICAL STEPS FOR DEVELOPING AN INTERVIEW PROTOCOL

1. Write out all of the questions that you might want to ask.

2. Write down the demographic information about the interviewee that you want to collect (whether from him or her or from background research).

3. Review the questions for clarity, considering how you might ask them.

4. Ensure that you are not asking any leading or loaded questions.

5. Read the questions out loud to yourself and listen carefully to how they sound as you read them.

6. Consider what questions are most important and which ones are the least important, marking them accordingly.

7. Develop probing questions—follow-up questions—for the important areas so that you can get as much information as you can.

8. Prepare a welcoming introduction speech.

9. Sequence the questions you will use and write out how you will ask them.

10. Write down your thank-you comments—and a reminder to yourself to ask for other persons that he or she might suggest that you interview—in detail.

11. Sequence the questions in an order that builds momentum, using some easy questions first to build trust and encourage the interviewee to talk.

12. Prepare your thank-you comments.

13. Add the key last questions (often called the golden questions): "What have you not told me that you want me to know?" and "Who else do you think I should talk with?"

14. Review the entire script and make revisions as needed.

When you've written out all the possible questions, put them away for a while (for a few days, perhaps) and then review them again, reading them from the bottom of the list to the top so that you read each question carefully and pay attention to the wording. Reading them aloud will increase your ability to hear them clearly and imagine what a person might hear as you use them in an actual interview. If something does not seem clear, revise it to improve its clarity and focus. Often at this point, you can notice that some questions—called *leading questions*—seem to be calling for a particular response and that you may be unaware of how biased they seem, especially if you are deeply involved in the research project. These questions need to be changed in order to eliminate this form of bias from entering the interview process. The other form of question you want to avoid are *loaded questions*, which contain emotionally powerful words that indicate the correct answer or which are structured to evoke a response that the interviewer wants to hear (Iarossi 32–36).

Examples of leading questions include: "What do you think of having to pay extra for food on planes?" or "Don't you think that collective bargaining agreements in professional sports favor athletes?" or "Do you think that allowing millions of tourists to visit fragile World Heritage sites will ruin the integrity of the sites? Loaded questions would be: "How do you feel about being treated like cattle on the plane trip?" or, "Why would people want to use their vacation time and pay their own expenses to rebuild a community center?" or, "Why would you want to pay the inflated costs of food and beverage at baseball games?" or, "What wonderful sustainable practices have you implemented at your hotel?"

If you can't detect some of the potential problems in a question or set of questions, try giving them to a colleague, a fellow student, or someone who knows little about what you are trying to accomplish. They may be able to note the errors, the bias, or problems with the structure and sequence of your questions.

Once you have revised the questions, reworded them, and resequenced them, it is time to prepare the beginning and ending information needed to make an interview successful. That means writing down how you will introduce the interview, the information you need to review at the beginning of the interview—such as confidentiality, note taking, use of information, purpose of the project, and time frame—as well as how you will start the first question.

Preparing your concluding remarks is just as critical, since many interviewers remember to say thank you but forget to remind the interviewee of the purpose of the research, the call back that may be necessary to check on specific information when your notes are not clear, or the use of quotations and specific statements. Toward the end of the interview, you may also want to ask the most important questions:

- "Is there anything else about this topic that you want to tell me?"

- "Is there anything you want to add to or correct before we complete the interview?"

- "Is there anyone else you would suggest I interview, and would you be willing to provide me with an introduction?"

These questions—sometimes called *doorknob questions* since they may occur when you have your hand on the door to leave—often produce very useful and insightful information about an aspect of your topic or purpose statement that you forgot, or did not know, to ask. Often doorknob questions can be a result of defective interview techniques since they can be last minute thoughts that come from poor planning. They can also be called "oh by the way questions" (Baker et al. 766). Doorknob questions can also be helpful for finding another person to interview and provide you with insightful new information or added depth to the knowledge you are acquiring through this interviewing process.

The last part of an interview protocol includes the thank-you comments and the final speech that you want to remember to say when the interview is over. The penultimate question may well be "Is there anything about this topic that you want to tell me and which I have not asked?" or, "Is there anything that you want to review with me or explain in more detail?" The last question should always be "What other people would you recommend I interview?" and "Can you provide an introduction to them?" These questions make sure that something is not missed. At the end, you want to remind the interviewees that the information is strictly confidential and that you will contact them to ensure quotes are correct. You will also want to thank them for their time and their insights, which have been so helpful to your research.

Remember that, at its best, an interview protocol is like a script; it should contain all of the information that you need and in the correct sequence. If you know it well, you might not have to refer to it. However, if you never write out all of the pieces, then you will collect information from various people but maybe not the right information or not in the correct sequence for the project that you have in mind. (For more specific suggestions, see the box **Practical Steps for Developing an Interview Protocol**.) As a reference tool, a comprehensive interview protocol can be very helpful for you as an individual. If you are using a team of interviewers and you want to compare information from a variety of interviews, then a standard protocol becomes essential to your success.

Whether you are conducting the interviews yourself or using volunteers or paid staff members, considerable preparation is required before conducting an actual interview.

CONTACTING THE INTERVIEWEE

One of the most difficult parts of the entire interview process involves locating possible interviewees, obtaining their consent, and arranging a time and space for the interview. The process begins with deciding whom you want to interview—either by name or by position—and when you want to interview them, and then contacting them.

When you have made contact, you need to remember to explain a number of items:

- The purpose of the research project in some detail

- Your name and affiliation

- The confidentiality that you will practice

- The method of recording the interview—your notes or a recording device

- The use of the information—will it be shared in the aggregate, characterized by position, or will the person be contacted before being quoted?

- What will you do with the interview transcript and/or tape after the research project?

PREPARING FOR THE INTERVIEW

If you have not had much experience in conducting interviews, you can benefit from considering the following tips and practicing before you interview a person. If you have had some experience, reviewing these points may help remind you of what you need to consider.

One of the best talents you can bring to the process of interviewing is your own curiosity. If you are not fascinated by the topic and the person that you will interview, then most likely the interview will not go well. Therefore, think a lot about the person you will interview, review the information you have collected, and reflect on what he or she is like as a person and as a professional. Consider how the person works, what pressures the individual faces, and what opportunities have been presented. If you are having trouble with these questions, then try imagining yourself in that person's shoes and contemplate what you would do, what your world would be like, what challenges you would face, and how you would handle them. Your own curiosity will provide you with lots of follow-up questions that often encourage individuals to say more than they intended and provide you with all kinds of unintended insights. Your own curiosity about the persons and the subject will also carry you through awkward parts of the interview, helping you produce questions when there is a lag and making sure you get as much information as you can from the interview.

The most important skills involved in conducting an interview include listening carefully to what the interviewee says, pausing to let the interviewee think about a possible response, and recording carefully his or her statements. Part of listening involves asking the questions in the order that you wrote them, asking them clearly, and then waiting for the response. Any kind of indication of what you want the interviewee to say limits the validity of the answer since you are providing clues about what you want the person to say, and often, in research interview situations, the interviewee wants to help you out (called acquiescence bias).

Some key tips on how to keep the interview focused and objective include:

- Remain neutral throughout the interview—do not give away what you want to hear with your body language, sounds, or nonverbal clues such as when you start to write and when you're not writing.

- Do not suggest answers to the interviewee—wait for him or her to answer the questions; there is nothing wrong with some silence.

- Do not change the wording or sequence of questions—honor the interview protocol since it helps keep the interviews comparable and allows easier analysis of the results.

- Handle a hesitant interviewee with tact and wit; wait patiently and encourage him or her to answer the question alone. Sometimes, restating the question helps the interviewee answer it.

- Probe when the interviewee has said something that interests you or suggests an area you have not considered.

- Do not set or form expectations for the interview—you are there to gather information, whatever it is—let the interviewee talk and tell you what he or she can.

- Do not rush the interviewee—patience in this situation is a virtue. (Adapted from *Demographic and Health Survey Manual* 9–11.)

Although you may need to practice your listening skills, the other critical skill to use in interviewing is the use of filter questions and probing questions. *Filter questions* are ones that are used with some individuals and not others, depending on the depth and range of information that the interviewee provides, on the one hand, and the relevance of their experience and knowledge, on the other. If you are asking questions about hotel service of a person who has had limited experience in staying at hotels, there may not be much reason to ask him or her several questions. Interviewing a person about poverty tourism when they have never stayed in anything but a luxury hotel would also be a useless endeavor. Conversely, a person who is an avid sports fan and season ticket holder may be able to provide extensive information that you want to acquire; as a result, you may ask him or her a number of detailed questions.

One of the most unproductive types of questions are *yes/no questions*, which many people write out thinking that the question is a comfortable way to conduct an interview. The difficulty with yes/no questions is that they do not prompt the interviewee to respond thoughtfully. Often, the individual will overlook the form of the question and talk about the topic. However, if the person takes you literally, the only answer to a yes/no question is yes or no. For example, if you asked someone, "Can you tell me about the challenges you face as a front desk agent?" the real answer to the question is "yes," "no," or "maybe." It would be far more productive to ask, "What are the challenges you face as front desk agent?" Instead of, "Have online reviews encouraged you to patronize of avoid a restaurant?" ask the question in this format: "In what ways have online reviews influenced your decision to patronize or avoid a restaurant?" Or try, "In what ways have the new season ticket packages affected your purchase of tickets?" instead of, "Have the new season ticket packages affected your purchase of tickets?" The broader question will produce better responses than the simple yes/no question.

Prompting questions are used to encourage individuals to talk. They are used to motivate persons to say more, to support their desire to answer the questions that you are asking. Sometimes, persons being interviewed are reluctant to talk without some encouragement or evidence that you are really interested. Prompting questions such as "Tell me something interesting about the challenges of that assignment." Or "Say some more about that issue." Or "I am sure you have lots to tell about your work as a concierge, bell captain, dining room host, or sales person" or "What was the most important part of the activity?" Asking the original question and then adding some positive statements, some prompting questions, will produce more information and typically a higher level of detail.

Probing questions are used to follow up on something, either to find out more information or to pursue a topic that the interviewee opened and did not complete. There are several probing methods:

- Waiting patiently for a response with your pen poised to take notes. Often this clue provides an impetus for the interviewee to talk some more.

- Asking specific questions about a part of the answer. This practice will invite them to say more about that topic, especially when you ask: "Can you explain that more fully?" "I am not sure I understand what you are saying." "Is there any other aspect to that situation that you can remember?" These additional questions invite interviewees to say more without giving them any leading questions.

- Waiting for them to respond to a question and not indicating that the answer is finished. Often, they will provide more information—and very insightful comments—thinking that you want to know more.

- Repeating the question a second time. Sometimes the repetition helps the interviewee to say more, especially when the question might be complicated or the interviewee's mind has wandered.

Practice listening skills—it is about waiting for the interviewee to talk, encouraging him or her to talk and not talking too much—and taking good notes if you want to be a good interviewer, since the quality of your notes is critical to your success. Often, using an expectant pause is one of the most effective methods of probing (Zikmund 440). Many interviewers use the expectant pause, also called *white space*—the use of silence to prompt a person to continue talking—as a powerful tool in discovering additional information. Sometimes, it is valuable to just pause and listen to the interviewee talk. Even if he or she has completed the answer to a question, refraining from immediately providing the question may encourage, sometimes out of nervousness and sometimes out of a desire to share more knowledge, the interviewee to expand on what was just said or to amplify ideas. Often, the individual will just start talking and the information you can acquire can become very insightful. Since it takes practice to be comfortable with white space, you might try it with friends or in comfortable interview situations so that you become patient and relaxed with waiting. Then you can use it in a wide range of interviews.

Interviewing is a fine art and takes a lot of practice. Part of that involves designing an effective interview protocol, part of it includes asking the right questions in the right order, and part of it involves considering the stages of an interview.

STAGES OF A RESEARCH INTERVIEW

When you actually conduct a research interview, you might find it helpful to consider the *stages of the interview process*: beginning, building trust, information gathering, checking and rechecking, and concluding. These stages, while common to many types of interviews, are slightly different in a research interview since the purpose is gathering information and ensuring its veracity. It is not about making a sale, getting a job, making a change in the person that you are interviewing, or deciding who to hire.

Of course, the initial contact with the person in establishing the purpose, time, and place of the interview sets the tone, but you want to reinforce that tone and maintain it throughout the process. First, you want to come to the interview well dressed and professional in appearance. Even if you are interviewing college students who might wear very casual clothes, you want to show that you are conducting a professional interview and select your clothing appropriately. If you are interviewing a professional in the field of hospitality or tourism, a suit, dress, or other professional outfit would be most appropriate. In the sports field, your outfit might vary according to the location and the individual you are interviewing. One recommendation is to check ahead of time on the dress code where you are going to meet with the individual. (You may find that administrative assistants are very helpful and generous with this advice.)

Research interviews—unlike hiring interviews or networking interviews—are structured to gather information and to ensure that the information is useful and appropriate to the purpose statement of the research. In order to accomplish that goal, you need to find a way to help your interviewee relax and trust you during the process (Cannell and Kahn 337–40). Helping him or her relax involves three different factors:

1. Building trust

2. Ensuring confidentiality

3. Establishing rapport

When you meet the individual—whether in a neutral location or in his or her office or workplace—use a direct and sincere approach to set a professional tone. Remember that you are trying to build trust in this initial phase of the meeting, and some small talk might be a way to establish rapport. Establishing rapport with the people you interview will allow you to collect more information and more useful information (Sedorkin and McGregror 229–30; Fontana and Frey 366, 367).

Establishing trust can be done with the way you handle the materials you bring, the way in which you reinforce and state, clearly, the purpose of the research interview, and how you organize the interview. Other ways to establish trust with your interviewee include honoring the statements and commitments that you make, producing evidence of your professionalism—as necessary and appropriate—and demonstrating your professionalism. It also involves being clear about the way or ways—taking notes, checking back, recording with a tape recorder or a video recorder—that you will conduct the interview. At this beginning stage of the interview, you may also want to reinforce the confidentiality of the meeting, indicate what you will do with the transcript of the interview, and explain to what extent you will quote the individual or just characterize his or her statements. Will you provide the individual with a copy of the typed transcript? How will you use the video record of the interview? Will you keep copies of everything or destroy the record after your project is completed? In terms of using quotes, will you check with the person before you quote him or her directly or will you only aggregate the comments from all of your interviews? Often this information is not clear to the interviewee; being explicit and giving the individual a chance to ask about these issues at the beginning of the meeting will build trust and improve the quality of the interview.

Since the primary reason for the interview is collecting information, asking clear questions becomes an essential skill and one that can make or break an interview (Robson 243–245; Biemer and Lyberg 184). Of course, there are some people who really enjoy being interviewed and will talk about their work, the situation, the team, the company, their policies, the employees at great length without much encouragement. Others may be reticent about discussing the topic you are asking about. In either case, since you have a clear and focused set of research questions, you can shape the conversation by asking specific questions. As the interviewee answers the questions, you can proceed to the next one or probe for more information whenever something interesting comes up.

Remember that individuals often do not remember correctly what happened, and you can often find out more detail through methods other than interviewing. However, asking what they saw or remember can often help you deepen your understanding of a situation or event—such as a major conference, a change in business practices, or a trend that you want them to analyze.

As you conduct the interview, you may find the individual providing you with ideas or insights that contradict what you have think happened or what you have read about. This phenomenon should inspire you to check and recheck what you heard and review what you wrote down to make sure that you have correctly captured the paradox. Sometimes, it can be useful to ask the interviewee if you have recorded his or her remarks correctly. Other times, a probing or follow-up question can clarify the possible confusion. In this situation, it is important to ensure that you have recorded the individual's statements; therefore, ask more specific questions and invite the interviewee to elaborate.

There might be other information that you want to check as well, such as dates, numbers, or particular aspects of what was said. While it is often true that individuals remember things differently than what actually happened, it is also difficult to capture all of the information in an interview. Overcoming *interviewer error*— mistakes made by not recording what was actually said or falsifying answers during an interview—is essential to the validity of your research (Biemer and Lyberg 167–173; Oliver, Serovich, and Mason 45). The best way to ensure that you do not make these mistakes is to take notes and record the interview at the same time. Another way to conduct interviews involves doing it in pairs with one person asking the questions and one person taking notes. Transcribing the interview afterward ensures that you have not missed anything and also provides you with a document to analyze for content—key concepts, phrases, ways of explaining events, and attitudes as well as information (Rubin 71).

During the interview, you may also find answers that do not seem to ring true to you. Some of them may be due to a number of bias factors that often affect the results. *Auspices bias* can affect responses due to the organization (department, college, university, or corporation) that is supporting the research project. In this situation, individuals will answer in a way to support—or contradict in some cases—the work of the project due to their feelings about the sponsor. *Social desirability bias* occurs when an interviewee gives the interviewer the answers that he or she thinks will provide a favorable impression.

The last phase of the interview involves summarizing what has happened, thanking the interviewee, explaining possible follow-up, reviewing the purpose of the research, and inviting the individual to contact you with more information or other ideas that come up after the interview. It is also a chance to ask for other recommendations of people to interview. Often this technique—called *snowballing* or going from one person to another based on the suggestion of the first person—provides you with access to individuals who you would not normally consider or who may be difficult to meet. Remember to end on a positive note, thanking the person for his or her time and interest in your research project and leaving your card or contact information.

Although all of these comments apply to person-to-person interviews, when people are sitting down in the same room, there are other variations on interviewing: telephone interviews, group interviews, and door-to-door interviews.

UNUSUAL INTERVIEW FORMATS

Telephone interviews actually fall into two categories: interviews set up in the same way as an in-person interview but conducted on the telephone for reasons of distance or scheduling, and blind interviews that were not prearranged. Phone interviews should be arranged with the same care as in-person interviews. While a phone interview may be shorter and more anonymous than an in-person interview, the person being interviewed has allotted a significant amount of time for the interview and is willing to talk at some length about the event, activity, policy, program, or organization.

Telephone interviews come in a wide variety, and how you prepare for them varies with the arrangements you've made for either interviewing an individual or making blind calls to a sample of the population. There is, however, a limit to the length of time that persons are willing to be interviewed by telephone; thirty minutes is about the maximum length of time most individuals will pay attention (Puleston 560).

Telephone interviews done by research or polling organizations such as the Quinnipiac College poll, the Siena College poll, the Marist College poll, Zogby International, or the Gallup Organization are conducted by interviewers who are trained to ask questions, record responses on computer terminals, treat everyone they poll the same way, and pronounce everything clearly in order to ensure accuracy in the polling process. Best practices of opinion polling can be found through the American Association for Public Opinion Research (AAPOR, "Best Practices").

GROUP INTERVIEWS

Sometimes it is useful and productive to interview a number of people at once in a situation different than a focus group. (For more information on focus groups, see **Chapter 12, Research Techniques: Observations, Focus Groups, and Other**

Techniques.) *Group interviews* involve collecting a number of individuals, asking them their opinions, perceptions, or knowledge about a situation, event, activity, or policy while everyone is sitting in the same room. Group interviews cover a range of topics, provide a way of collecting several individual opinions at the same time, and are often conducted in this format to save money and time (Fontana and Frey 365; Creswell 133). A group interview differs from a *focus group*, which is a structured format designed to encourage individuals to react to each other's comments and to focus on one topic, product, or situation. Focus groups are most often used for marketing and product development purposes, although they are used occasionally for research as well (Fontana and Frey 364–65; Morgan 3).

Conducting a group interview takes an additional set of skills from in-person interviews since asking the questions, enabling each person to answer, and listening carefully involves a group dynamic absent in one-on-one interviews. The task of recording can be significantly challenging as well since it is critical to record who said what and when as well as the overall impression of the group, while also capturing the nonverbal behavior. Group interviews are rarely used in research due to the complex skill set needed to conduct them carefully as well as the challenges in recording them. This factor is also a complication that occurs in conducting door-to-door interviews.

DOOR-TO-DOOR INTERVIEWS

Interviewing people by stopping by their house or dropping in on them can provide excellent information and can be used as way of gathering regional information or opinions from the general public. These interviews provide very different data than the information that can be acquired from prearranged individual interviews based on a set of well-established parameters, such as a person's knowledge base, experience, or position in a company or organization (Bryman and Bell 214–16).

Door-to-door interviews are often part of such major research projects as census taking, other forms of polling, and marketing research. It takes some training and skill to prepare the interviewers to approach strangers and ask for their willingness to answer questions. The cultural climate in the United States has made this approach of knocking on doors in homes and apartments fraught with danger, especially if the interviewer comes from a different age group or ethnic background from the person being approached. In some cases, this model is used in situations where interviewees provide a captive audience—travelers waiting for buses, trains and airplane, for example. In these situations, *intercept interviewing*—finding people to answer questions by using locations where individuals congregate—can provide very useful information, especially if the location tends to attract the individuals you want to interview. In these settings, interviewers are dressed in uniforms and present organizational identification as they approach individual travelers asking for their participation in the interview process.

Once the person has agreed to be interviewed, however, the challenge has just begun. Asking the questions, hearing the answers clearly, and recording them in a short time frame—individuals are sometimes willing to provide 10 to 15 minutes for this interview, but no more—can be very difficult (Seidman 57). The time limit includes the hello, getting permission to interview, stating the purpose of interview, asking questions, and saying thank you, which leaves little time for the entire process. To assist in this challenge, door-to-door interviewers often use very structured interview formats and software with which to record the answers to the interview questions.

Since the ratio of willing respondents to persons approached varies dramatically with the situation, this interview method requires the awareness of many factors and is often a fairly sophisticated organizational structure to implement. It also focuses on the general public, which may or may not always be the right audience. Consequently, this method is generally used only for large-scale surveys and polls.

FOLLOW-UP INTERVIEWS

Sometimes, you will discover that you have not taken careful notes or that you have discovered new information and you want to conduct a second interview with an individual. In this case, observing the same protocol about contacting the person, arranging a time and place, preparing the questions, practicing them, taking notes, and thanking them still apply. The time may be shorter, the location may be different—second interviews are often conducted by telephone for ease and convenience—and the persons are the same, but since there is a pattern of trust and rapport, these interviews can proceed more smoothly and quickly. If you do conduct a second interview, do not forget to thank the person again and, if the individual had recommended that you talk to someone else, share what happened in that interview, without, of course, betraying any confidentiality.

Good preparation for the initial interview often precludes the need for a second interview, but do not hesitate to go back to an individual if you discussed that possibility during your first interview if you need more information or if it is critical to your research project.

SUMMARY

While interviews are excellent sources of gathering information for a research project, they provide such challenges as arranging, preparing, conducting, and recording. Analyzing the information involves another set of challenges (see **Chapter 13— Analyzing Data and Other Information**) in order to make the information useful to you in your research. Since interviews, as all data-gathering techniques, have strengths and weaknesses, you should consider their appropriateness for the research you want to conduct.

An alternative technique—the use of questionnaires—is the subject of the next chapter. Since they can be executed more efficiently and are easier to analyze than interviews, they are the most common form of collecting data.

KEY TERMS

Acquiescence bias	Interview fatigue	Research interviews
Auspices bias	Interview protocol	Semi-structured interviews
Courtesy bias	Interview schedule	Social desirability bias
Door-to-door interviewing	Interviewer error	Stages of interview process
Doorknob questions	Leading questions	Status bias
Filter questions	Loaded questions	Structured interviews
Focus groups	Order bias	Unstructured interviews
Group interviews	Probing questions	White space
Intercept interviewing	Prompting questions	Yes/no questions

WORKS CITED IN THIS CHAPTER

American Association for Public Opinion Research. "Best Practices." *American Association for Public Opinion Research.* 2010. Web.

Bernard, H. Russell. *Research Methods in Anthropology: Qualitative and Quantitative Approaches.* 2nd ed. Walnut Creek: Sage Publications, 1995.

Bessinger, RE and Bertrand, JT, "Monitoring Quality of Care in Family Planning Programs: a Comparison of Observations and Client Exit Interviews". *International Family Planning Perspectives,* 27.2 (2001): 63–70.

Biemer, Paul P., and Lars Lyberg. *Introduction to Survey Quality.* Hoboken, NJ: John Wiley & Sons, 2003.

Bryman, Alan, and Emma Bell, *Business Research Methods.* 2nd ed. Oxford: Oxford University Press, 2007.

Cannell, Charles F., and Robert L. Kahn. "The Collection of Data by Interviewing." *Research Methods in the Behavioral Sciences.* Eds. Leon Festinger and Daniel Katz. New York: Holt, Rinehart and Winston, 1966. 327–80.

Crawford, I. M. *Marketing Research and Information Systems.* Rome, Italy: Food and Agriculture Organization of the United Nations, 1997. Web.

Donalek, Julie. "The Interview in Qualitative Research." *Urologic Nursing* 25.2 (2005): 124–25.

Fontana, Andrea, and Frey, James. "Interviewing: The Art of Science." *Handbook of Qualitative Research.* Eds. Norman Denzin and Ivonna Lincoln. Thousand Oaks, CA: Sage Publications, 1994. 361–76.

Guest, Greg, Arwen Bunce, and Laura Johnson. "How Many Interviews are Enough? An Experiment with Data Saturation and Variability." *Field Methods* 18 (2006): 59–82.

Hiller, Harry, and Linda Di Luzio. "The Interviewee and the Research Interview: Analyzing a Neglected Dimension in Research." *Canadian Review of Sociology and Anthropology* 41.1 (2004): 1–26.

Houtkoop-Steenstra, Hanneke. *Interaction and the Standardized Survey Interview: the Living Questionnaire.* Cambridge, UK: Cambridge University Press, 2000.

Hoyle, Rick, Monica Harris, and Charles Judd. *Research Methods in Social Relations.* New York: Wadsworth, 2002.

Iarossi, Giuseppe. *The Power of Survey Design: A User's Guide for Managing Surveys, Interpreting Results, and Influencing Respondents.* Washington, DC: The World Bank, 2006.

Katz, Daniel. "Do Interviewers Bias Poll Results?" *Public Opinion Quarterly*. 6 (1942): 248–68.

Metzler, Ken. *Creative Interviewing: The Writer's Guide to Gathering Information by Asking Questions.* Boston: Allyn and Bacon, 2000.

Molitor, Fred, Richard Kravitz, Yue-Yun To, and Arlene Fink. "Methods in Survey Research: Evidence for the Reliability of Group Administration vs. Personal Interviews." *American Journal of Public Health.* 91 (2001): 826–27.

Oliver, Daniel., Julianne Serovich, and Tina Mason. "Constraints and Opportunities with Interview Transcription: Towards Reflection in Qualitative Research." *Social Forces* 84 (2005): 1273–288.

Olson, Kristen, and Andy Peytchev. "Effect of Interviewer Experience on Interview Pace and Interviewer Attitudes." *Public Opinion Quarterly* 71 (2007): 273–86.

ORC Macro. *Demographic and Health Survey Interviewer's Manual.* MEASURE DHS Basic Documentation 2. Calverton, MD: ORC Macro, 2006. Web. 24 October 2010.

Puleston, Jon. "Improving Online Surveys." *International Journal of Market Research.* 53 (2011): 557–60.

Polsa, Pia. "Comparability in Cross-Cultural Qualitative Marketing Research: Equivalence in Personal Interviews." *Academy of Marketing Science* 8 (2007): 1–18.

Presser, Stanley, and Shanyang Zhao, "Attributes of Questions and Interviewers as Correlates of Interviewing Performance." *The Public Opinion Quarterly.* 56 (1992): 236–40.

Rubin, Herbert J., and Irene Rubin, *Qualitative Interviewing: the Art of Hearing Data.* Minneapolis: Sage Publications, 2004.

Sedorkin, Gail, and Judy McGregor. *Interviewing: A Guide for Journalists and Writers.* Crows Nest, Australia: Allen and Unwin, 2002.

Sekaran, Uma. *Research Methods for Business: A Skill Building Approach.* 4th ed. New York: John Wiley & Sons, 2003.

Seidman, I. E. *Interviewing as Qualitative Research.* New York: Teacher's College Press, 1991.

Shapiro, Michael J. "Discovering Interviewer Bias in Open-Ended Survey Responses." *Public Opinion Quarterly.* 34 (1970): 412–15.

Sin, Chih Hoong. "Communicating Interviews: The Experience of Research with Minority Ethnic Older People in Britain." *Quality in Ageing.* 5 (2004): 21–29.

Strauss, Anselm, and Juliet M. Corbin. *Basics of Qualitative Research: Techniques and Procedures for Developing Grounded Theory.* 2nd ed. Thousand Oaks: Sage Publications, 1998.

Trochim, William M.K. *Research Methods: the Concise Knowledge Base.* Mason, OH: Cengage, 2005.

Zikmund, William G. *Business Research Methods.* (7th ed.) Mason, OH: Thomson, South-Western, 2003.

CHAPTER 11

Research Techniques— Questionnaires

INTRODUCTION

The most useful and commonly used form of collecting data in applied research involves questionnaires. They are prevalent in everyone's life—how many of you have been asked to complete one recently—due to the breadth of marketing research, polling, and now electronic sampling on many websites. Questionnaires are present in a wide range of applications, from banks asking for customer opinions upon logging into online banking, to travel sites such as TripAdvisor engaging its subscribers to produce its annual travel trends survey, to hotel companies offering loyalty points to members for completing surveys, to common website third-party pop-up advertisements asking you to take a survey.

Although widely used, questionnaires are not simple to develop, design, and administer. Since selecting a sample and obtaining a decent response rate is also an important aspect of good research, this chapter provides an explanation about the types of questionnaires, the advantages and disadvantages, and advice about creating and administering questionnaires.

The chapter also contains information about confidentiality, privacy, and permission letters as well as a discussion of incentives to encourage a high response rate.

PURPOSES OF QUESTIONNAIRES

There are many reasons to use questionnaires as a method of gathering information for a research project. In situations where you want to compare information across a wide range of respondents, questionnaires enable you to collect a lot of information in a relatively short period of time so that you can draw conclusions with some credibility. Because of their standard format and scored items, they provide data that can be analyzed to assess correlations and other statistically significant conclusions. When trying to test a hypothesis or retest one with a different population, questionnaires provide a strong data set to use since the numbers can be analyzed from a variety of perspectives.

In situations where you want to sample a specific population, questionnaires can provide a wider range of data and a larger number of responses compared to interviews and focus groups, which typically involve smaller numbers of respondents or participants.

When you are not trying to prove something in a quantitative manner, questionnaires can still provide a range of opinions or information to help you support a vague notion or open the possibilities of research in a particular area or topic. Although some scholars find this use of questionnaires to explore and develop information about a topic to be suspect, the only real use being quantitative, that opinion is slowly changing (Robson 232–34). However, in using a questionnaire for qualitative purposes, the nature of the questions you use and the quantity of answers can help you to determine if there is a pattern of responses to confirm or alter your intuition of what might be happening. The pattern can assist you in exploring possible explanations for an activity or event.

Perhaps the most common reason to use questionnaires is their malleability. If you ask the right questions and enter the data into a useful and powerful software program, you can analyze patterns of responses in subsets of the respondents. That way you can draw more useful and qualified insights. (For more information about conducting a cohort analysis, see **Chapter 13, Analyzing Data and Other Information**.)

When questionnaires are used in a quantitative study and are structured in a manner where you can analyze the results statistically, the responses can provide you with data to correlate responses and detect patterns of responses. In this situation, you need to be careful about constructing your sample. In quantitative research, ensuring representative samples is essential to be able to draw significant and valid conclusions. (See **Chapter 7, Sampling Issues in Research**.)

In their simplest form, questionnaires can provide information that you can examine by cohorts—groups of persons who completed the questionnaire. For example, you can compare the response of women with men, of amateurs with professionals, of persons with little or no specific experience to those with much experience, or of business travelers with leisure travelers.

REASONS TO USE QUESTIONNAIRES

- Provide statistical information.
- Enable correlations.
- Test or retest theories, prove a hypothesis.
- Sample a specific population.
- Support a notion, even if ill-defined.
- Obtain patterns of responses.
- Compare responses over subsets of respondents.

Considering that there are many reasons to use questionnaires, it is essential to understand the range of types of questionnaires.

TYPES OF QUESTIONNAIRES

There are many types of questionnaires, but they can usefully be divided into self-administered and interviewer administered, among other categories. *Self-administered questionnaires* include mailed questionnaires, ones distributed at meetings or events, and online questionnaires. *Interviewer administered questionnaires* include telephone questionnaires, in-person individual questionnaires, and in-person group questionnaires.

Mailed questionnaires used to be the most commonly used since they were easy to develop, print, and distribute. They could be coded on the form and were relatively inexpensive to print and distribute; often, respondents could add more information to the questionnaire, which helped in editing and coding. However, the response rate was often low when they were distributed without any connection between the researcher and the respondent, and successive mailings to produce a good return rate were costly and time-consuming (Fox, Robinson, and Boardley 132–33). Sometimes, the responses on the questionnaire were hard to read or decipher, and even when simple forms were used that could be scanned by machine, often individuals did not complete them accurately or marked several answers at the same time. In addition, once received, each questionnaire had to be entered into a database in order to analyze and compare answers across questionnaires, and there was plenty of room for errors in reading and typing answers into that database.

Personally distributed questionnaires—at meetings, malls, workplaces, theater, sporting events, and other locations—produce higher response rates, especially when individuals are asked to complete them at that moment. This *intercept method* of distributing questionnaires as people arrived at or were leaving a location such as a grocery store, concert, or airplane terminal used to produce high response rates, but the willingness to respond has decreased with the number of organizations using this technique as a sales gimmick and the growing reluctance to chat with strangers. Typically, the response rate from an intercept survey is higher due to the interaction between the survey administrator and respondent. In fact, the intercept method of distributing questionnaires at the end of a meeting or conference is a common method of collecting evaluation information. (For more information about program evaluation, see **Chapter 6, Forms of Qualitative Research**.) Normally, face-to-face distribution of questionnaires can often produce a higher response rate of completed questionnaires: 70 percent, compared to 67 percent for telephone and 61 percent for mail (Hox and DeLeeuw 335). However, Internet surveys are now replacing intercept surveys; depending on the nature of the questions and the type of questions and the nature of the survey, either method can produce a high response rate (Maronick 330).

An advantage of personally distributed questionnaires comes from the ability of the persons distributing the questionnaire to answer any questions about the purpose or format of the questionnaire and to ensure that the individuals complete it by themselves. Although this method does not cost postage, having the persons there to distribute and collect the questionnaires represents significantly higher personnel costs. In addition, the same difficulty of editing, coding, and entering the responses into a database remains.

Online questionnaires, also called e-questionnaires, are being increasingly used due to the ease of developing and administering them as well as the low cost involved. In fact, they are perhaps the most common of questionnaire formats in current use due to their ease of administration and the prevalence of social media as vehicles to reach individuals. In addition, they can be organized using a URL or other vehicle that provides prompt, easy-to-administer formats using the Internet for distribution. Sometimes they are located on a server and individuals are given the URL to access the questionnaire. Other times, the questionnaires are distributed electronically with requests to return. One of the challenges with this form of questionnaire is the assumption that the individuals being asked to respond to your questionnaire have a computer or tablet and are comfortable with and used to completing online questionnaires and other documents. While that phenomenon is becoming increasingly common, it is by no means universal in certain subgroups—age or ethnic, or geographically defined—therefore, you may be limited in the respondents that you can reasonably expect to complete your questionnaire.

In using any of these three forms of questionnaire, you make several assumptions, the first and most important being that the individuals who respond to your questionnaire are being honest in answering the questions and actually have the knowledge and experience to answer the questions. The second assumption you make is that the individuals are actually completing the questionnaires themselves and not asking someone else to complete it for them, a common practice among executives and busy persons who have staff members complete their forms. The better the quality of your letter explaining the purpose and intent of your research, the more honest the responses will be and the higher the likelihood of them coming from real intended respondents. If potential respondents see the value of what you are doing and the merits of completing the questionnaire, they are more likely to complete it, accurately and promptly. (For more information about what to put in the letter or introduction to a questionnaire, see the section on **Privacy and Permission**.)

Telephone questionnaires are typically an interview conducted over the telephone where the person who calls records the answers into a software program as the respondent answers the questions orally. Telephone discussions can be interviews or questionnaires depending on the goal and structure of the questions or the interview protocol. (For more information about telephone interviews, see **Chapter 10, Research Techniques: Interviews**.) Sometimes, incentives can encourage a higher response rate as well. (See the section on **Incentives**.)

Telephone questionnaires need to be very simple since it is hard for respondents to remember the structure of a question or the five to seven possible responses (strongly disagree, disagree, no opinion, agree, strongly agree) to some questions. Professionals who make these calls need to be well trained at articulating clearly the questions and responding very patiently to the individuals that they call. Normally, the persons who place the calls and ask the questions are well trained, ask for more explanation of a response, and ensure that the responses are correct and thorough.

Clearly, this form of questionnaire is costly to administer, but it has the advantage of reaching a wide range of potential respondents. However, it has become increasing difficult to administer due to both the high percentage of persons who hang up immediately, thinking it is a marketing ploy, and the high number of unlisted or do-not-call telephone numbers. Polling organizations use this format for most of their work since they can gather and analyze information quickly, and electronic telephone directories, or electronic digital dialing, make the process easy.

Doorknob questionnaires are instruments left at people's homes or places of work in hopes that they will answer the questions and return the form or mail it to the administrator in a self-addressed, stamped envelope (SASE). Although not a popular form of questionnaire administration since the response rate tends to be very low, it is often used to acquire information. A common form of doorknob questionnaire is practiced by the U.S. Census when there is no response from e-mail or postage-mailed questionnaires or in locations where there is undependable mail delivery. With some audiences, such as senior citizens and persons staying at home, these questionnaires are popular since the doorknob questionnaires provide a welcome activity for these individuals. Other individuals are often scared or anxious about these instruments and reluctant to complete them, mostly due to issues of privacy and confidentiality. Recognizing these concerns can help you improve the response rate of doorknob questionnaires because you can adapt your message or delivery techniques accordingly (Singer, Mathiowetz and Couper 479).

Administering *in-person questionnaires* can be very costly, time-consuming, and difficult, but they have some of the same advantages as telephone questionnaires. The person administering the questionnaire can ask for clarification or review answers. The responses get recorded immediately and clearly so that the analysis can proceed during the process of collecting response, and there is no question that the person answering the questions is the person providing the responses.

Whatever format of questionnaire you use, it is important to consider the benefits and challenges of using questionnaires and the skills of writing questions since you want to gather the right information to conduct your research successfully.

ADVANTAGES AND DISADVANTAGES

There are many advantages and a number of challenges in using questionnaires. They are hard to draft and design in ways that provide the information you need to collect, but they are much easier to score than most other forms of data gathering, such as observations, in-person interviews, and focus groups. They can be administered relatively cheaply, compared to interviews, and take little training to manage. There are various ways of administering questionnaires, and each has its advantages and disadvantages.

Advantages of Questionnaires	Disadvantages of Questionnaires
Provide a lot of detailed information relatively quickly	Take significant skill to write good questions
Collect a lot of information from a wide range of respondents	Contain incomplete answers or answers filled out in a manner that is hard to code
Enable comparison of answers across several respondents	Require professional format and appearance to improve respondent rate

(Continued)

Advantages of Questionnaires	Disadvantages of Questionnaires
Make it possible to collect and analyze answers easily and quickly	Provide no chance to follow up on unclear answers
Enable use of statistical software to analyze patterns of responses	Provide no nonverbal behavior to interpret responses
Compare information and answers across subcategories of respondents with the right software	Allow respondents to misinterpret or over-analyze questions
Do not require recording and transcribing answers	May be difficult to interpret with some answers

DEVELOPING QUESTIONNAIRES

Although many people may think that questionnaires are easy to write, they are, in fact, very complex documents and difficult to create. There is a range of types of possible questions to consider, and formatting the questionnaire can make a big difference in the response rate. The sequence of questions can dramatically affect the results as well.

The process of preparing a questionnaire starts with clarifying the purpose of the research—to discover or investigate a topic, to test a hypothesis, to confirm, or to retest something. Once you are clear what you are trying to ascertain, you can start to create the questions that you want to develop (Robson 241). Often that process takes some time and several iterations since it is a complicated process to ensure that you are collecting the right information and that you do not lead the respondent to answer questions in a certain way. This issue is called respondent bias. (See **Chapter 10, Research Techniques: Interviews**.) Asking questions and considering them from the perspective of the person completing the questionnaire will also open your mind to understand how they see the problem or issue that you are investigating (Corbin and Strauss 70).

There are normally six steps in the process of preparing a questionnaire:

1. Clarifying and reviewing the purpose of the research project

2. Writing out the questions with appropriate answer formats

3. Revising and editing the questions to make them clearer

4. Sequencing them in a way that makes sense to the respondent

5. Trying them out with colleagues

6. Rewriting and formatting them

In some ways, the first step—writing out questions—is the most difficult since it is important to consider what information you want to collect and what types of questions are most likely to provide that information—rating questions, ranking questions, category questions, etc. (see the next section on **Types of Questions**). The challenge is to select the structure of the questions and write them in such a way that they encourage the respondents to answer honestly and provide the information you seek.

When writing questions, remember that your goals include obtaining the information you want and encouraging the respondent to give you complete and accurate answers. Therefore, writing questions carefully can make a big difference. Some of the key principles for developing clear questions include:

- Make the questions simple and straightforward so that the respondent does not have to decipher what you are asking (Fanning 7; Horst 27–28).

- Limit the number of open-ended question since they take more time and slow down respondents, most of whom have a limited amount of time to devote to completing your questionnaire.

- Group similar types of questions together so that they are easier for the respondent to answer at the same time.

- Ask positive—not negative—questions since they are easier to answer and are less likely to confuse the respondent.

- Limit questions to 20 words or less (Iarossi 31).

- Craft short questions rather than long ones—they should not be longer than one line of type if at all possible (Fanning 7; Horst 27).

After writing out the questions as best as you can, put them away for a while and go on to other tasks that you need to or want to do. Letting the questions sit overnight or for several days will help you read them fresh. To see them afresh, try the following three strategies:

1. Read them backward from the last question to the first.

2. Read them aloud so that you can hear them clearly.

3. Read them out of order.

Another way to obtain help in seeing them clearly is to give them to a colleague to read and see if the questions are clear, the sequence makes sense, and the questionnaire format is easy to understand.

If you are going to administer the questionnaire to persons for whom English is not the primary language, you should have the questionnaire translated into the language with which the potential respondents are most comfortable. After translating it yourself, if you can, or having it translated by someone else, it is important to arrange for a back translation. A *back translation*, the process of translating the new questionnaire into its original language, involves having the questionnaire in the foreign language translated back to English by a person different than the original translator. (Brace 203–205). What you will find is that the process of double translation picks up errors in the understanding of the questions, and it may lead you to revise the wording or the structure of the questions.

Remember to read the questions from the perspective of a person reading them for a first time and consider the sequence of the questions, which can encourage persons to complete the questionnaire or lead to questionnaire fatigue or confusion, especially if you shift frequently among types of questions. This task is important since the actual question format or context can dramatically affect the results (Kenett 406; Sekaran 243). Using certain types of questions can also make a huge difference in the effectiveness of the questionnaire.

TYPES OF QUESTIONS

When writing a questionnaire, you may find it helpful to reflect on the types of questions that you want to use. They all have their own particular advantages and beneficial uses. They are divided into closed-ended and open-ended. *Close-ended questions* have one answer and are much easier for a participant to answer since they take only a moment to check or click (in the case of an online questionnaire). They are also much easier to score and code, and consequently, analyze in a software program. In addition, they help respondents to complete the questionnaire and reduce incomplete documents, which become a problem to analyze and interpret. *Open-ended questions* invite the participant to provide a lot of information and require the individuals to take time to consider. They can provide a wider range of information but can be much more difficult to score.

The most common form of closed-ended question to gather demographic information is a *category question*, which requires a person to check into which category the individual belongs. The most prevalent example is gender—male or female—or marital status—single, partnered, married, divorced, separated, or widowed. In tourism and hospitality, an often-used category question is one that asks the purpose of a trip and provides four opinions: business, leisure, family and friends, or a combination. However, novices at developing questionnaires often ask more demographic information than they will use in analyzing the results—a situation to avoid. *List questions* are ones that ask a person to check all of the items that apply, such as, "What are the reasons for undertaking this particular trip?" and provide a number of possible responses for the respondent to check, such as:

- Conducting business
- Enjoying some leisure time
- Combining business and leisure
- Visiting family and friends
- Taking advantage of favorable exchange rates
- Responding to advertised special rates
- Doing what I always wanted to do but never had the time before
- Completing my bucket list

EXAMPLES OF DEMOGRAPHIC QUESTIONS

Age

Gender

Educational background

Hometown

Purpose of trip

Occupation

Marital status

Citizenship

Annual income

Some of the problems in writing questions derive from inexperience when persons write loaded or leading questions. *Loaded questions* are ones that show a bias from the question writer toward possible answers. An example of a loaded question is: "In what ways do you see that boutique hotels are just a passing fad?" or "Don't you agree that there are too many World Heritage sites and that they are mismanaged?" or "Isn't it horrible that concussions are destroying sports?" *Leading questions* contain the answer that you are seeking. Many married individuals know what leading questions are when a man or woman asks, "Honey, do I look good in this outfit?" to which the clearly expected answer is "Yes, of course." In questionnaires, a leading question might be: "What do you think has provided the low RevPAR in hotels?" or "How have museum blockbuster shows changed the way in which visitors experience going to a museum?" or "Have personal seat licenses changed the pattern and range of season ticket holders?"

Ranking questions ask the participant to place items in a priority order; for example, asking the priority of various aspects of their satisfaction with the hotel with the instructions being, "Please indicate which of the following factors you find most important in your satisfaction with this hotel. Use a one for most important and a nine for the least important," the options being:

• Brand of hotel

• Cleanliness of the facility

• Ease of making reservations

• Effectiveness of housekeeping staff

• Quality of the food and beverages

- Relationship between quality and value

- Safety of the hotel

- Service of the wait staff

- Welcome at the front desk

While ranking questions ask the participant to put the items in an order, often using a number or percentages, *rating questions* ask the person to evaluate the statement or the situation as in the following examples.

Please rate the following aspects of service at this hotel on a scale from 1 to 5 (with 1 being very poor and 5 being very excellent):					
	Very Poor	Poor		Good	Very Good
	1	2	3	4	5
Friendliness of staff	1	2	3	4	5
Greetings from staff members	1	2	3	4	5
Promptness of service	1	2	3	4	5
Quality of service	1	2	3	4	5
Smiles from staff members	1	2	3	4	5
Use of your name from staff	1	2	3	4	5
Welcoming attitude of staff	1	2	3	4	5
	1	2	3	4	5

The most common form of rating question uses the *Likert scale*, developed by Rensis Likert in 1932 to distinguish among various levels of disagreement or agreement (Likert 42). The Likert scales provide numbers, which can be counted and scored. The most typical Likert scale ranges from one for strongly disagree to five for strongly agree; sometimes, it is more effective to use a seven-point scale. Either way, odd numbers produce a broader spread and one that is more useful than an even number of options (Robson 294). Typically, Likert scales go from negative to positive and from a lower number to a higher number since people read responses from left to right. An example is listed below:

Please indicate your agreement with the following statements:					
	Strongly Disagree				Strongly Agree
1. I liked the service at this stadium.	1	2	3	4	5
2. The ushers were friendly and welcoming.	1	2	3	4	5
3. The facilities were clean and well-kept.	1	2	3	4	5
4. The food was good.	1	2	3	4	5
5. The beer selection was good.	1	2	3	4	5

ELECTRONIC QUESTIONNAIRES

When developing electronic questionnaires, there are a range of types of questions and tools to use. The most popular and important is the *status bar*, a statement or figure at the bottom of the page that indicates the amount of questionnaire left to complete. A clearly visible status bar tends to increase the likelihood that respondents will complete the questionnaire since it indicates how much more of the questionnaire is still in front of them. This friendly assurance often improves your response rate of completed questionnaires. Therefore, when designing an electronic questionnaire, consider the design of your status bar.

Other electronic devices include the *push button*, which indicates what the respondent is supposed to do next. The most common form of push button is the sign $\boxed{Next}$ at the bottom of a page or after a question. Most respondents who are familiar with online purchasing understand the push button and know to click on it so that the software moves to the next page. Other examples of push buttons are buttons that enable a respondent to move to the $\boxed{bottom\ of\ page}$ or the $\boxed{top\ of\ page}$ or to $\boxed{Go\ Back}$.

Other software tools include, but are not limited to, drop-down boxes, radio buttons, pop-up boxes, and check boxes. A *drop-down box* is one in which several answers appear when the question is clicked; a common use of drop-down box in an electronic questionnaire is a question about gender or home country or age. You have created the categories and the person can choose them by opening the drop-down box and clicking on the most correct answer. *Radio buttons* are often circles or squares that show a check mark or fill in when the respondent clicks on the button. They are typically designed so that a respondent can only answer one question in an array.

Pop-up boxes are boxes that contain questions or information that pop up in response to other questions or where the respondent may need more information in order to understand the question. *Check boxes* are the same on electronic and paper questionnaires; they require that a respondent indicates which of the following answers is the most correct, and they are all shown on the electronic page just as they are on a paper questionnaire. The drop-down box does not show the answers until the box is clicked; check boxes are visible all the time. Check boxes are often used in list questions when more than one answer is possible.

Currently, there are a number of software products available for designing questionnaires. Some of them include SurveyMonkey, Qualtrics, SurveyGizmo or SurveyPro, or SurveyGold. A Google search will show you a wide range of other options. Some will let you use the software on a pilot basis and some may already be available where you study or work. Using these software packages can be very helpful once you have already developed your questionnaire. Developing the questions while involved in the software leaves you with the challenge of making many decisions about layout and format while you still have not decided what questions you want to ask and in what order. The simpler and more effective way involves creating a questionnaire in a Word document, playing with layout and format and sequence, checking the design with colleagues, and then placing it into software that you will use to administer the questionnaire.

SEQUENCING QUESTIONS

Sequencing questions becomes a critical task since the prejudice created by the structure and sequence of questions can influence the answer of succeeding questions. This problem, called *order bias* can be forestalled by carefully considering what earlier questions would influence later ones (Ferber 177–78). The most common practice, called the *funnel approach*, involves starting with general questions and those easier to answer, followed by questions that are more specific and take more thought (Cannell and Kahn 348–49).

STEPS IN SEQUENCING QUESTIONS

- List the questions you want to ask and then try to sort them into categories of similar questions. Then consider the sequencing of categories.

- Start with general questions and then move to specific ones.

- Provide clear instructions before each different section.

- Place similar-type questions in the same section of your questionnaire to prevent respondent fatigue from shifting from one type of question to another; it can affect the quality of the responses.

- Place open-ended questions at the end of the questionnaire since they are harder to complete and respondents are more likely to complete them when they have finished most of the questionnaire.

- Make interval scales consistent by providing equal intervals for each category (e.g., ages 21–25; 26–30; 31–35; 36–40; 41–45; 46–50; 51–55; 56–60 instead of 21–30; 31–35; 36–40; 41–50; and over 50) since unequal intervals might indicate a bias on the part of the researcher.

- Watch the use of terms. Some words, like "short term," "sustainable," "luxury," might mean one thing to you and something quite different to the respondents completing your questionnaire.

- When using a list of items as possible answers to a question, put the items in alphabetical order so that you do not lead respondents by making some items more important than others.

- Consider all of the categories when you are writing category questions so that participants do not feel excluded. (For example, single, married, widowed, partnered with a significant other is a more inclusive list than *single* and *married* only).

- Ensure that there are no grammatical or typographical errors in your questionnaire.

DEMOGRAPHIC DATA

There is a debate about demographic questions, often called *classification data*—the personal information that you collect in order to subgroup your respondents for analysis. Some scholars think that the questions about age, gender, income, job, purpose of trip, and other demographic data belong at the beginning of a questionnaire and others believe they belong at the end (Sekaran 243). Since classification data questions are relatively easy to answer, do not require much thinking, especially categorical questions, and help respondents warm up to the process of completing a questionnaire (Cannell and Kahn 349–50), some researchers like placing them at the beginning of questionnaires. They also feel it increases the respondent's likelihood of completing the questionnaire.

Others favor putting classification questions, especially those asking about income, or other information that a respondent might be unwilling to disclose, at the end of a questionnaire (Sekaran 242). Those that recommend placing these questions at the end point out that individuals are often reluctant to share private information—especially information about income—but they will if it is at the end of the questionnaire since they want to complete it (Dillman 123–25). A third opinion suggests that most classification data questions should be placed at the beginning of questionnaires but that more controversial questions such as income belong at the end, thereby benefiting from both theories (Oppenheim 37). The decision is up to you since all of these strategies work.

However, be wary of asking for more classification data than you will use in your analysis. Collecting a lot of information that you will not use, either because it is not relevant to your research purpose or because it has nothing to do with the hypotheses that you are trying to prove, is simply a waste of respondents' time and yours as well. Therefore, think carefully about what information is relevant to collect and analyze.

QUESTIONNAIRE ADMINISTRATION

Distributing and collecting questionnaires, whether through meetings, mail, or electronic means continues to be one of the most critical aspects of data gathering since the response rate can make a significant difference in your ability to analyze data and to provide insights with some validity.

The most common factors that affect response rate include clarity of purpose, professionalism of appearance, format or structure, and follow-ups. Persons are more likely to complete your questionnaire if the purpose is clear and if you ask for their help in a professional and friendly manner. Follow-ups are critical to ensuring an appropriate response rate, and more reminders typically produce a higher response rate (Iarossi 149). Both mailed and electronic questionnaires often require several follow-up reminders since busy people often want to complete the questionnaire but put it off due to the pressure of other business. There is a recommended system commonly used called the Dillman Total Design Method that sets out to identify and shape the aspects of the survey to obtain the best possible responses, and then to "organize the survey efforts so that the design intentions are carried out in complete detail" (Dillman 12). Basically, regular, professional and friendly reminders tend to increase the response rate of mailed or electronic questionnaires.

Providing a clear description of the purpose of your questionnaire can improve the likelihood that a respondent will complete the questionnaire and provide accurate information. Many individuals appreciate being asked for their opinion and want to help with serious research. Therefore, consider carefully how you will describe your research at the beginning of a questionnaire or in a permission letter sent to prospective respondents. The following examples illustrate ways to demonstrate clarity of purpose to a person considering your questionnaire:

Example One

As a university student born between the ages of 17 and 25, you are invited to participate in a research project examining the role of advertising within the sphere of youth tourism. The study was developed to investigate advertising's ability to influence Generation Y student travelers' perceptions of escorted group travel. Specifically, it explores Generation Y student travelers' feelings toward escorted group travel, and whether advertising is an effective medium for tour operators catering to Generation Y university students. This study is part of a student research effort on Generation Y Student Travelers' Perception of Escorted Group Travel.

Example Two

As an MLB fan who has recently attended a game, and by completing the following questionnaire, you are participating in an applied special research project investigating fan motivations for attending MLB games. Specifically, this study will explore the likeliness that specific factors will help or hinder fans' likelihood to attend MLB games.

Example Three

Thank you for your participation. This research study focuses on Filipino Americans and their travel to the Philippines, as well as the attitudes of Filipino Americans toward the Philippines as a tourist destination. This questionnaire should take about 15 to 20 minutes to complete. Your responses will be anonymous and will only be used for our research purposes. Please mark your responses by clicking on your choice as appropriate.

Example Four

As a recent guest of a hotel offering self-service technologies to aid in service exchanges, you are invited to participate in a research project on self-service technology in the hospitality industry. The study was developed to investigate consumer preferences and behaviors toward self-service technology in the hospitality industry. Specifically, it explores the effect of implementation of SST on a consumer's willingness to pay more to stay at a hotel. It is part of a student research effort on self-service technology in the hospitality industry.

Example Five

Thank you for your participation in our survey. The research study measures the travel motivations and culinary preferences of tourists on leisure vacations. There are three sections. Please complete all sections. The survey should take approximately 15 minutes to complete. Your responses will be anonymous and confidential and will be used only for research purposes.

All five examples provide a clear reason for the questionnaire and invite respondents to assist with significant research. They also indicate that the responses will be kept confidential and only used for research purposes.

Response rates to questionnaires vary, and it is increasingly difficult to obtain responses to requested questionnaires (O'Connell 27). Research on expected response rates varies widely. Several factors that influence response rates include: the randomness of the sample, a preexisting relationship with the respondent, the type of questionnaire and information being asked, and the design of the questionnaire. However, the format of the questionnaire can make a difference as well; web surveys produce a faster response rate than mail or fax surveys, depending on the audience involved (Cobanoglu, Warde, and Moreo 450). In fact, the range of response rates can vary from 1 to 70 percent. With mailed questionnaires to a cold audience—that is, respondents who have no connection to the researcher or his or her organization—a very modest response rate can be considered significant and very productive. However, if you wish to be able to generalize from your survey, a response rate of above 60 percent is considered acceptable, 70 to 85 percent is very good, and over 85 percent is excellent (Bryman and Bell 144). However, often surveys with much lower response rates are only minimally less accurate (Holbrook, Krosnick, and Pfent 528). It depends a lot on the purpose of your questionnaire and the characteristics of the population you are sampling.

Due to the ease of responding and the prevalence of immediate response capability in the contemporary electronic setting, it is possible to obtain higher response rates than mailed questionnaires, although research also varies as to the effectiveness of electronic surveys over mailed surveys (Cook, Heath, and Thompson 821–36). In the case of a mailed questionnaire or one that is distributed in person, including with the questionnaire a self-addressed and stamped envelope (SASE)—first-class postage—can make a real difference in the response rate (Paxson 71; Robson 249–50). Providing the envelope also allows you to code the responses in a specific way so that you know what cohort the respondent is in, information that can be useful in your analysis as well as in organizing a follow-up reminder.

QUESTIONNAIRE PRESENTATION

The first part of a questionnaire typically contains information about the purpose of the research and the reasons for requesting the participation of the respondent. Often, respondents are told that their responses will be kept confidential, none will be attributed to individuals but only reported on categories, and that the original questionnaires will be destroyed after being coded and entered into appropriate databases. The clarity of that information and the way in which it is presented provides the first method to encourage respondents to complete the questionnaire, improving the response rate. If you provide information about how long it will take to complete the questionnaire and how the information will be used, you will build trust with your potential respondent. Giving them detailed information about how to reach you also helps encourage them to trust you and complete the questionnaire.

The second way to encourage respondents to complete the questionnaire involves creating a favorable impression when they look at the document, whether in electronic or print form. One of the most critical aspects of a questionnaire includes the format, design, layout, and appearance (Paxson 69–71; Sekaran 245; Robson 249). In fact, respondents are most likely to respond to questionnaires if they are well organized, professionally presented, and clearly organized. After all, few people want to take precious time to complete a questionnaire that looks like someone has not even taken the care to make sure it looks good, has correct grammar, and contains no typographical errors. Even the formatting of the pages—in either an online or printed questionnaire—makes a difference in the willingness and ability of a respondent to provide accurate answers (Iarossi 18). Even minute details such as ensuring that questions and answers are not spread over a page break or that font size is consistent and easily readable can make a difference.

The clarity and size of the font, the ease of understanding and following the directions, the layout of the boxes to check or the lines to fill, and the presentation make a significant difference in the respondents' impression of your project and their willingness to participate (Sekaran 245). In the case of a captive audience, who must fill out the questionnaire in a contrived setting under supervision, the formatting may not be so important. However, it still contributes to the professional appearance of what you are doing and the attitude of professionalism or responsibility that the respondents will bring to providing the answers you request (Fanning 1–2; Brace 154).

PRIVACY AND PERMISSION

One of the most critical aspects of administering questionnaires involves the process and necessity of requesting permission. First, you want to invite the potential respondent to take the time to answer your questions and encourage him or her to do it thoughtfully so that you have good and usable responses. Second, you want to state the use to which you will put the information. Third, you want to indicate the breadth and range of your research and its institutional support. Doing a private project may yield very different responses than one associated with a company, well-known industry organization, association, or college/ university.

Since you are involving a human being in your research process, you need to be clear that the individual will not be harmed by completing the questionnaire. That information should include details about how you will handle the questionnaires after they have been analyzed—will you shred or otherwise destroy them? Will you hold them for later research possibilities? Will you destroy any personally identifying material? You also want to inform the potential respondent about your ethical stance around confidentiality and privacy in general.

In addition, when you are collecting data from questionnaires and want to use quotations from the responses to open-ended questions, you need to indicate that you might do that when you are requesting the respondent to participate. Simply indicating that any information from the questionnaire will be used without attribution in any research publication will cover your situation, but providing that information indicates what a respondent might expect. In an interview situation (see **Chapter 10, Research Techniques: Interviews**), you may need to check with the person interviewed about the exact wording of a response and obtain his or her permission before using a direct quotation in a document. In the situation of questionnaires, there are often very few written comments to use, and the general permission request at the beginning of the questionnaire may suffice. Since the questionnaire is anonymous, there is no other way to actually request permission to use what is written on the questionnaire.

A typical phrasing for permission might include the following sentences:

> Thank you for your willingness to complete the following questionnaire as part of a research project on xxxx. You must be 18 years of age or older to participate in this research effort, and there are no known risks associated with your participation in this research.

> All individual responses will be kept strictly confidential and used only in aggregate (or by category), to accomplish the study's purpose and to report the findings. If your response to any open-ended question is quoted, it will not be attributed to any individual and will be used only to clarify the results of the research.

> Although you will receive no direct benefit from this research, your voluntary participation is very much appreciated.

> Thank you for your help.

When conducting research as part of an institution, you may need to request permission from the company or organizations' committee on research with human subjects. Most companies, universities, or large organizations that conduct research have such a review board in order to ensure that research involving people protects their safety and security. Checking with your organization's policies on research with human subjects may save you a lot of pain later and ensure that you are conducting your research in an appropriate and professional manner. In some cases, you may need to expand the permission statement and add information about whom a potential respondent can contact if there are questions about the instrument or the research project. In most college courses that involve research, the faculty member has already obtained permission for the research, but it is always useful to check.

When using a postal or electronic questionnaire, you can place this information in your letter encouraging them to complete the questionnaire. However, you need to consider all the possible questions that might arise since you will not have a chance to answer them other than with the information on the form. When using a telephone or in person questionnaire, you can make these statements orally and answer any questions. Especially, if you intend—or think you might want—to actually quote the responses to any open-ended questions (often a great way to add color and vitality to your analysis), then you need to indicate that possibility to potential respondents. In that case, you may want to state that you may use the statements but without providing any personal or identifying characteristic.

INCENTIVES

Response rates are sometimes improved by *incentives*, gifts, tokens, or rewards provided for completing a questionnaire, offered to respondents. Simply providing a reason for the respondent to complete the questionnaire, without a gift, often increases the likelihood and promptness of the response. Sometimes, just explaining the reason for the research is sufficient. In fact, it is the most common incentive and works very well, especially when the format of the questionnaire looks very professional. The most common encouragement for mailed or distributed questionnaires is a self-addressed and stamped envelope (SASE) since it saves respondents from having to locate those things before mailing the response back (Paxson 71). However, the research on incentives has been limited and inconclusive (Brennan, Benson, and Kearns 66).

In other cases, researchers have found that providing a modest reward—a copy of the results, a gift certificate, a chance to win something in a drawing, or a donation to a charity—have all been used to increase response rates (Edwards et al. 4). If you are developing an incentive or providing a reward, ensure that it is consistent with the purpose of your search and appropriate for your audience. Providing a gift certificate for McDonald's or Burger King is not likely to encourage people to respond to a questionnaire on healthy diets or the quality of service in white tablecloth restaurants.

The other challenge involves offering participation in a raffle or drawing. If you are promising the respondents privacy and confidentiality, but asking for their email address or other identifying information, that request may raise questions about the extent of the privacy. Therefore, you need to find a way to collect that information without associating it with the questionnaire.

SUMMARY

This chapter on questionnaires has provided a broad background about their purposes, their strengths and weaknesses, the issues in developing questions, the challenge of administering them to obtain a high rate of response, and the continuing concerns of privacy and confidentiality. It prepares you to create questionnaires and use them in your research.

The next chapter, **Chapter 12, Research Techniques: Observations, Focus Groups, and Other Techniques**, will focus on observation and focus groups as methods of collecting data for applied research purposes.

KEY TERMS

Back translation	Drop-down box	Interviewer administered
Category questions	Funnel approach	questionnaires
Check box	In-person	Leading questions
Classification data	questionnaires	Likert scale
Closed-ended questions	Incentives	List questions
Doorknob questionnaires	Intercept method	Loaded questions

Mailed questionnaires	Pop-up box	Self-administered
Online questionnaires	Push button	questionnaires
Open-ended questions	Radio button	Status bar
Order bias	Ranking questions	Telephone
Personally distributed	Rating questions	questionnaires
questionnaires		

WORKS CITED IN THIS CHAPTER

Brace, Ian. *Questionnaire Design: How to Plan, Structure, and Write Survey Material for Effective Market Research*. London and Sterling: Kogan Page, 2004.

Brennan, Mike, Susan Benson, and Zane Kearns. "The Effect of Introductions on Telephone Survey Participation Rates." *International Journal of Market Research* 47 (2005): 65–74.

Bryman, Allyn, and Emma Bell. *Business Research Methods*. Oxford: Oxford University Press, 2003.

Bush, Alan, and A. Parasuraman. "Mall Intercept versus Telephone-Interviewing Environment." *Journal of Advertising Research*. 25 (1985): 36–43.

Cannell, Charles F., and Robert L. Kahn. "The Collection of Data by Interviewing." *Research Methods in the Behavioral Sciences*. Eds. Leon Festinger and Daniel Katz. New York: Holt, Rinehart and Winston, 1966. 327–80.

Cohanoglu, Cihan, Bill Warde, and Patrick J. Moreo. "A Comparison of Mail, Fax and Web-Based Survey Methods." *International Journal of Market Research* 43 (2001): 441–52.

Cook, Colleen, Fred Heath, and Russell L. Thompson. "A Meta-Analysis of Response Rates in Web- or Internet-Based Surveys." *Educational and Psychological Measurement* 60 (2000): 821–36.

Corbin, Juliet, and Anselm Strauss. *Basics of Qualitative Research: Techniques and Procedures for Developing Grounded Theory*. Los Angeles: Sage Publications, 2008.

Dillman, Don A. *Mail and Telephone Surveys: The Total Design Method*. New York: John Wiley & Sons, 1978.

Edwards, PJ, I. Roberts, M.J. Clarke, C. DiGiuseppi, R. Wentz, I. Kwan, R. Cooper, L.M. Felix, and S. Pratap. "Methods to Increase Response to Postal and Electronic Questionnaires (Review)." *Cochrane Library* 3 (2009): n.pag. Web. 1 November 2010.

Fanning, Elizabeth. "Formatting a Paper-based Survey Questionnaire: Best Practices." *Practical Assessment, Research and Evaluation* 10.12 (2005): 1–14.

Ferber, Robert. "Order Bias in a Mail Survey." *Journal of Marketing* 17 (1952): 171–78.

Fox, Christine M., K. Lynne Robinson, and Debra Boardley. "Cost-Effectiveness of Follow-Up Strategies in Improving the Response Rate of Mail Surveys." *Industrial Marketing Management* 27 (1998): 127–33.

Holbrook, Allyson L., Jon A. Krosnick, and Alison Pfent. "The Causes and Consequences of Response Rates in Surveys by the News Media and Government Contractor Survey Research Firms." *Advances in Telephone Survey Methodology*. Hoboken, NJ: John Wiley & Sons, 2007. 499–528.

Horst, Paul. *Personality: Measurement of Dimensions*. San Francisco: Jossey-Bass, 1968.

Hox, Joop J., and Edith D. DeLeeuw. "A Comparison of Nonresponse in Mail, Telephone, and Face-to-face Surveys: Applying Multilevel Modeling to Meta-Analysis." *Quality and Quantity* 28 (1994): 329–44.

Iarossi, Giuseppe. *The Power of Survey Design: A User's Guide for Managing Surveys, Interpreting Results, and Influencing Respondents*. Washington DC: The World Bank, 2006.

Kenett, Ron S. "On the Planning and Design of Sample Surveys" *Journal of Applied Statistics* 33 (May 2006): 405–15.

Maronick, Thomas. "Pitting the Mall Against the Internet in Advertising-Research Competition: Internet Panels Are More Popular. Are they More Effective?" *Journal of Advertising Research* (2011): 321–31.

O'Connell, Andrew. "Reading the Public Mind." *Harvard Business Review* (2010): 27–29.

Oppenheim, Abraham Naftali. *Questionnaire Design and Attitude Measurement*. Great Britain: Gower Publishing, 1966.

Paxson, M. Chris. "Increasing Survey Response Rates: Practical Instructions from the Total-Design Method." *Cornell Hotel and Restaurant Administration Quarterly* 36 (1995): 66–73.

Robson, Colin. *Real World Research*. 2nd ed. Malden: Blackwell, 2002.

Roster, Catherine A., Robert D. Rogers, and Gerald Albaum. "A Comparison of Response Characteristics from Web and Telephone Surveys." *International Journal of Market Research* 46 (2004): 359–73.

Sekaran, Uma. *Research Methods for Business: A Skill Building Approach*. 4th ed. Hoboken, NJ: John Wiley & Sons, 2003.

Singer, Eleanor, Nancy A. Mathiowetz, and Mick P. Couper. "The Impact of Privacy and Confidentiality Concerns on Survey Participation: The Case of the 1990 Census." *Public Opinion Quarterly* 57 (1993): 465–82.

Research Techniques: Observations, Focus Groups, and Other Techniques

CHAPTER 12

INTRODUCTION

The two previous chapters reviewed the challenges and opportunities provided by interviews and questionnaires, some of the most common research techniques used in applied research. This chapter will discuss four more research techniques: structured observations, focus groups, expert panels, and content analysis. The first three methods involve a special form of gathering data from people whose behavior or insights and commentary provide information for your analysis. The fourth method provides a nonobtrusive way of analyzing information and does not involve the observation or recording of comments by human beings. Unfortunately, these four methods are often misunderstood and assumed as easy ways to gather and analyze data. As you have learned by now, however, maintaining objectivity while using research techniques remains a continuing challenge.

This chapter will review the definition and benefits of each of these four methods, discuss the challenges and ways to overcome them, and provide special information relevant to each research technique.

BENEFITS OF OBSERVATIONAL RESEARCH

Structured observation can provide a useful and very productive method of gathering information if you are clear about what you are observing and how you want to observe it. Observing consumers has its roots in focus groups for product testing (Abrams xix–xxiv) and understanding pedestrian traffic patterns in public spaces, parks, and centers (Underhill 22–23).

Structured observation is perhaps the most commonly misunderstood method of collecting data since it seems to be so easy and so subjective. After all, people observe behavior all the time and think that they have analyzed it carefully. Newton's apocryphal observation of an apple falling can even be considered observational research (Crowther and Lancaster 108). Observation is something that most of us do all the time; however, using observation as a research technique involves a lot of careful planning to clarify what is being observed and how it will be noticed, recorded, and analyzed. Observational research is almost an ethnographical study that examines people in everyday environments (Abrams xxi–xxii).

There are several benefits to using observational research techniques. You can identify and count or measure actual customer behavior and actions rather than hear about them from others who may have a particular point of view about customer behavior. Observational research is more accurate than focus groups, which rely on participants' memories or perceptions of products or services, while observing them provides insight into their actual experience (Abrams 6–7). By counting and measuring, you can also discover patterns of behavior that you, or others, may not have seen or been aware of, given all the other reading and work you have done on the topic (Sharp and Tustin 1590–592). Perhaps the most vivid examples of patterns of behavior that have been discovered by careful and systematic observation is what we know about the behavior of shoppers due to the work of Paco Underhill. His team of researchers has created the science of shopping and illuminated behaviors that no one noticed before, not even professional sales persons. For example, Underhill and his fellow researchers noticed in observing fast-food restaurant drive-through situations that approximately 10 percent of customers park in the fast-food parking lot and eat after passing through the drive-through (91). Without some systematic observation, this pattern of behavior would not have been recognized.

Observing others can also produce some interesting potential notions or ideas that might yield theories to test using a different research technique. Observing the behavior of persons entering a restaurant or waiting in a food concession line at a stadium can tell you a lot about what they will buy and how they will treat servers. Developing these ideas and understanding customers better are only a few of the many reasons for careful structured observations (Abrams 24–48). Sometimes even professionals do not realize what is happening in their companies. Observing how customers interact with each other or their environment and the effectiveness of various strategies has led to the development of models of service recovery and the prevalence of acronyms in many hotels so that staff can be trained to use a certain model.

Another function that observation can play is to liberate researchers from their limited perspectives. Since some scholars and other industry professionals tend to see the world through the eyes that they have trained to look a certain way, they may not notice or be aware of certain customer or managerial behavior. Being forced to look at what managers actually do rather than assume behavior on the basis of self-reports or perceptions of others can provide real insights and overcome research blindness (Gram 399). This form of *research blindness* can be diminished by using structured observations in the same way that careful observation of a job candidate can eliminate the often erroneous assumptions about them made on the basis of how they appear, what they say, and how they say it, in short, from all the ways that they act in an interview situation. Most professionals cannot get beyond their previous assumptions about persons and often make snap judgments in interviews. However, the more carefully structured the observations, the more likely you can get beyond your lack of ability to really see who is in front of you.

A third benefit of careful observational research is the ability to notice behavior without disturbing others. Most people who know they are being observed react to the observation in self-conscious ways. That reality changes what you can learn from observing behavior. One of the fascinating insights of Underhill's work is that he and his researchers learned that people do not notice they are being observed if someone is beside them; they are very aware of persons who are in front of them and behind them; so observers stand in the person's peripheral vision and can record behavior without disturbing shoppers (Underhill 14).

Since there is a real difference between seeing and noticing, observation requires a structured and coherent plan which includes what you will observe, how you are going to record your observations, and how you will analyze the records that you collect. It takes a lot of careful organization and planning to conduct objective observations.

BIAS IN CONDUCTING OBJECTIVE OBSERVATIONS

When conducting a research observation, several forms of bias can enter into the situation: selective attention to activities and events or behavior, perceptual flooding from past memories or triggers, inability to observe consistently, the seduction of topic or behavior being observed, stress and anxiety affecting perception, and individual intrapersonal and interpersonal reactions. Other bias comes from the system or the structure of the observation, including poor sampling models, poor record keeping, lack of clarity about purpose, and symbol confusion.

Selective attention can create real difficulties in observing the behavior of individuals or groups because the observer, no matter how well trained, may come to the situation with a particular interest in one type of behavior and not another, or the individual may not have the skills and the perspective to only observe what you have requested and not be drawn to all of the other fascinating things that are happening at the same time. It is critical to have selective attention in some situations, but the real question remains as to whether the person conducting the observation can and will be able to follow your specific instructions and count only the units of measured behavior that you consider important. When observing the behavior of tourists at a theme park, selective attention can impair your discipline if you only focus on souvenir and ride purchases but ignore food and beverage purchases. Observing fan behavior at a tailgating party requires a focus on the behavior of the individuals; it means ignoring the food and beverages being served.

There are two ways in which perceptual flooding can disrupt the best-trained observers. In some situations, observers find that their past experience triggers emotions so that they have difficulty noticing and recording what they are supposed to be watching. Persons attending baseball games sometimes cannot avoid looking at the game and tend to observe behavior differently based on the scores, the excitement of fans, or their attitude toward the winning or losing team. If they are expected to observe fan behavior, they need to be especially oriented and trained not to participate in that fan behavior but to notice everything that they see and record it using an established system.

The other challenge comes from the anxiety and stress that a situation may place on the observer. Observers who are being asked to watch what managers do in staff training sessions may get involved in the subject matter of the training or worried about whether they could learn the material, neither of which is relevant to their observing the behavior of the trainer and the student-participants. In addition, if the observer is tired or stressed because of some other aspect of his or her life, then the person may not be able to pay close attention to the subjects being observed. Called *observer drift*—the practice of forgetting, not noticing, or decreased interest in keeping good records and watching carefully—this process can cause real difficulties (Boice 11). The mind can wander; daydreams or worries of other situations affect the discipline of careful objective observation so necessary to this research technique.

Other individuals find that they experience some inability to observe consistently since the situation or the topic can be so seductive. Finding individuals to observe shopping behaviors without getting intrigued by the merchandise, or observing fan behavior without wanting to watch the game, or managerial behavior without thinking of how they might handle the situation can be difficult. Sometimes, observers have an emotional reaction to the individuals they are observing and cannot see the behavior or actions of the individual clearly. Often careful training will overcome this difficulty, but sometimes observers need to be shifted to another assignment since interpersonal and intrapersonal issues affect their ability to observe fairly and dispassionately.

There are many ways to overcome these forms of bias, and the range of those techniques and the other challenges of conducting objective observations are the subject of the next section.

CHALLENGES AND RECOMMENDATIONS FOR CONDUCTING OBJECTIVE OBSERVATIONS

Most of the challenges in observation revolve around issues of objectivity, which involves clarifying your goals, establishing the unit of analysis or observation, determining the time frames for your observations, creating a consistent recording system, and assuring inter-rater reliability. Of course, the first difficulty is deciding who you want to observe and obtaining access to the persons that you want to observe.

Conducting a research observation begins with the process of determining what or who you want to observe. When you are conducting a research observation as opposed to just noticing for the pleasure of it, you need a clear focus on certain behavior, actions, and symbols. If you are watching a baseball game, you may or may not notice what is happening in the dugouts or among the fans since you are watching the players. If you are observing in a lobby, you may not notice the behavior of the doormen or bell staff since you are focused on the front desk. Simply clarifying what you are observing brings focus to the effort. And your research questions help you identify what you are looking for. However, the research questions may be too general; in this case, you will need to specify the goal(s) of your observation.

Without access to the persons or groups or activities that you want to observe, you cannot use this method unless you are observing persons in public settings where there is no problem with access. Observing the patterns of traffic in an airport, train terminal, or visitor center does not require you to obtain permission. However, it is a good idea to obtain the manager's approval. If you are observing behavior in a private setting, you must ask for permission to gain access and to observe. As part of that challenge, you need to obtain permission to observe the individuals before you begin your endeavor. Obtaining permission can involve asking managers and others to observe the behavior of staff members or it can involve working with human resource managers since they are often concerned with the welfare of the individuals working at that company. You may also need to obtain permission from the Committee on Research Involving Human Subjects (or similar body) at your institution since you are, in some ways, invading the privacy of people you are watching. (For more information on the roles observers can play see the following section on **Observational Roles**.)

The second task involves determining the time frame or periodicity of your observations. Since it is virtually impossible to observe all the behavior of an individual or a group of individuals, you must decide what behavior you will observe—the *units of behavior*—and what *periodicity*—how often you will notice and record that behavior. If you want to watch the behavior of customers arriving at the front desk, it is not likely that you can capture all of the guests or even all of their actions. Therefore, you need to decide to observe every third person or every fifth person or organize your observations to collect all the data you can every 15 minutes. Selecting an individual or a time frame becomes an important decision for your research and should be driven by the research questions that you have developed as well as the skills of the observers you are using. If your focus is the behavior of guests in a restaurant, college football spectators, or persons on a guided tour, you need to select which individuals to observe and how often. Making this decision is a sampling issue. Underhill's work trailing shoppers and recording their every behavior relies on a decision point when the observers decide to follow a shopper; often this decision is arbitrary, but they collect enough information about lots of shoppers that their insights are valid. They also observe the customers in a store at very specific times to capture behavior across a wide range of periods and day parts (Underhill 13). If you are conducting a more limited number of observations, you may want to be more intentional about who you decide to observe and how often you conduct the observations. (For more information on sampling, see **Chapter 7, Sampling Issues in Research**.)

One of the ways to be successful at objective observation is to practice. Most individuals get better at conducting objective observations by conducting them and taking notes. Try watching some event or person and notice how hard it is to record what you are seeing. See how important determining the unit of observation is, see how critical it is to have a clear coding system, and notice how many decisions you have to make. Given all of those issues, when you decide to conduct a structured research observation, you need to decide on the unit of observation—what will you observe, and what will you record. Once you have that clear and prepare a coding manual and coding sheets, you can start to make some careful observations.

The third task—once you have decided what you are observing—involves recording your observations in a manner that they can be counted and analyzed. That means defining the *unit of observation* and developing a way to record it. Some people use charts and codes to register observations; others use a form of shorthand. Either way, you need to establish a common method of recording that is clear to all the persons doing the observing since it will become essential to combine and analyze the observations. Some of the ways that you can help your observers is to provide them with a training program, a coding manual, and a system for taking notes of behaviors, and then practice with them so that all of the observers can demonstrate a certain amount of consistency, or inter-rater reliability, about what they notice and how they record it. One of the challenges involved in this aspect of the training is determining the symbols that you want to use and how to use them. If you are not careful, one observer will use a set of notes or symbols differently than others, creating a significant problem in interpreting the recorded notes and analyzing the observations.

To ensure that you are objective, try doing a pilot observation with another colleague. Using the same coding system and unit of observation, try observing the same event or action and then compare your notes. In this way, you can start to build your skills and determine whether the unit of recording, the periodicity, and the recording system work effectively to answer the research questions you originally proposed. It will also help you to consider which of the many observational roles you want to play in conducting your observations.

OBSERVATIONAL ROLES

When conducting observations, it is helpful to consider the range of roles that observers can play; some individuals operate as outside observers, others act as participant-observers, and there are a range of roles in between. There are also a number of perspectives that you can bring to observing, including descriptive observation, inferential observation, and evaluative observation.

Since observing someone's behavior may change what the person does or how he or she does it, part of the issue involves refining your role. There are three options: complete observer, participant as observer, and observer as participant (Gold in Cole 64). A complete observer, sometimes referred to as an *outside observer*, is a person who is not involved in the activity and has a clearly defined role as observer. Sometimes that role is explained to the persons who are being observed since you are present in their space. If you are observing the training of a new housekeeping staff member, it is fairly obvious that you are observing since you have a clipboard or notebook to record your observations, and you are not doing the training. Outside observers can provide a lot of useful information and insights. For example, Underhill's work determined the conversion rates of customer traffic to sales purchases, analyzed the waiting times at checkout, discovered the interception rates of shoppers who interact with store employees, and found out the average amount of time a shopper spends in a store (35–38).

The clearest example in our industries of a complete observer whose identity and role is not provided to the persons being observed is a mystery shopper. *Mystery shopping*—the practice of observing unknown to the staff—which is prevalent in hotels, restaurants, and other retail or service companies, has three major purposes: one, to provide information about what is happening so that it can be used as a diagnostic tool; two, to motivate staff to do well since their performance is being measured by some outsider; and three, to determine how the operation measures up to the competition or to industry benchmarks (A. Wilson 414). Examples of the range of issues observed in a hotel include:

- Are your employees building rapport and emotional connections with guests?

- What could you do to ensure fewer customers leave with a neutral or negative brand image?

- What is your competition offering that your customers wish you offered and vice-versa?

- Are your employees taking the time to sympathetically listen and respond to guests' needs?

- Are your employees correctly informing customers about your products, services, and/or policies?

- Are customers of every age, ethnicity, and gender receiving the same exceptional level of customer service?

- How engaged are your employees, and how can you optimally improve their engagement?

- Are promotional signs, displays, and other types of marketing materials present and correctly positioned within your hotels?

- Which locations within your organization are consistent shining examples of offering customer delight, and what are their best practices?

(*Bestmark*)

Ironically, some organizations announce the arrival of a mystery shopper, which tends to cause an improvement in overall performance; others do not. In fact, some companies indicate that they use a mystery shopper to improve employee performance when no one ever conducts the observation and analysis. (For a list of several companies, see **Some Mystery Shopping Companies**.) Most mystery shoppers operate on a checklist of issues to observe and rate such as the set below used in observing restaurant wait staff behavior:

1. Does the server smile?

2. Does the server establish eye contact easily and often?

3. Does the server initiate conversation outside of the order taking at any time?

4. Did the server compliment any orders when taking them?

5. Did the server use positive words consistently? (Please/Thank You/Wonderful!)

6. Did the server listen well to the guests when ordering?

7. Did the server appear to be enjoying the work?

8. Would you return and ask for the server?

9. Did the server ask any/all under 30 guests for ID before serving drinks?

10. Did the server check back on food quality (apps/entrees) within five minutes?

11. Did the server present fresh silver on a side plate with clean napkin?

12. Did the server use pen with no logo and carry a wine key?

13. Did the server have a clean, standard uniform?

14. Was the server organized and consolidated in work area?

(adapted from Quality Assurance Consulting).

SOME MYSTERY SHOPPING COMPANIES

Coyle Hospitality Group

Bestmark

QACi

LRA Worldwide

Although the work sounds intriguing, it can be grueling since you need to observe and analyze every single operational aspect of a hotel or restaurant.

Other times, that role is not clarified and you can be a participant as observer, sometime called a participant-observer or an observer as participant. A *participant observer* is a person who belongs to the group being observed but who takes a special role in taking notes and recording a complete set of observations. An *observer as participant* is an individual whose primary function is to observe but who might participate to cover his or her identity, to reduce the barrier between him or her and the persons being observed, or to be able to gather more comprehensive information by participating. Participant observation is a centerpiece of ethnographies (Cole 64).

There are three ways to consider what you observe: descriptive observation, inferential observation, and evaluative observation (Boyd and DeVault 535–37). If you are trying to describe what a person is doing or what is happening in a restaurant, an office, a meeting—called *descriptive observation*—you need clear criteria about what you are looking for and a way to take notes that accurately reflect what is happening. It is almost like being a camera that records an event or an activity. If you are trying to conduct an *inferential observation*, then you are gathering information and interpreting it in the situation and taking notes accordingly. In an *evaluative observation*, you are trying to make a judgment about what you are observing by applying preestablished criteria while you observe it. In the process of observing the front desk operation of a hotel, or the work of a hotel manager, you may be looking to see what is happening and how well it is being done (Chareanpunsirikul and Wood 555). Are the front desk staff members responding with the appropriate forms of welcome that the hotel has established, and is the tone warm? Have they checked in guests within the prescribed time period and used the appropriate greeting? What does it mean when a hotel general manager answers the phone in a particular voice? Are there standard expectations that are not being met? Are individual guests being treated appropriately—and how does one define and notice the appropriateness of the behavior—when being checked in or welcomed? As you can see from these examples, the evaluative observation involves matching the performance being observed with established criteria.

Another technique that is powerful to use in applied research involves participants in focus groups where they contribute to creating information and insights.

FOCUS GROUPS

Focus groups provide a powerful way of gathering information and conducting research in a structured format. *Focus groups* typically involve a group of individuals carefully selected for a specially structured form of meeting in which verbal and nonverbal language is observed, recorded, and then analyzed carefully. Most of the groups include from 6 to 12 similar participants and last for approximately two hours (Massey 21). One of the earliest definitions indicated that focus groups were really group depth interviews (Goldman 61). Although a relatively recently popular form of research, focus groups can provide a powerful set of insights since the development of ideas and reactions from the group setting creates a wealth of information to analyze (Hartman 402). Focus groups have been used in the field of marketing, and more recently, in political arenas and communication although they have been productive as a research tool for years.

BENEFITS OF FOCUS GROUPS

Some of the benefits of focus groups include the possible generalizability of conclusions, their contribution to new knowledge, the depth of information available, and their efficiency and ease.

In most focus groups, the goal is to obtain a variety of opinions and thoughts and use the power of the social dynamic of a group to increase the quantity and depth of the ideas generated. The structure of a focus group enables the generation of many ideas, especially when it is well moderated and the recording system provides a comprehensive set of data about the discussion. In fact, just the discussion in the group of participants often produces more spontaneity and candor than other forms of data gathering; there is something about the presence of others that makes a difference (Goldman 62). In fact, the presence of a talented *facilitator*—who can be an acquaintance of the members of the group or a stranger—can enable the group to produce more effective, insightful, and useful, but not more in quantity, ideas than the same number of members working without a skilled facilitator (Fern 9).

A second benefit of a well-organized and conducted focus group is the creation of new ideas and insights. Often a focus group is used as a qualitative research technique when the goal involves trying to understand a new situation or the ways that individuals think about a particular situation. If you want to investigate the reason those individuals tailgate or entertain so lavishly and regularly at football games, you could use a group of tailgaters to discuss that activity. Wanting to know what people think about when they consider deciding on a cruise or voluntourism trip might lead you to organize focus groups on those topics. Investigating why certain guests prefer boutique hotels could be done with a focus group of frequent visitors to boutique hotels. There may not be enough literature yet to enable you to develop clear and well considered hypotheses, but a focus group might provide the information that could lead to a more systematic investigation that tests certain ideas. A focus group helps develop the ideas; the survey will test their applicability and validity.

Beyond the creation of new ideas and new comments and reactions from partici-pants, focus groups can also produce a depth of insight and range of information that other techniques cannot. One of the reasons is the ability of the facilitator of the focus group to ask more questions and find out the reasoning behind the comments. That ability to probe makes a big difference. And the new forms of focus groups—online groups instead of group meetings, for example—are producing a wider range and a larger quantity of ideas; computer or software mediated focus groups generate more ideas per participant than face-to-face focus groups (Reid and Reid 154).

In addition, since a focus group involves verbal and nonverbal behavior, you can obtain a lot of information using this technique. Sometimes the verbal behavior indi-cates one set of options and the non-verbal behavior provides a different impression. Noticing that difference and being able to ask about what the non-verbal behavior means provides focus group facilitators with a real advantage.

A fourth benefit to focus groups is the relative ease and efficiency of this tech-nique. Compared to an exhaustive survey or a large number of interviews, a focus group or two of anywhere between 6 and 12 individuals is easy to organize, facilitate, record, and analyze. Since you are assembling individuals to discuss a topic, you can have some influence on how they are chosen and bringing them together does not represent a huge challenge, especially if individuals opt in or out based on a schedule that you have established before you invited them.

CHALLENGES AND RECOMMENDATIONS FOR CONDUCTING FOCUS GROUPS

There are several challenges in using focus groups: selection process, quantity and background of members, facilitator's skills, recording issues, and analyzing the data.

Selecting participants for a focus group involves some careful thinking. Participants need to have a background relevant to the situation you are investigat-ing, but if they have too much expertise, they may dominate the group and you would not be able to access the ideas of the group. For instance, including some marketing experts into a focus group about why and how people buy season tickets would cor-rupt the discussion and the practice. On the other hand, inviting persons who do not attend sporting events to participate in this focus group would also make no sense. Therefore, consider carefully the individuals you want to invite to a focus group and word the invitation—whether in person, electronic, or other—carefully. The clearer you are about your selection criteria and the method of sampling—simple random, judgment, stratified random, snowball, or volunteer—the more effective your choices will be and the more likely that you will be able to draw useful conclusions that can generalize to other situations (Hartman 405).

The range of backgrounds of focus group participants represents one of the key valuable sources of information. Some focus groups involve homogenous groups of participants so that people feel comfortable expressing their thoughts. Others include people with a range of experience and backgrounds that add richness to the discussion and often contributes to the quantity and quality of the ideas expressed. In most focus groups, whether the participants know each other before the event or not makes little to no significant difference in the quality and quantity of the ideas expressed and discussed (Fern 10).

It also takes a skilled facilitator—a professional who can conduct the session to encourage maximum interaction and new ideas while preventing anyone from monopolizing the conversation—to make a focus group effective. The individual needs to know the topic and be able to start the conversation with open ended questions so that no one feels restricted in what they want to say, but the facilitator needs to also follow up on reactions, call on more reserved or reticent group members, and then proceed with closed ended questions to get specific ideas and details. If the group is passive, he or she needs to be more active; if the group is active, the facilitator can be more passive since there is no need to provoke the group (Goldman 64). Since one of the advantages of using focus groups is the ability to follow up on comments and determine the thinking behind statements, the facilitator needs to be skilled in using probing questions, (For more information about probing questions, see **Chapter 10, Research Techniques: Interviews.**) Ironically, focus groups with skilled facilitators do not produce a higher quantity of ideas than focus groups without skilled facilitators, but poorly facilitated focus groups can go astray and produce irrelevant information that will not help your research. You want to be able to probe and follow up with relevant and useful thinking, a role that a facilitator plays in the group (Fern 9).

Recording issues can be a real challenge since the purpose of a focus group is to record individual and group thoughts, opinions, and reactions as expressed verbally and also nonverbally. Most often marketing research focus groups include one way mirrors or the use of cameras to capture both individual and group nonverbal behavior. You can also use some recorders in the room although for them you need a systematic way for them to observe and take notes on the behavior they notice. Often, this task is done by a video camera or a series of still photographs taken by trained staff and kept so that they can be analyzed later. In fact, arranging for a recording set up and determining how to keep notes are some of the major decision documenting challenges in planning for a focus group. Aside from recording issues, there are five steps in setting up a focus group:

1. Clarifying the purpose of the focus group, which means returning to your research question.

2. Selecting the participants.

3. Developing the questions to be asked in the focus group.

4. Deciding on whether you will be the facilitator or do you need to find someone else.

5. Finding a comfortable location where the discussion can be watched (Hartman 404).

Once you have all the records of the discussion and the images or recorded notes, the task becomes analyzing the data that you have collected. As with all analysis, the process returns to the research questions and how this information reflects answers or aspects of answers to those questions. If the goal of the focus group is to uncover a number of ideas and factors that influence behavior, then the process of analyzing the data involves mining for themes and corroborating those results with the work of other people who also read and analyze the documents and notes. Working with this data, however, becomes increasingly difficult depending on its quantity; longer focus groups with more members create a lot of verbal and nonverbal data to analyze. The number of members in a focus group does not, however, affect the analysis.

SIZE OF FOCUS GROUPS

One of the unusual issues in working with focus groups involves determining the size of the groups. While there is no ideal size, it is important to create a focus group that is large enough to generate lively and useful debate but not so large that the discussion cannot be controlled or carefully recorded. There should not be so few that there is no real group discussion, either. There can be anywhere from 5 to 20 members, but most commonly, focus groups contain between 6 and 10 members (Fern 2). In his research, Fern found that groups of eight focus group members generated many more ideas than groups of four (Fern 12). Therefore, when setting up your focus group, consider that you may want more than one focus group but each focus group does not need any more than ten members to be functional and effective.

This discussion of focus groups has reviewed the benefits and challenges of one form of group; another use of groups involves panels of professionals and experts.

EXPERT PANELS

The use of expert panels in research, also known as *Delphi panels*, was originally developed during the middle of the last century by Norman Dalkey, at the Rand Corporation, as a way to bring together the opinions of a number of experts without holding a meeting where individual personalities and group dynamics could sway opinions (Van de Ven and Delbecq 606). They have often been used to predict future trends, analyze the impact of certain events, or define the expectations of a program's success. They provide a way to capture important information and insights in a relatively short period of time and with a minimum of effort.

The process of using an expert panel involves several detailed steps:

- Clarifying the goals of your research

- Selecting the participants based on their expertise on the subject

- Organizing the process to maintain objectivity

- Developing a series of structured questions

- Eliciting answers to the questions and other comments from the experts

- Combining their initial responses into a coherent document designed to elicit more comments and test for consensus

- Circulating the document to the panel to obtain further insights

- Combining the second round of responses into a coherent document designed to elicit more comments and test for consensus a second time

- Circulating the document again

- Integrating all the comments into a coherent document.

The traditional format for the Delphi technique is two iterations although sometimes, more iterations are needed (Van de Ven 606–607). Since individuals need time to respond to the documents, the process often takes several months, and it is critical to obtain a commitment from the experts to participate fully in the entire process (Pollard and Pollard 148). Delphi panels are a powerful way to collect opinions and conduct research.

BENEFITS OF EXPERT PANELS

There are several reasons to use expert panels in research. You can collect a lot of significant information from experts who operate anonymously from each other and are, therefore, not influenced by other opinions or the dominance of strong personalities, something that can happen in discussion groups or group interviews (Dalkey and Helmer 459). For example, a Delphi panel on the future of boutique hotels or personal seat licenses would gather opinions from people who know the hotel field or sports management. Keeping them from interacting with owners and operators of boutique hotels or stadia can free them up to see the situation from a broader perspective and share their insights without outside pressure. A discussion about boutique hotels by professionals operating them would produce a positive report; professionals marketing personal seat licenses would only see the possible growth in sales and not consider other aspects of this relatively new practice in sports management. Professionals opening a new museum will only see the positive aspects of this new venture.

A second advantage is the relative efficiency of the method. Collecting a wide range of opinions on future trends, possible difficulties in policies or programs, or long-term developments can be done relatively easily. Interviewing the members of the panel individually would take a lot more time and would not provide the opportunity to reiterate and test ideas with the individuals who agreed to serve on the panel. In addition, normally, the information would be hard, if not impossible, to obtain in other ways. In fact, the Delphi technique has been used for long-term forecasting when there are no data available or when regular trend analysis does not seem applicable. When you are trying to forecast future events or trends, combining the wisdom of a number of experts can be a useful way to collect opinions from persons who have some insight and knowledge but who cannot easily be brought together (Van de Ven and Delbecq 606).

Another benefit is the quality of the ideas generated by the Delphi technique. Delphi panels generate significantly more ideas and often a broader range than in-person meetings aimed at the same purpose (Van de Ven and Delbecq 615). In addition, the ideas tend to be more focused and specific since there is no group pressure to make common and broad generalizations that are neither productive nor insightful (Van de Ven and Delbecq 617). A Delphi technique can also be used productively to combine experts who represent a wide range of fields and who might not know each other.

Given the need to develop a special panel of experts, you may find a lot of challenges in conducting a Delphi panel.

CHALLENGES AND RECOMMENDATIONS IN CONDUCTING EXPERT PANELS

The most critical challenge in conducting a Delphi panel involves finding the professionals with the expertise, convincing them to participate (anonymously) on the panel, and keeping them on a tight timetable. Most of the possible panelists are busy professionals with lots of projects and many business challenges; ironically, those individuals are the ones you want since their daily work provides them with the information and reflection that provide good insights and comments for your project. Obtaining access to those individuals can be difficult. Recognizing their participation in a publication can help, as can other incentives, but they need to commit to participating and not be looking for attribution for their ideas. Sometimes, the anonymity you can provide encourages them to participate on the panel.

A second challenge involves managing the questions and the documents. It is critical to be clear what you are asking since simple, open-ended questions will not produce useful information (see **Chapter 11, Research Techniques: Questionnaires**). Therefore, you need to know a lot about the topic about which you are asking the panelists. Sometimes, the best way to prepare for the process involves developing a pilot questionnaire and trying it out on a different group so that you can make changes and improve it before sending it to the panelists.

A minor, but sometimes awkward, challenge, is handling panel members' requests for different formats of questionnaires. Some want it faxed and will hand-write responses; others want an electronic form to complete online, and some want a document appropriate for typing. Making sure that the form works on all situations and contains similar information can be a challenge, but it is critical to provide the panelists with the format that they are most comfortable using since you want their thoughtful and prompt responses.

Given the reality of busy schedules of panel members, maintaining the timetable and finding ways to remind them to return questionnaires to you with comments is critical to the process. Since you need at least two iterations of the questionnaire or other document, you need people to respond to one version before you send out the next one. Therefore, a clear and realistic timetable is important; sticking to it is even more critical to the success of the process.

Another challenge to your success is discouraging the panelists from discussing their responses with each other. Operating a confidential panel so that individuals do not know who else is on the panel can help, but often the experts that you have invited to participate know each other and there is always the opportunity for them to corroborate with each other and share common opinions. The cooperation and discussion can start to develop a seeming consensus thereby inviting you to think that there is agreement when it may only be due to collaboration before completing the questionnaire. Ways to overcome this challenge include ensuring that all participants sign an agreement not to discuss the panel or the topics until the project is completed, maintaining the confidentially of panel members from each other, monitoring the interaction among panel members, and requesting panel members to report on any conversations with colleagues.

These challenges, however, do not diminish the value of expert panels when trying to determine aspects of the future. In trying to understand or investigate the past, you may find content analysis, a very different technique, to be the most productive research technique.

CONTENT ANALYSIS

One of the most powerful and least obtrusive ways of conducting research involves the examination of what has been said, written, or shown. As opposed to most other research techniques, which involve interaction with the behavior of human beings, content analysis is a document oriented research model. Not unlike historical research and statistical analysis of data that has already been collected and reported, content analysis relies on materials that have been produced for a variety of purposes as the primary data for counting, recording, and analyzing. Interviews, questionnaires, observations, and focus groups involve the interaction of human beings and introduce all kinds of bias into the research process. Content analysis does not raise those issues.

Conducting a careful objective review of the symbolic meaning of words, texts, images, and other forms of media is the main purpose of content analysis (Kolbe 243). As Berelson, one of the first scholars to write about content analysis, said, "Content analysis is a research technique for the objective, systematic and quantitative description of the manifest content of communication" (18). It is a carefully conducted and objectively organized process that involves decisions about how to analyze the material being reviewed. *Content analysis* has also been described as "A research technique for making replicable and valid inferences from texts (or other meaningful matter) to contexts of their use" (Krippendorf 18). Content analysis goes far beyond reviewing a few texts and drawing wide generalizations because it requires a systematic approach to research. Although some scholars do not consider it a very productive research technique, it provides a special way to collect and analyze data so that you can make valid and insightful comments about the use of words, phrases, or images (Bryman and Bell 193).

Perhaps the most important element in content analysis is understanding the role of the researcher in selecting texts to review and organizing the process of reviewing them in order to draw conclusions that do not exceed the limits of the investigation. Making these decisions affects, dramatically, the level of objectivity and the validity of the conclusions. The process of conducting a careful content analysis requires a number of elements to ensure its usefulness as a research method: a systematic approach to coding (which includes a coding manual and a coding system), a common definition of the unit(s) being coded, and the careful training of coders to establish inter-rater reliability. The systematic approach is essential to avoid the insertion of personal judgments into the system and diluting the objectivity of the coding and counting. These elements are essential so that the study can be replicated or expanded into a different area or topic. However, the technique also has a lot of merits.

BENEFITS OF CONTENT ANALYSIS

There are many advantages to conducting a content analysis: the usefulness of quantitative results, the systematic nature of the process, its nonintrusive quality, and the depth of content that can be analyzed.

Since content analysis involves counting words or phrases, the results provide solid numbers, quantitative data that can be very useful in interpreting the nature of the audience, the purpose(s) of the documents or the unintended relationships among concepts. Often the numbers provide insights that other research techniques might not uncover. For example, the number of times that certain words are used to describe tourists may indicate some of the thinking behind the advertisements, the quantity of certain pictures of cruise ships may indicate their assumptions about future purchasers or their desire to increase those types of cruise passengers. Elegant dinner outfits and elaborate jewelry on cruise passengers will not encourage fun-loving and party-going younger passengers to consider that ship or that cruise line. Since it is a transparent form of analysis, the tables, graphs, and other mechanisms used to record the counts add validity and veracity to what you are doing.

A second benefit derives from the structure of content analysis. The systematic nature of the process involving decisions about what to count, how to count it, and when to count it produces objective analysis of various terms, phrases, or images— depending on the unit of analysis and the research questions involved. Since the steps to ensure objectivity are so clear and well structured, the results carry a level of clarity and truth that can eliminate misunderstandings or correct commonly held assumptions (Kolbe and Burnett 244). For example, interviewing webmasters about their websites might create more positive impressions than are warranted by a content analysis review of the images and phrases on the websites. Conducting a content analysis of the websites makes the results more clearly objective and less influenced by key players. In fact, the content analysis may well provide insights about the differences between what the website providers think they are projecting and what the users perceive. (Choi et al. 127).

A third benefit of content analysis is it nonintrusive quality. Since content analysis does not involve surveying, observing, or interviewing individuals, there is little or no impact on human beings. Therefore, the many types of bias that can occur while using those methods are eliminated (Kolbe and Burnett 244). In fact, the nonintrusive aspect of content analysis means that the materials used do not get affected nor does the actual conduct of the research affect what has already happened. Counting the words used and their context tends to be a more objective form of research, which is less likely to be affected by bias. For example, although there is a general assumption of much profanity in video games and the topic may well trigger lots of personal reactions, a recent study found little evidence of profanity in most games (Ivory et al. 459). A review of the language used in various proposals for funding new stadium construction can indicate the actual arguments made rather than what people want to think was said or what public officials want people to assume.

Another advantage of conducting serious content analysis is the opportunity to differentiate between the manifest content and latent content of certain documents (Lombard, Snyder-Duch, and Bracken 589). *Manifest content* denotes the meanings of words and images that can be taken at face value; the content is clear to anyone reading the words or phrases. In fact, much content analysis is focused on this level of analysis and helps to point out how often certain words were used and how many times certain words are used instead of others. The Ritz Carlton motto of "Ladies and Gentlemen serving Ladies and Gentleman" is only one indication of the value of the manifest content of the words. *Latent content* refers to the connotations of the words and the meanings behind them. For example, referring to individuals who stay at a hotel as patrons, guests, members, or customers may indicate some latent assumptions about how the hotel views and treats the individuals who visit. Only through the analysis of the language would you notice this possibility and what it indicates about the hotel.

There are some disadvantages of content analysis as well. It can be difficult to locate documents, interpreting the context or meanings of words can be difficult if not impossible, the process can be very time consuming, and researchers often make erroneous assumptions in organizing coding schemes. However, content analysis lends itself to many situations where you have limited access to individuals. You can discover insights by analyzing what they said and wrote; reviewing public documents can often provide even more insights than interviews. Given these benefits, conducting a content analysis carries a number of challenges.

CHALLENGES AND RECOMMENDATIONS IN USING CONTENT ANALYSIS

Conducting a valid content analysis means facing some of the same challenges as doing structured observations—determining what you want to analyze, how you want to analyze it, when (for what period or periods) you want to analyze the documents, and how you can maintain objectivity in the process. These questions are critical to answer before undertaking this type of investigation since they affect the objectivity of the work and the validity of the conclusions.

Deciding on what documents you will review is the first question. Are you examining published documents such as newspaper stories, magazine articles, annual reports, training manuals, promotional materials, and public statements, or are you reviewing private documents such as company memoranda, letters, contracts, and training manuals? This decision will be critical to the value of your results since your analysis is limited to these documents. It is a sampling question that demands real thought and consideration. (For more information on sampling, see **Chapter 8, Sampling Issues in Research**.) The choice of what documents you will analyze should be informed by your original purpose statement and research questions and the depth and breadth of your research scope.

Clarifying what you will look for in your review of various documents or media is perhaps the most fundamental challenge and the most important one to ensure the usefulness of your findings. Do you want to count words, phrases, sentences, images, or something else? Do you want to use a short time frame or a long one? Do you want to capture the tone of words and images or only their appearance? Deciding on the actual words that you will count demands significant knowledge of the subject in order to determine the appropriate words and cognates to count.

A related aspect of content analysis involves what you are looking for in the words, phrases, or images. Since so much of printed communication contains nuances and tones, you may want to capture the *disposition*—the tone used with the words (Bryman and Bell 201). Are the words being used in a reporting sense or an editorial sense? Is the article, news item, or image part of a campaign, a commentary, or a piece written by a columnist? Often, authors use words in a particular manner to make a point, and watching for the disposition is a critical aspect of determining that tone and context. In addition, you may want to consider whether you are trying to discover the manifest meaning of various documents, or whether you are interested in what assumptions lie behind the use of words.

Another dimension of content analysis involves time frame and periodicity, very much like structured observations. What time frame of documents will you analyze? Will it be a period of years? If so, which years, and why? How do you determine the right time frame, given your research questions? Should the time frame be determined by actions of the individuals or organizations you are examining, industry events, or a chronological year? The time frame will affect your results and may distort the numbers you develop so you need a clear rationale for selecting the period within which you will analyze the selected materials. If you are examining words used to describe player's contracts, which contracts and which players would be one of the questions and then time frame would be the next. For example, not recognizing the annual phases of contract negotiations and releases would diminish the importance of your content analysis.

The fifth challenge involves maintaining objectivity. One of the most critical tools in developing objectivity and consistency is a coding manual and schedule, which are described below. However, training the persons involved in doing the coding is also a critical aspect of maintaining objectivity. They need to know what you are looking for, why you are looking for it, and how to avoid interpreting and bringing their own perspective to the task of counting and recording. That aspect of the work is most essential. One way to build consistent counting behavior involves coding a common document and then comparing the records. If there are significant discrepancies, this opportunity to discuss what happened will lead to increased inter-rater reliability in the future, which is your ultimate goal. If you cannot depend on the various coders to do their work consistently and clearly, then your research will not be valid. If you are conducting the coding, you need to be a participant in the same training and compare your records with the other coders. In fact, training coders and ensuring their independence and objectivity are three of the five most common steps of ensuring objectivity: rules and procedures, training of judges, pretesting or measures, independence of judges from authors, and independence of judges from each other (Kolbe 245).

CODING IN CONTENT ANALYSIS

Since *coding*—the process of recording what you find in a document or set of images in a consistent and reliable manner—is such a critical aspect of content analysis, researchers have developed systems to increase objectivity. The process of analytical coding as a research technique for content analysis entails assigning words or phrases to pieces of data in order to arrange them into categories of useful information (Saldana 8). Sometimes the coding process reduces the quantity of information to a manageable quantity. Other times, it expands the information and makes the analysis phase more difficult. If you have the data in hard copy, this coding process may take a long time; inputting documents or images into data banks or software packages where it can be easily manipulated and coded will save a lot of time.

As a first step in the coding process, you need to establish parameters about what you are seeking to count. The first step is determining the unit of analysis that you will use. *Unit of analysis* refers to the words, phrases, or images that you want to count. The second step involves developing, for coding purposes a coding manual, the document that provides advice to coders about what to look for, how to record information, and what labels to use. Providing a coding manual and training all of the research team to use it will help improve your validity and ensure that the team brings a common approach to its work. It is essential to ensure inter-rater reliability and to enable you to draw valid insights from this data analysis.

Once you have determined the coding unit that you want to count, you must decide on the documents you will analyze and the time frame of their creation or publication. (This decision is a sampling decision; for more information, see **Chapter 8, Sampling Issues in Research**.) From this point, you are ready to establish the *coding manual*—a document that contains all the rules for what to count, what to notice around the unit of analysis, and how to record that information. Most coding manuals have clear rules and lots of illustrations and examples. It is a way of ensuring that each person doing the coding operates with the same understanding of the process and will do similar work. Theoretically, any person who has been trained to count and record words and phrases in the manner that you establish can use the coding manual for reference, and his or her work will be consistent with all of the others.

Determining how you want to count the words, phrases, or images is both a matter of frequency and coding. Will you count each mention of a word in a document and code it in some particular manner or are you only looking to see if a word or phrase is used at least once and that mention is enough? Either decision can be valid, depending on your goal; the task involves determining exactly how you want the coding and counting to be done so that you get the numbers you need that match your research questions. Persons doing the counting will use a coding schedule.

A *coding schedule* is the form used to record the information that you are collecting. It can be a very complicated document or a simple one, depending on what you want the raters to record and how you will use the data collected. What it must contain is space and a method to report all of the information that you want recognized about the units of analysis in the document. For example, if you are conducting a content analysis of the descriptions of hotel managers in trade publications, you might want to record information about gender, age, position, hotel, action or reason for mention, quoted or not, type of story (news item, press release, editorial commentary, or advertisement), and many other aspects of the mention. In a study of boutique hotels, you might want the coding schedule to include information about adjectives used, size of hotel, location, part of chain, age of facility, type of story (news, editorial, or advertisement), services provided, designer, amenities, positioning, price, image, and other aspects of the hotel. Of course, each of these elements would be explained in the coding manual.

These tools make content analysis doable; developing them carefully is one way to ensure objectivity in the counting and recording. Since content analysis provides good numbers when done in this manner, it can produce interesting information and make significant contributions to the industry.

Following your research questions and carefully planning the use any of the four techniques discussed in this chapter—structured observation, focus groups, expert panels, and content analysis—will make developing your research proposal much easier and the quality of your research will be much improved.

SUMMARY

This chapter has reviewed the benefits and challenges of four major research techniques commonly used in applied research: structured observations, focus groups, expert panels, and content analysis. In many ways, they are similar in that they involve collecting data from persons or documents in a manner that demands a carefully disciplined approach. Observations and content analysis enable you to gather data and analyze them in a nonobtrusive manner; they also demand careful planning. All four techniques require careful and systematic record keeping in order to produce valid results. Although content analysis is often considered a qualitative and quantitative method, all four of these research methods contribute understanding and insights; they are more often used in a discovery mode than as a way to test theories and hypotheses that have already been developed.

They are great research techniques; once you have used them, or interviews, questionnaires, or other research methods, you have collected a lot of information. Having that information and collecting it in a form that helps you analyze it becomes the next challenge. Ways to analyze data and the importance of interpreting information carefully is the subject of the next chapter—**Chapter 13, Analyzing Data and Other Information**.

KEY TERMS

Coding
Coding manual
Coding schedule
Content analysis
Delphi panel
Descriptive observation
Disposition
Evaluative observation
Facilitator

Focus group
Inferential observation
Inter-rater reliability
Latent content
Manifest content
Mystery shopper
Observer as participant
Observer drift
Participant observer

Perceptual flooding
Periodicity
Research blindness
Selective attention
Skilled facilitator
Unit of analysis
Units of behavior
Units of observation

WORKS CITED IN THIS CHAPTER

Abrams, Bill. The Observational Research Handbook: *Understanding How Consumers Live with Your Product*. Chicago: NTC Business Books, 2000.

Berelson, Bernard. "Content Analysis in Communication Research." In *Media Studies: A Reader*. 2nd ed. Eds. Paul Marris and Sue Thornham. New York: NYU Press, 2000.

Bestmark. "Hotel & Lodging Industry: Mystery Shopping, Compliance & Customer Experience Solutions." Bestmark.com. Web.

Boice, Robert. "Observational Skills." *Psychological Studies* 93.1 (1983): 3–29.

Boyd, Robert D., and M. Vere DeVault. "The Observation and Recording of Behavior." *Review of Educational Research* 36 (1966): 529–51.

Bryman, Alan, and Emma Bell. *Business Research Methods*. Oxford: Oxford University Press, 2003.

Chareanpunsirikul, Suchada, and Roy C. Wood. "Mintzberg, Managers, and Methodology: Some Observations from a Study of Hotel General Managers." *Tourism Management* 23 (2002): 551–56.

Choi, Soojin, Xinran Lehto, and Alastair M. Morrison. "Destination Image Representation on the Web: Content Analysis of Macau Travel Related Websites." *Tourism Management* 28 (2007): 118–29.

Cole, Stroma. "Action Ethnography: Using Participant Observation." In *Tourism Research Methods: Integrating Theory with Practice*. Eds. Brent W. Richie, Peter Burns, and Catherine Palmer. Oxfordshire, UK: CABI Publishing, 2005.

Crowther, David, and Geoff Lancaster. *Research Methods: A Concise Introduction to Research in Management and Business Consultancy*. 2nd ed. Oxford, UK: Elsevier, 2005.

Dalkey, Norman, and Olaf Helmer. "An Experimental Application of the Delphi Method to the Use of Experts." *Management Science* 9 (1963): 458–67.

Ellet, William. *The Case Study Handbook: How to Read, Discuss, and Write Persuasively About Cases*. Cambridge: Harvard Business Press, 2007.

Ezeh, Chris, and Lloyd C. Harris. "Servicescape Research: a Review and a Research Agenda." *Marketing Review* 7 (2007): 59–78.

Fern, Edward F. "The Use of Focus Groups for Idea Generation: The Effects of Group Size, Acquaintanceship, and Moderator on Response Quantity and Quality." *Journal of Marketing Research* 19 (1982): 1–13.

Goldman, Alfred E. "The Group Depth Interview." *Journal of Marketing* 26 (1962) 1–68.

Goodwin, Eric. "Shopping for a Mystery Shopper." *Restaurant Hospitality* 1 (2006): 80–82.

Gram, Malene. "Self-reporting vs. Observation: Some Cautionary Examples from Parent/Child Food Shopping Behavior." *International Journal of Consumer Studies* 34 (2010): 394–99.

Hartman, Jackie. "Using Focus Groups to Conduct Business Communication Research." *Journal of Business Communication* 41 (October 2004): 402–10.

Ivory, James D., Dmitri Williams, Nicole Marins, and Mia Consalvo. "Good Clean Fun? A Content Analysis of Profanity in Video Games and Its Prevalence across Game Systems and Ratings." *CyberPsychology and Behavior* 12 (2009): 457–60.

Krippendorf, Klaus. *Content Analysis: An Introduction to Its Methodology.* 2nd ed. Thousand Oaks: Sage Publications, 2004.

Kolbe, Richard H., and Melissa Burnett. "Content Analysis Research: An Examination of Applications with Directives for Improving Research Reliability and Objectivity." *The Journal of Consumer Research* 18 (1991): 243–50.

Lombard, Matthew, Jennifer Snyder-Duch, and Cheryl Campanella Bracken. "Content Analysis in Mass Communication; Assessment and Reporting of Intercoder Reliability." *Human Communication Research* 28.4 (2002): 587–604.

McCabe, Scott, and Elizabeth Stokoe. "Have you Been Away? Holiday Talk in Everyday Interaction." *Annals of Tourism Research* 37 (2010): 1117–140.

Massey, Oliver T. "A Proposed Model for the Analysis and Interpretation of Focus Groups in Evaluation Research." *Evaluation and Program Planning.* 34 (2011): 1–28.

Morgan, David L., and Richard A. Krueger. "When to Use Focus Groups and Why: Successful Focus Groups: Advancing the State of the Art." *Sage Focus Editions* 156 (1993): 3–19.

Neuenforf, Kimberly A. *The Content Analysis Guidebook.* Thousand Oaks; Sage, 2002.

Pollard, Constance, and Richard Pollard. "Research Priorities in Educational Technology: A Delphi Study." *Journal of Research on Technology in Education* 37 (2004–2005): 145–60.

Quality Assurance Consulting. "Dining Room Sample" QACinc.com. Web.

Reid, Donna J., and Fraser J. M. Reid. "Online Focus Groups: An In-depth Comparison of Computer Mediated and Conventional Focus Group Discussions." *International Journal of Market Research* 47 (2005) 131–62.

Saldana, Johnny. *The Coding Manual for Qualitative Researchers.* London: Sage, 2009.

Schmidt, Marcus. "Quantification of Transcripts from Depth Interviews, Open-ended Responses and Focus Groups: Challenges, Accomplishments, New Applications and Perspectives for Market Research." *International Journal of Market Research* 52 (2010): 483–509.

Sharp, Anne, and Michelle Tustin. "Benefits of Observational Research" ANZMAC 2003 Conference Proceedings Adelaide. Adelaide: ANZMAC, December 2003.

Underhill, Paco. *Why We Buy: The Science of Shopping.* New York: Simon & Schuster, 1999.

Van de Ven, Andrew H., and Andre L. Delbecq. "The Effectiveness of Nominal, Delphi, and Interacting Decision Making Processes." *Academy of Management Journal* 17 (1974): 605–21.

Wilson, Alan M. "The Role of Mystery Shopping in the Measurement of Service Performance." *Managing Service Quality* 8 (1998): 414.

Wilson, Valerie. "Focus Groups: A Useful Qualitative Method for Educational Research?" *British Educational Research Journal* 23 (1997): 209–24.

CHAPTER 13

Analyzing Data and Other Information

INTRODUCTION

The previous three chapters reviewed the benefits, challenges, and opportunities of various research techniques—interviews, questionnaires, structured observations, focus groups, expert panels, and content analysis. All of them focused on collecting information in an objective and valid manner. However, once the information is collected, the question becomes what to do with the data, how to organize them, how to summarize them in useful ways, and then how to interpret and analyze the data appropriately.

This chapter will address the important distinctions among collecting data; organizing, interpreting, and analyzing it; and reporting the results. The next chapter will discuss the challenges of preparing a comprehensive research proposal and the importance of understanding the audience.

STEPS IN ANALYZING INFORMATION

When conducting any quantitative or qualitative research, you can find yourself with a lot of data from a variety of sources such as interviews, observations, diaries, logs, testimonials, organizational or personal documents, and reviews by others. The challenge becomes what to do with that data. Often beginning researchers think carefully about how to collect information but are less thoughtful about what to do with it once it has been acquired. When collecting material, it is important to have a plan for examining it and analyzing it, but it is hard to think through the analytical steps. However, even good plans go awry; sometimes, the initial plans do not work when confronted with actual data.

The purpose of your research and the range and type of data that you collect will make a significant difference in the ways in which you will analyze them. If you conduct interviews of restaurant managers, then you will need to find a way to organize the transcripts and find patterns in what they said. If you conduct a quantitative analysis of RevPAR patterns in various cities in the United States, you will need to consider what kind of statistical analysis you will conduct on the data. If you observe fans at basketball events, then you need to determine what you can do with your observation notes and how to find relationships between various factors that might influence fan behavior.

One way of looking at the process of analyzing data is the three-step method of: coding or categorizing data, combining the data in various structures, and displaying and comparing the results (Creswell 148). However, the following seven steps are the most common and most useful description of all the processes involved in analyzing data:

1. Collect the data

2. Immerse yourself in the data

3. Align the examination with your original research goals

4. Organize the data

5. Identify relationships and patterns

6. Review the data

7. Interpret the information in light of broader concepts (Adapted from Miles and Huberman 10).

The following sections will explain these seven steps and suggest ways to proceed. Collecting data has been the subject of the previous three chapters so it will not be discussed in detail here (see **Chapter 10, Research Techniques: Interviews**, **Chapter 11, Research Techniques: Questionnaires**, and **Chapter 12, Research Techniques: Observations, Focus Groups, and Content Analysis**).

COLLECTING THE INFORMATION

One of the critical tasks in collecting data is to determine how you will collect them in a way that provides you a chance to report them, systematize them, and put them into perspective. Many new researchers collect extra amounts of information without considering what they will do with the data collected. The result is an abundance of data and no way to benefit from all the time it took to collect, code, and sort them. Analyzing why customers select luxury hotels by interviewing general managers, observing guest and staff behavior in lobbies and public rooms, interviewing front desk attendants, and surveying guests is an example of collecting too much information that does not provide answers to the questions that the research originally posed. Assessing the merits of various marketing campaigns by interviewing directors of marketing, holding a focus group with season ticket holders, distributing questionnaires to fans as they leave a particular game, meeting with concessionaires, and conducting a content analysis of all the printed and visual advertisements may provide you with too much information to analyze carefully.

It takes careful planning and good decision making to determine what to collect and how to collect it in a format that makes it easy to analyze. Persons who conduct surveys using pens or pencils have to take the time to enter all of the responses into a software program that can then analyze the data collected. This step invites all kinds of administrative errors in typing, copying, entering incorrect responses, and misinterpreting. It also adds an additional step in copying the original source documents so that they can be reviewed and analyzed again. Since source documents are the primary documents in your research, they need to be handled carefully so that they are not lost or misplaced and so that they can be retrieved easily (Alreck and Settle 255). Using a software package or an electronic form of questionnaire collection obviates this step and makes a big difference in what can be accomplished, without error, and in an easier manner.

In some survey situations, notebook computers or electronic tablets have made it easier to collect data and transmit that information directly into a software package. Using them for tourists who have a short time to spend completing surveys while they wait for their luggage or ground transportation can yield a large quantity of responses in a short period of time and save enormous effort in copying all of the responses since the responses can be directed to a data collection bank. Conducting the same surveys in a verbal manner with administrators writing responses would produce fewer responses and invite errors of recording, collecting, and copying.

A different challenge in collecting data arises when you are using secondary data that have been organized or found by others. Often, research involves reexamining data that others have used or developed and reviewing it from a different perspective or conducting an alternative analysis of that data. Examples include using census data and other government data in various combinations, examining STR data about hotels, and analyzing information from Forbes or Smith and Streeters about sports teams.

Other challenges in data collection involve ensuring that the research team follows the original plan for selecting the persons to interview or survey. Changes made during implementation introduce another level of possible error into the data themselves, which raises questions about the quality of the analysis that follows the collection of the data. Therefore, you must ensure that your research design is followed, regardless of what happens in the process of collecting information and coding it. Changes often have to be made during the data collection process, but they need to be made very carefully and documented thoroughly since sloppy administration of a good plan can render your research invalid. (For more information on validity, see **Chapter 9, Validity, Reliability, and Credibility in Research**.) The next step after collecting data is viewing and absorbing them.

IMMERSING YOURSELF IN THE DATA

When you have a collection of information, it is often hard to sort it out and examine it in a serious manner unless you have a real understanding of what it contains and what is missing. Therefore, good research involves an early review of the information, developing a sense of what is there, considering what you might be able to do with it, and determining if any important pieces are missing. Although often avoided or ignored, this step can provide you with a general overview of what you have collected, suggest to you other information that you might need to find, and start the process of noticing what the material contains.

During this step, it is critical to avoid coming to conclusions or interpreting data; it can, however, be a useful time to consider some options about ways to organize the data and show their significance. One of the most important aspects of this immersion stage involves reviewing and checking data for accuracy and completion before preparing them for analysis.

If you have planned carefully and followed your plan consistently, your information may be easy to examine and prepare for analysis. The first step involves reviewing each of the questionnaires, interview transcripts, observer notes or whatever documents you have for accuracy and completeness. If there is some information missing from this raw data, then you have to decide what to do. That might involve rechecking the interview transcript with the tape, correcting errors in the transcript, or requesting more information in the case of an incomplete document. In some cases, where a questionnaire has only been partially completed, you may have to put the form aside and analyze it and ones like it separately. Ignoring the blank questionnaires, however, means that the analysis of the other data is subject to *nonresponse bias*, the distortion of results due to persons who do not complete the questionnaire (Little 287). If there are missing questionnaires, then the number of responses indicates the difference between administered questionnaires and completed ones, and that information provides useful insights.

If you need to work with a questionnaire for which there are some blanks but it is mostly complete, you are then facing the challenge of *imputed data*—determining how to accommodate the gap of missing elements of data by substituting some number—in order to have a full set of responses to all of the questions. Although it needs to be done carefully, often supplying imputed data into your research involves reviewing the other responses to that question carefully and then choosing the midpoint in the scale for that item for that questionnaire since it will affect your data analysis the least (Little 288; Sekaran 302–303).

Adding these numbers, however, assumes that the lack of a number or an answer is due to random factors and not due to a specific decision not to answer (Allison 301). Many people choose not to answer questions about income due to privacy or discomfort. These answers are not due to random factors. However, a lack of an answer to one of a series of questions where all the options have been answered is more likely to be the result of an oversight.

The process of imputing data can provide you with a more complete and a better set of data than simply eliminating all of the missing responses—called *listwise deletion*—which changes the total number of responses and may distort your results. There is a wide variety of statistical methods to compensate for lack of data or to impute missing data, and you should consider consulting them if you find a large quantity of missing responses. Alternatively, you may need to continue collecting data to improve the number of responses to your questionnaire.

In rare situations, you may be able to recollect data and bring it back to be prepared for analysis. Sometimes, the process involves checking out gaps in the responses and deciding on another administration of a questionnaire or conducting interviews to supplement the survey results. In the cases of interviews, you may just decide to continue interviewing. Returning to the sample population, or a similar set of respondents, to distribute questionnaires or interview individuals can be a productive way to gather more in-depth information. The opportunity provided by an interview to discuss responses to questions and to ask follow-up and probing questions may be essential to your research. (For more information, see **Chapter 11, Research Techniques: Interviews**.) In fact, this form of mixed method research has become increasingly common.

CODING DATA FOR PRIVACY AND RECORD KEEPING

Coding demographic and psychographic data are essential in order to protect the privacy of your respondents and to provide a picture of the population surveyed or interviewed. It is a process that should happen as data are collected since it provides a way to process the information. It is important to code interview and observation records so that you can find them again while ensuring that no individual names are included in the final analysis, unless the person has indicated that he or she is willing to be quoted. And that means ensuring you have the permission document accurate and completed. In many cases, you do not want to quote individuals, but if in your scan of the information in front of you, you notice some quotes that look very useful or indicative of something important, then you may want to check on the accuracy of the quote at this point in your work while you have time for the individual to respond to your request.

With questionnaires, you do not need to code for privacy. However, coding all of the responses provides you with a way to access information. Called the first step in the *cycle of coding*, this step is essential to ensure that the data can be reviewed and analyzed easily (Saldana 45).

Often investigators or scholars keep a full set of the original data—both hard copy and electronic—which they can always return to if needed, and they work with complete coded copies of all the information collected. In this manner, you will protect the safety and integrity of the information that you have collected.

Once this initial coding to protect a person's identity is concluded, you can start to create the portrait of the respondents you surveyed, interviewed, or observed, since this information will be critical to the validity of your findings. In published research, these demographic data are described in a paragraph or two and often also portrayed in a table. Often, the sample is characterized by information about the typical respondent, and usually it requires a table that lists the various demographic categories, the number of respondents in each category, and the percentage that number represents of the whole. A hypothetical example is shown below.

Demography of the Sample

Category	Number	Percentage
Males	252	59%
Females	175	41%
Total	427	100%
Business Travelers	185	43%
Leisure Travelers	95	22%
Visiting Family and Friends	47	11%

Once this step is completed, you can move to code the data as a part of content analysis (see **Chapter 13, Research Techniques: Observations, Focus Groups, and Other Techniques**) or use these codes to review the data and make decisions about next steps.

REVIEWING THE RESEARCH QUESTIONS OR OBJECTIVES

When new researchers are confronted with a quantity of data, they sometimes get excited about the information and want to see what the information contains and forget the original purpose statement. Reviewing the original purpose statement and research questions or objectives will give you suggestions for how to sort and collate the information that you have. They will remind you why you set out to collect the data that you did, and help you structure the ways in which you want to sort and analyze the information that you have collected. If you have several research questions that lead in varying directions, then you may want to consider multiple ways to sort and organize the data in the early stages of analyzing them. If you are examining the various factors that influence baby boomers' choice of travel destination and type of travel, then you may want to organize some of the data by age and gender and then reorganize the data by location or mode of transportation—car, bus, train, ship, ferry, or plane. Each way of sorting it might produce different insights, but try various methods based on the original questions that impelled your inquiry. If you are evaluating the impact of various frequency marketing programs on guest purchase decisions at a specific hotel chain, you may want to sort by category of guest, level of loyalty program, or frequency of hotel stay. In the case of evaluating sport concussions, you may want to sort data by athlete, position on the team, frequency of concussion, type of concussion, return to the field, or doctor or trainer involved.

Once you have reviewed the data you collected, you may need to ponder new strategies or techniques of sorting data that are different than ways you might have considered at the beginning of this journey. Comparing two or three ways of organizing information may provide you with new insights that you might not have otherwise considered. It can also be useful to reshape the original research questions in order to take into account other ways of organizing the information you have collected.

This particular step will help you avoid losing sight of the original purpose and encourage the process of organizing data in line with your original research questions or objectives. The next section explains how to organize and sort information to make it usable and easier to analyze.

ORGANIZING AND SORTING INFORMATION

Organizing the data is a powerful step to help you analyze them. Although it may be seductive to start analyzing data as soon as you collect them, remember that you can distort your examination and bring all kinds of bias into the process unless you carefully organize all of the information that you have collected and give it all equal treatment. Although not all of the data will provide you with significant insights, you never know what part will be most critical. There are many ways to sort the data that you have collected.

To ensure that you will analyze data fairly and objectively, you need to organize them in such a manner that you can find the information and access it in a usable format. Before computers and database programs, the process of organizing information was more difficult than it is today, but current database systems still require careful thinking about what categories you want to use and why. Therefore, after immersing yourself in the information that you have collected, you need to consider what categories will best organize it. Do you organize information by who said or wrote it or do you organize it by themes? Do you organize it by tone, style, or influence? For example, if you are examining the responses of tourists to a UNESCO World Heritage Site, do you organize the comments by site? By age of the tourist? By home country of the tourist? By the season or time of year of the visit?

Since the categories you use will directly affect what you notice in your reviews, it is critical to think about them ahead of time. Not unlike the categories and units of analysis you establish before conducting formal observations or reviewing the contents of a range of documents, the process of establishing categories before you start will improve the ease and quality of your analysis. One simple method is to set up categories on a spreadsheet program, the most common of which is probably Excel.

Entering the data into various types of software, such as Excel, or other common data base makes this task quick and easy. Electronic survey software, such as Survey Monkey or Qualtrics, can also provide an easy way to sort the data. When respondents complete their questionnaires using these, and other, software, the responses are immediately organized so that you can call for reports that sort by various indicators and in real time. Sorting during this initial process of data analysis will help you since you can begin to see patterns and notice that you may have very few responses of one category which might mean you need to continue collecting data or it might mean something significant about your sample. It also gives you a way to describe the common characteristics of your sample—an important aspect of what you need to prepare to do in the final report. In some ways, the easiest data to work with are numerical, but they are not always the best for your research objectives of questions.

In the case of qualitative data, the use of software packages may be less helpful, but using them to collect and display common words or patterns of behavior can provide a way to highlight important issues and cause you to notice them in ways that might not be evident when just reviewing the data in large doses. The more that you can use some kind of coding of interviews and observations, the clearer you can be about what the data show and the less dependent you will be on your own intuition and limited perspective.

IDENTIFYING RELATIONSHIPS AND PATTERNS

One of the key ways to analyze information is to look for patterns in any set of data. In either case, the challenge is to create pictures of the data so that you can begin to see common patterns—similar themes, perspectives, or ways of perceiving acting—in the information that you have collected. *Pattern analysis*—the evaluation of information or data to notice common tendencies, insights, responses, or thoughts—provides the most critical aspect of any research project. Often, it is the hardest since the details are obvious but not some of the common tendencies buried in the details. Creating a graph or diagram of common responses can be one way to highlight patterns in qualitative situations; various software programs will produce information about patterns when you are using large amounts of data in quantitative research.

One of the most difficult aspects of most data collection plans is the overwhelming quantity of information that can be collected and the lack of planning of what to do with it. There are several strategies for ferreting out patterns and relationships; they include describing numbers, conducting statistical analyses, reviewing documents from various perspectives, and using outside readers. However, the task remains a challenge for both quantitative and qualitative research. Of course, identifying relationships among quantitative data differs strongly from working with qualitative data (LeCompte 147). Both remain important to understand.

The most common way to analyze quantitative data is to use descriptive statistics to portray the numbers. The ability to describe the range of numbers, the commonalities in the numbers, and the quantity of sources provides a perspective on the numbers which can begin to highlight possible patterns. Just representing numbers in various tables and charts or in various diagrams indicates areas where there are a number of common tendencies and areas with few responses. Noticing these groups enables you to begin to perceive relationships and similarities, a critical aspect of the analysis of patterns.

The most common way to analyze qualitative data is the *data analysis spiral*, an iterative process of moving from collecting data, categorizing it, sorting it, and interpreting it to finding patterns to recategorizing, resorting, reinterpreting, very much like the seven steps mentioned at the beginning of this chapter (Creswell 151). The final step involves visualizing and representing the patterns and findings. Since this process is complex, often qualitative researchers talk about learning the analysis by doing it, a process also common to quantitative researchers (Creswell 150).

Whether qualitative or quantitative, an important part of any research challenge is acknowledging the number of questionnaire respondents, observations made, persons in focus groups, documents analyzed, or persons interviewed. These numbers enable the most critical step in examining patterns—conducting a *cohort analysis* in which you compare the responses made by various demographic categories to certain questions as opposed to determining the overall, or aggregate, responses of the group of persons you have surveyed, interviewed, observed, or analyzed. For example, noticing how women versus men answer questions about purchasing sports paraphernalia, or younger groups compared to older groups behave as tourists, or persons from certain ethnic backgrounds compared to other ethnic groups select restaurants provides far richer insights. In fact, analyzing data in this manner provides you with more useful information than simply reporting aggregate data. While an *aggregate analysis*, a description of the entire data, provides an overall picture of the entire sample, it is more interesting to know more detailed information. While it is relevant to realize that social media users spent three times as much time on Facebook than any other social media site, it is even more insightful to know that 29 percent of Facebook users are 25 to 34, and 10 percent are older than 55 (Nielsen 7). Numbers, however, are always easier to review for patterns.

QUANTITATIVE ANALYSIS OF PATTERNS

Sometimes, it is possible to identify relationships by examining elements that can be highlighted by key statistical concepts such as mean, median, mode, frequency distribution, standard deviation, correlation, regression analysis, and analysis of variance. *Mean* refers to the average of a set of numbers, *median* denotes the number for which half the scores are above and half below; and *mode* is the most common number in a set of numbers. A *frequency distribution* indicates the number of times that individuals responded to each of the items on a scale, and the *standard deviation* indicates the way in which numbers are arranged around the mean.

Standard deviation measures the extent of the breadth of the numbers in a collection. A higher standard deviation indicates a broader spread of numbers since one standard deviation indicates that approximately 68 percent of the numbers in a group lie between one standard deviation above and below the mean, and 95 percent lie within two standard deviations above or below the mean. Therefore, with a higher standard deviation, the spread is wider. Understanding the standard deviation can provide a sense of the information and how many responses fit into the central section of a standard curve. Analyzing dimensions of central tendency such as the shape of the bell curve, its *kurtosis*—peaks or flatness—or its skew—symmetry or lack of it—can also indicate the pattern of responses. *Correlation* provides a measure of the relationship between to variables in a single number ranging from -1.00 to $+1.00$. A high correlation means that changes in one variable match changes in the other one. *Regression* is a calculation of the power of the influence of one variable upon another. *Analysis of variance*—often referred to as ANOVA—is a statistical examination of the effects of several variables on the behavior being observed and analyzed.

If you have compiled data on amounts of money that sports fans spend at an event, you can examine those numbers using statistics and show what the average person spent compared to the highest spender and lowest spender. Comparing the mean scores with the median scores will also tell you additional information about the patterns of expenses. However, you may need to segregate certain categories of expenditures to establish smaller but more insightful patterns so that you can distinguish between season ticket holders and daily visitors or between persons in the luxury boxes and persons in the bleachers. If you are examining the amounts spent on conferences and special events by an organization, then you may want to do an analysis of the means of all the events and then segregate them by category so that you can compare large-scale events and celebrations such as awards dinners with small-scale events such as board and committee meetings. Putting all of the events together in one statistical report will mask the very real differences among various different categories of special events.

If you are using numerical data or other information that can be coded into numerical form, then you can use Excel (or other similar software) to organize and reorganize the numbers by moving columns to rows and rows to columns, thereby illustrating information that was not evident in parallel column format. You can also add different rows for columns and columns for rows showing different sets of information and providing potential insights. If you have not learned how to use pivot tables, try working with them on any Excel spreadsheet that has rows and columns; you will see how easy using the mouse to drag and drop columns or rows can be and how insightful the resulting spreadsheets can be. (You also may want to save these new spreadsheets under a new label so that you have them to refer to and analyze in the future.)

With quantitative data, patterns can be discovered by employing a number of these statistical methods or software tools to identify influences of one variable on another. When there are fewer numbers to analyze, finding patterns can be more complex. The work of finding patterns and analyzing them in qualitative research is, however, still important.

QUALITATIVE ANALYSIS OF PATTERNS

Although seeing patterns can be a more difficult challenge when dealing with qualitative information, it remains critical in analyzing any set of data. The increasing growth of some software packages has made the process of analyzing qualitative data easier, but they are still not completely successful (Romano et al. 216–17). In situations where you have been collecting qualitative information, it is often harder and more complex to recognize patterns and relationships. Although it might seem more difficult to interpret narrative data since it lacks the built-in structure found in numerical data, it can be done with care and an objective perspective.

One common method requires comparing the results with what you expected to find so that you have a clearer sense of what you have collected. If you thought that most of your respondents or interviewees were going to agree with several statements about cultural heritage sites and they disagreed or disagreed strongly, you are more likely to notice their scores; the discrepancy will most likely cause you to think about why they rated their comments as they did since you expected something different. If you thought that women would react differently from men in what they want in a hotel room, and you found that they all wanted the same things, then you have noticed a pattern that is not what you expected.

Another method is to compare the information you have collected with other information that you have read in your literature review. Noticing that there were differences in responses to questions that you administered or interviews you conducted compared to what other authors have reported is another way to notice a pattern of responses that seems unusual to you. Reviewing the studies of customer loyalty that indicate that how people are treated and what they feel about a hotel chain makes a big difference in their behavioral loyalty and finding that the most common response in your data set is brand recognition and there are no mentions of affective commitment at all will cause you to look closely at those responses and see what possible new pattern might be there (Matilla 175). Alternatively, finding that your responses among sports fans reflect what you have been reading may show you the enduring consistency of the research findings.

The prior task of organizing information can also help a great deal—in fact, it can mask or uncover patterns, depending on the ways in which you organize the information. Therefore, it is important to try various ways of organizing the information in order to ascertain patterns. The following strategies may also be helpful when analyzing narrative data. One way of analyzing interview transcripts is to provide a column to the left of your notes—whether observations, interview transcripts, or focus group records—and record interesting ideas or highlights on the left-hand column. Once you have completed that task, then you can review the information in the left-hand column and determine how often certain key words, or synonyms, appear and where they occur.

Looking at the repeated words and phrases provides a start on noticing patterns. After you have analyzed one or two documents, then you can continue with other documents to see if those words occur again or if other words are more common. Reading the interview transcripts, focus group notes, and observation records more than once will be important if you want to ensure that you do not miss anything. Also counting the number of times that certain words or synonyms and concepts are mentioned is also a critical part of this process.

Another way to notice patterns in qualitative situations with narrative reports is to read common interview questions or focus group questions horizontally across all of the interview transcripts instead of reading one person's interview all the way through. If you read all of the answers to the same question and take some notes of common insights, you may see some interesting common examples or themes. Once you have examined one question throughout all of the transcripts or other documents and taken some notes, then try reading a different question, often scrambling the order of the interview notes so that you are not always reading the same person's comments first and the same persons last. Reading in this horizontal manner, you have a chance to see what patterns might lay in the data you have collected.

A fifth way to analyze notes and narratives is to group them as you organize them and read them in specific groups to see if there are several common themes or mentions of certain events, activities, or facts among group members. Deciding on the membership of various groups may distort this analytical process, but it is the first key decision in undertaking this analysis. Documents can be grouped according to the characteristics of the persons who were interviewed or observed; alternatively, they can be grouped by themes that they cover or concepts that emerge from your perusal of the information. Reading all of the comments made by season ticket holders and then all of the comments by persons who are at the game for the first time might show patterns among different groups of spectators. The same can be true of tourists divided into first-time visitors to a destination and those who have come several times. With word processing software, you can copy and paste parts of documents to make new documents to analyze. (The important part is making sure that you keep track of where the parts came from so that you can review the statements again in their original context to ensure that you have not misinterpreted something or inappropriately brought your own frame of reference to the comment.) In each of these strategies, ensuring that you always review and re-review the data becomes critical so that you do not make assumptions not supported by the information you have collected.

REVIEWING THE DATA

Once you have developed a set of patterns, it is important to review the data you have collected and see how those patterns fit the data (LeCompte 151). It becomes essential to determine if you missed something from your original coding or note taking and need to incorporate it into your ongoing analysis. Alternatively, you may have misread some of the responses to interviews, questions on a survey, observation notes, or words in documents. Reviewing the responses with a fresh perspective will help ensure that you have not brought any preconceived bias to your review of the data.

Comparing information with what you expected to find can be a strategy to take in reviewing the data. It can serve as a good test of the original hypotheses or questions that you were asking and help you determine if you have been able to answer them carefully and objectively or whether you are just seeing patterns in the data because you want to see them. One challenge in conducting objective research is carefully reading interview transcripts, documents, notes from meetings or focus groups, and other sources of data and not adding patterns that you want to see. Remembering that the purpose of your research is to understand and discover can help you separate from the need for the data to show what you want, but keeping an objective distance is not easy. Reviewing information with other individuals can help as can reviewing information in different order. Shuffle the interview transcripts so that you do not always read the same interview first or mix up the notes from various observations or focus groups and you may find that you see things afresh when you mind does not follow the same pattern.

Another strategy is to have a different person take the patterns you have identified and see if that person sees the same patterns in the data. In this situation, you need to provide the outside person with the full interview transcripts, questionnaires, or observation notes so that the individual can determine if the patterns are really there. This process is one way to establish *inter-rater reliability*—the determination of consistency of analysis among several independent readers. Do you and the other person see the same common words, mentions, reactions, and ideas in the documents? Does the statistical analysis seem to reflect the responses in the questionnaires? If so, then you have improved the reliability of your analysis. Sometimes this process involves one person reviewing the responses from questionnaires or interviews and then making them into categories while a different individual take the categories and reapplies them back to the data. The use of both the inductive and deductive method helps to ensure inter-rater reliability (Burla et al. 114–15).

Conducting these various reviews of the data by using several different strategies and using a set of fresh eyes is one way to ensure that you protect the reliability of your analysis. Especially in situations where you have several possible ways of recognizing patterns in data, it is important to have more than one individual review and analyze responses for themes or categories.

INTERPRETING THE FINDINGS

Once you have the patterns, it is critical to interpret them and determine what they mean in terms of the research that you have conducted. Analyzing the data collected involves a number of issues: reviewing your original purpose statement, presenting information, presenting data, and examining implications of your research findings. The first part involves connecting the findings as you have them at this point to your original purpose statement and research questions as well as rereading the findings from your literature review to structure the interpretation of the data you have collected and analyzed. The second part of the process involves analyzing the collected summaries of the data, which was discussed previously. The third part of interpretation requires assessing the applicability and limitations of the findings (Leedy and Ormrod 284–85).

Interpreting findings involves reviewing and restating the purpose of the research, the research questions or objectives, and your literature review. If you have done a careful literature review, you will find that parts of it will provide you with insights useful in interpreting the findings that you have developed. If you read about various concepts of fan behavior and models of fan avidity, then you can use them to interpret the patterns of responses about how and why sports fans buy the tickets that they do. If you found various insights about the impact of brands on customers, then you can use that information to interpret the responses guests made to why they are staying at the hotel they chose. If you recognized patterns of lack of sustainable practices in cultural and heritage sites, then you can use that information to analyze the responses of tourists who have visited these sites.

Sometimes, key parts of the literature review or your awareness of what you expected to find can help you make sense of the patterns that you have noticed and force you to look for additional patterns. Others may point you to questions in your survey or interviews that you might not have examined before. For example, in examining NBA or NFL collective bargaining agreements, you may initially focus on the role of contracts in your data analysis, but a review of the literature on management may inspire you to also look at stakeholders, communication patterns, and negotiation strategies as part of the negotiation process. If you expected to find that hotel guests rated cleanliness the most important quality in a hotel and you found little recognition of that factor, you might be drawn to closely examine all the interviews and the way that you have coded them. If your literature review pointed out that older tourists were only interested in authentic tourist experiences, but you found that they were really interested in a wider range of reasons to travel, you might want to consider their reasons more carefully.

Looking at how the answers to certain questions vary by demographic groups or elements of the sample population also gives you a sense of the patterns involved and how to interpret them. Patterns are important, but they are only part of the analysis. The real thinking comes with placing the patterns in a context and explaining how they reinforce insights from previous research or suggest a new approach or a new understanding. For example, simply listing responses from hotel guests about what they desire in a hotel does not have the same impact as analyzing the range of responses, assigning numbers based on the number of people who checked each response, and then matching it with other studies of the same topic. Showing that persons who are traveling on business answer one way on certain questions while persons who are traveling for leisure answer another way provides a more insightful finding.

When interpreting the findings, one thing you might consider doing is using quotes from various survey instruments (if you have open-ended questions), interviews, focus groups, or expert panels to illustrate the patterns and provide a deeper sense of what some of the responses might mean. When making the selection of quotes to include, consider who made them and how else they might be interpreted so that you only use quotes that contribute to your findings. Remember also that you will need permission to use the quotes; now is a good time to review the contents of your permission letters given to interviewees or members of your focus group. If you promised to quote only by classification, now is the time to check the code and provide a descriptor such as older tourist from the United States, or director of marketing at a major hotel, or season ticket holder. If you have permission to quote the person directly, then you may want to review the record closely to make sure that you have the exact quote correct.

Sometimes, pointing out paradoxical quotes can provide a dimension of depth to the findings that you are explaining and interpreting. Other times, quotes do not help you. When planning this part of your research project, consider which sources you might want to quote so that you will make plans to ensure that you obtain good quotes and that you corroborate the accuracy of your notes or recording with the person who made the statement. It may also be important to explain the quotes and interpret them since an individual may not have given you a quote that is directly related to a point you want to make. Sometimes, going back to an interviewee to check that you copied a quote correctly will lead him or her to improve the quote in a way that helps you use it with more impact. Other times, the changed quote loses its effect in supporting what you want to say. In either case, the integrity of your research means that you honor the actual quote and explain it in your report.

Data analysis and interpretation is the process of assigning meaning to the collected information and determining the conclusions, significance, and implications of the findings. The steps involved in data analysis are a function of the type of information collected and the software used, if appropriate; however, returning to the purpose of the analysis and the evaluation questions will provide a structure for the organization of the data and a focus for the analysis. For example, reviewing transcripts of interviews to determine the themes or categories of insights can organize the process of research and enable the assessment to proceed more clearly. An example is the analysis of detailed interviews from persons who had taken group tours (Morais, Kerstetter, and Yarnal 381).

DISPLAYING INFORMATION

One of the most critical aspects of a research report involves displaying information after the analysis has been completed. In any report, you will want to identify and explain, clearly, the patterns that you identified and the impact of certain forces on other forces or events, persons, and activities. However, it is also true that you need to organize the data and patterns in such a way that they support your conclusions. Sometimes, software can provide the displays, and the visual images are one of the many benefits of using software packages to analyze data whether they are qualitative or quantitative (Cambrar-Fierro and Wilson 19). That might mean using graphs, charts, or diagrams.

When constructing a graph, there are lots of dimensions to consider. The primary one is to honor the integrity of the information and not distort the numbers by showing them in an inappropriate scale or presentation. The second is to provide a clear visual portrayal of the numbers involved. Sometimes, the presentation involves a graph, table, or a chart. Either way, it is important to label the information appropriately with a title to the graph, chart, or table and indicate the source of the data. If you are comparing data you have collected with data from other published sources, it is critical to clarify the origins of the other data. If you are only presenting your data, then the structure and labels of the presentation need to be clear so that the reader can understand the data presented.

In making graphs, remember to try several scales for either the x or y axis to make the information understandable and visually appealing. Place the independent variable on the horizontal (x) axis and the dependent variable on the vertical (y) axis, label the horizontal (x) axis and the vertical (y) axes appropriately, and indicate the source of the data. Often a graph is used to illustrate comparative data; in that case, select the markings (color or pattern) for the various lines to make them legible and clear. A graph comparing RevPAR with occupancy rate when the numbers are so close to each other needs a scale of the vertical (y) axis that makes the difference in numbers clear. The presentation of ticket sales may need to be separated among season ticket sales, box seat sales, distribution channel sales, and individual game tickets to illustrate the differences in quantity and profit for the various sales strategies.

Using frequency tables, bar charts, histograms, pie charts, and other devices to display information that has been collected and analyzed provides an easy way to demonstrate differences, trends, and outliers of data.

A *frequency table* is a chart that indicates categories of persons, behaviors, or events, the actual number of the persons, behaviors, or events, and the percentage of each category.

Guests at XXX Resort for the Month of YYY

Ages	Number	Percentage
0–20	250	17%
21–30	125	9%
31–40	90	6%
41–50	570	38%
51–60	325	22%
61–70	50	3%
71–80	65	4%
81 and over	10	1%
Total	1485	100%

A bar chart or histogram can also be used. *Bar charts* provide columns of nominal or ordinal numbers and indicate the number of items in each category on the y axis and the categories on the x axis while a *histogram* shows intervals of number on the x axis and the number on the y axis. While they look similar, they show different aspects of data. A *pie chart*, easily created from spreadsheets and other software, shows the percentages of a behavior—for example, a pie chart indicating the age ranges that visit certain resorts would demonstrate graphically, and more vividly, the same information that can be placed into a table (Bryman and Bell 241–43; Robson 119–24).

Showing data visually helps indicate what is important to the research; therefore, how you choose to present it makes a big difference in how it is interpreted. The major issue with data, however, derives from their significance. Numbers do not mean anything; interpreting numbers and discerning their meaning is what makes a research project worth doing. Perhaps the most essential aspect of that challenge is determining what is significant, the subject of the next section.

SIGNIFICANCE

A common issue in analyzing and interpreting numbers is the question of significance. The issue refers to the base connection or parameter when noticing some change and commenting on its significance. It is one thing to see that the number of restaurant brunch patrons has doubled over the past month since the restaurant started serving Sunday brunches; it is very different to point out that the number went from 10 to 20 persons in a 100-seat restaurant.

In determining significance, it is essential to differentiate among three important concepts in research: connection, correlation, and causation. *Connection* refers to the relationship of one thing to another; it can mean the relationship between guests at luxury hotels and their travel habits, or the connection between age and type of travel. It is something to look for in conducting research since discovering connections between two forces, demographic factors, or patterns of actions can help understand the process or procedure and shed light on something important. However, finding a connection does not necessarily mean that the two factors or forces directly, or even indirectly, influence each other.

Determining the nature of the influence of one factor on another or the patterns under which two forces operate in similar fashion is a matter of correlation, the relationship of one variable moving in a certain pattern or way with another variable. When persons with more free time and higher amounts of disposable income tend to stay in more luxurious hotels, one can say that there is a correlation. And much of quantitative research involves determining the nature of that correlation and the extent of its influence. There are a number of statistical packages, the most common of which is probably SPSS (Statistical Package for the Social Sciences), which can apply a number of tests of correlation and determine the extent of the effect of one variable on another.

Causation is a more difficult phenomenon or relationship to determine. In fact, most of the research that is conducted in this field does not purport to prove causation because it is so difficult to separate the power of moderating variables on the influence of one variable on another.

Noticing significant differences in numbers involves careful use of statistical techniques, since the challenge is to prove that the results could not have happened due to chance. The most common strategy to interpret this aspect of data involves tests of significance and analysis of variance, but the process of determining significance is as relevant to qualitative research as it is to quantitative research. In quantitative research, the level of confidence expected or established at the beginning of the process of undertaking the research sets the parameters for significance (Thompson np).

Since sharing the value or significance of your data is so critical, it needs your careful attention. Making sure that you really have something important to say depends on the quality of your original data and the carefulness of your analysis, the subject of this chapter.

SUMMARY

This chapter has explained the steps in collecting, reviewing, and analyzing information in order to interpret data in light of the original purposes of the research. The seven steps included collecting the data, immersing yourself in the data to appreciate it, aligning the examination of the information with your original research goals, organizing the data, identifying relationships and patterns, revising the data, and interpreting the information in light of broader concepts. The chapter also discussed the issues of presenting information, determining the significance of the findings, and incorporating data analysis into your research proposal.

The next chapter will review the challenges of preparing a full research proposal and the criteria against which a proposal should be measured or evaluated.

KEY TERMS

Aggregate analysis	Data analysis spiral	Listwise deletion
Analysis of variance	Deductive reasoning	Mean
Bar chart	Dependent variable	Medium
Causation	Frequency distribution	Mode
Coding	Frequency table	Pattern analysis
Coding manual	Histogram	Pie chart
Coding schedule	Imputed data	Significance
Cohort analysis	Independent variable	Source document
Connection	Inductive reasoning	Standard deviation
Correlation	Inter-rater reliability	Unit of analysis
Cycle of coding	Kurtosis	

WORKS CITED IN THIS CHAPTER

Allison, Paul D. "Multiple Imputation for Missing Data." *Sociological Methods and Research.* 28 (2000): 301–309.

Alreck, Patricia, and Robert B. Settle. *The Survey Research Handbook.* Homewood: Irwin, 1985.

Andrews, Richard. *Research Questions.* London: Continuum, 2003.

Bryman, Alan, and Duncan Cramer. *Quantitative Data Analysis with SPSS Release 10 for Windows: A Guide for Social Scientists*. East Sussex: Routledge, 2001.

Bryman, Alan, and Emma Bell. *Business Research Methods*. Oxford: Oxford University Press, 2003.

Burla, Laila, Knierim B, Barth J, Liewald K, Duetz M, Abel T. "From Text to Codings: Intercoder Reliability Assessment in Qualitative Content Analysis." *Nursing Research* 57.2 (April 2008): 113–17.

Cambra-Fierro, Jesus and Alan Wilson. "Qualitative Data Analysis Software: Will It Ever Become Mainstream?" *International Journal of Market Research*. 53 (2011): 17–24.

Creswell, John W. *Qualitative Inquiry and Research Design: Choosing Among Five Approaches*. 2nd ed. Thousand Oaks; Sage Publications, 2007.

Dwork, Cynthia. "A Firm Foundation for Private Data Analysis." *Communication of the ACMs* 54 (2011): 86–95.

Kolbe, Richard H., and Melissa S. Burnett. "Content-Analysis Research: An Examination of Applications with Directives for Improving Research Reliability and Objectivity." *Journal of Consumer Research* 18 (1991): 243–50.

LeCompte, Margaret D. "Analyzing Qualitative Data." *Theory Into Practice* 39.3 (2010): 146–54.

Leedy, Paul D., and Jeanne Ellis Ormrod. *Practical Research: Planning and Design*. 9th ed. Boston: Pearson, 2010.

Little, Roderick J. A. "Missing-Data Adjustments in Large Surveys." *Journal of Business and Economic Statistics* 6 (1988): 287–96.

Lombard, Matthew, Jennifer Snyder-Duch, and Cheryl Campanella Bracken. "Content Analysis in Mass Communication: Assessment and Reporting of Intercoder Reliability." *Human Communication Research* 28 (2002): 587–604.

Matilla, Anna. "How Affective Commitment Boosts Guest Loyalty (and Promotes Frequent Guest Programs)." *Cornell Hotel and Restaurant Administration Quarterly* 47 (2006): 174–81.

Miles, Matthew B., and A. Michael Huberman. *Qualitative Data Analysis: An Expanded Sourcebook*. Newbury Park: Sage, 1994.

Morais, Duarte B., Deborah L. Kerstetter, and Careen M. Yarnal. "The Love Triangle: Loyal Relationships among Providers, Customers, and Their Friends." *Journal of Travel Research* 44 (2006): 379–86.

Nielsen. *State of the Media: The Social Media Report Q3 2011*. The Nielsen Company. 11 September 2011. Web. 28 November 2011.

Qualtrics.com.

Robson, Colin. *How to Do a Research Project: A Guide for Undergraduate Students*. Malden: Blackwell, 2007.

Romano, Nicolas C. Jr., Christina Donovan, Hsinchun Chen, and Jay F. Nunamaker Jr. "A Methodology for Analyzing Web-Based Qualitative Data." *Journal of Management Information* 19 (2003): 213–46.

Saldana, Johnny. *The Coding Manual for Qualitative Researchers*. London: Sage, 2009.

Sekaran, Uma. *Research Methods for Business: A Skill Building Approach*. 4th ed. New York: John Wiley & Sons, 2003.

Survey Monkey. "View and Analyze Survey Responses in Real Time." SurveyMonkey.com Web. 18 December 2011.

Thompson, Bruce. "The Concept of Statistical Significance Testing." *Practical Assessment, Research & Evaluation* 4 (1994): PAREonline.net.

CHAPTER 14

Writing a Research Proposal

INTRODUCTION

For some people, the most daunting part of conducting research involves writing the proposal that explains the need for the research, articulates the research design, and makes a case for conducting the research. Any proposal—whether for approval in graduate school, for funding to conduct a program evaluation, or for support as a cooperative activity—is designed to convince the reader about the importance and *feasibility* of the proposal.

In many ways, the challenge is considering all of the aspects of a coherent proposal, including how to collect data, how to guarantee privacy, how to assure validity and reliability, and how to analyze the data collected and make sense of it. Some investigators find it challenging to write for a specific audience, which has the authority to accept, reject, or request amendments to the proposal. However, you can overcome these potential difficulties by writing your proposal carefully and providing the information that an outside reader wants to know.

This chapter discusses the reasons for a comprehensive and detailed proposal, the elements of a proposal, the importance of focusing on the *audience* and writing with a particular point of view, executive summaries, the range of documents that should accompany any proposal, and the criteria for evaluating a research proposal. The first section focuses on the reasons for a proposal; once you understand that issue, it can be relatively easy to put together a coherent, comprehensive, and well-written research proposal.

REASONS FOR A PROPOSAL

Any proposal should be designed to convince the readers that the purpose and plan to accomplish that purpose is sound and makes a lot of sense. The reason for developing a coherent research proposal is that the process provides you with the opportunity to think through all the aspects of the research, evaluate what has already been done in this area, and clarify what contribution you think you can make with your design (Heath 148).

The second reason is that you want to convince a potential supporter to fund the research, to work with you, to provide you with the time to conduct the research, or to approve the project as a valid enterprise. Therefore, in a research proposal, the reviewer will look for the clarity of the goal or purpose, the evidence of the need for the research, the feasibility of the design, and the coherence of the plan—including the budget—that supports the research design. Therefore, the details and comprehensiveness of the proposal are very important.

In a graduate program, the proposal should convince a faculty member (or faculty committee) of three things: one, that the research topic and purpose statement is worth pursuing; two, that you can complete the research in a reasonable period of time; and three, that you have the skills and experience to complete the project. The clarity and thoroughness of the proposal are key aspects that will convince the faculty member. In all three cases, your proposal needs to contain all of the information that the reader needs to make a determination about your proposal.

In these situations, you also need to provide information about all of the aspects of the research and have created a design that ensures you will be able to collect and analyze the data critical to your purpose. Some of the aspects that need to be included in your proposal include making sure you can:

- Obtain access to individuals, staff members, customers, hotel guests, tourists, or sports fans (whatever is appropriate for your proposal)

- Compile or acquire the documents, statistics or other data you will need

- Arrange material and financial support for the investigation

- Acquire approval to conduct research on human subjects

- Ensure the skill and experience base to complete the investigation

- Assure the significance of the results and their usefulness to others

By having read about other methods and assessed them in your literature review, you and your readers will recognize that the method you have chosen has a high likelihood of success. By considering the other research that has been conducted and pointing it out to your audience, you can assure that your research will connect to the work of others and make the contribution that you intend. It will also increase the likeliness of support, regardless of your audience.

Providing the clarity and assurance that you have thought through all the important parts of the research design will help your reader find it easy to support your enterprise in whatever manner you are requesting. Sometimes, that involves material support—facilities, equipment, paper—and sometimes staff time or access to computing facilities (Porte 15). If you have demonstrated that you have considered all the alternatives and have the best possible plan with the highest likelihood of succeeding, the reader will be even more likely to support you.

Writing out a complete research proposal also increases your likelihood of being able to conduct the project since you have demonstrated the need for the research, developed a way of collecting and analyzing the information, and considered all the challenges involved in making sure the research will be well done. It means that when you obtain the approval, you are prepared to undertake the project.

Having to write it out in detail also helps you consider all of the aspects of the significance of the research and the likelihood that your audience will agree with your proposal. To ensure that your proposal is accepted, you need to include all of the elements of a comprehensive proposal.

ELEMENTS OF A PROPOSAL

Depending on the audience of your proposal, there are many ways to consider the key elements. Your first step should be to inquire about the type of writing and the range of information required for the proposal you are preparing. If you are seeking foundation or government support, you need to consider the way in which the organization wants to receive the information, the forms required and the structure suggested. Giving them information in the proper format is essential to be taken seriously and to be considered for financial support. Not-for-profit organizations, nongovernmental organizations and universities also have their requirements for the content and form of the proposal. Be sure to inquire and obtain the most recent information about the necessary information and structure. The following general concepts and principles may be helpful, but they need to be adapted to specific situations, and some of the key elements may be irrelevant, or even superfluous, in the minds of some readers.

For independent research as part of a graduate program, the elements include:

- Executive summary
- Introduction
- Purpose of the research, including its significance and the research questions or objectives
- Literature review and insights
- Research design, including information about data collection method, sampling, and a plan for analysis of the data
- Expected findings
- Possible limitations
- Applications and next steps
- Conclusion
- Appendices of supporting documents

For research proposals that require funding, the structure is normally:

- Cover sheet
- Executive summary
- Introduction
- Purpose of the research and its significance or usefulness
- Literature review and insights from practice

- Research design, including information about data collection method, sampling, and a plan for analysis of the data

- Expected findings

- Strategy for disseminating the findings

- Possible limitations

- Next steps

- Conclusion

- Appendices of supporting documents, including budget, staff information, and letters of organizational support

There are three purposes for a proposal: communication, planning, and contracting. First, the proposal should explain the goals and purpose of the investigation to any reader whose support and approval are necessary for the research to be undertaken. Second, the proposal should provide the details about how the research will be conducted and implemented. That means that it must contain information about all aspects of the research plan and address all the possible difficulties in implementing the plan. The more comprehensive the proposal, the easier it will be to actually follow and the higher the likelihood of support to undertake and success in completing the research. Third, the proposal should provide a clear understanding—sometimes almost a memorandum of agreement—between the persons who approve the project and the ones who undertake it. It also indicates in what form the final results—thesis, dissertation, article, conference presentation, or white paper—will be disseminated and the audience toward which the report will be addressed (Locke, Spirdosuo, and Silverman 3–5).

In more detail, most research proposals contain the following elements and answer the questions associated with each section:

- Executive Summary
  - What is the proposal about?
  - What do you expect to find?
  - How it is significant?

- Introduction
  - What is the structure of the proposal?
  - How is it organized?
  - What are the critical aspects of this particular proposal?

- Purpose Statement
  - What is the overall purpose of the research? What is the problem you want to solve?

- Why is it important and significant?

- What are the questions you want to answer?

- What are the hypotheses you want to test? Or validate?

- Why is this work important for you to do?

- Why is this project important to the industry?

- What audience(s) will want to learn the results of your work?

- What difference will it make?

- Literature Review

  - What does the literature say about this and related topics?

  - What studies are you building on to make your case for the importance or significance of your research project?

  - What studies show the importance of your research design and validate the format and method that you have chosen?

  - What studies can help you interpret the findings you hope to draw if you were to conduct the research?

  - What are the patterns and gaps in the research?

  - What is missing in the literature?

- Research Design

  - How do you propose to investigate the problem you have identified?

  - What methods will you use to find out the answers to the questions you have?

  - What form of inquiry—qualitative or quantitative or mixed—will you use, and why is it the most appropriate one?

  - What data will you collect?

  - What sample selection process will you employ, and why?

  - How will you analyze and present your findings?

  - What statistical or qualitative analytical tools will you use, and why?

- Validity and Reliability

  - How does your design address questions of internal and external validity?

  - What would you like to do to ensure that what you find will be credible to others?

  - Will your research plan be replicable by others?

- Potential Results and Implications

  - What do you think you will find?

- What are the implications of what you will find?

- What new research or changes in practice do you think this research might suggest?

- Limitations

  - What are the problems posed by the research design?

  - What limits on the data collection or analysis come from the method proposed?

  - What other research would you recommend as follow-up?

- Applications

  - What suggestions for changes in policy or practice come from the expected findings?

  - How might the insights be used to make improvements in operations?

  - What are the implications of your expected findings for the industry?

  - What are the implications of the research methods that you used?

- Conclusion

- Bibliography or works cited, depending on the purpose (academic, consulting, or grant) of the proposal

- Appendices

  - What organizations support this research?

  - What business or organization will provide an administrative home and support services?

  - What forms will you use? Administrative budget forms, interview protocols, approvals for research on human subjects, permission letters from organizations, survey information?

  - What supporting documents can you provide? Letters of support from outside organization or partners in this research project?

  - What is the budget?

  - Who are the staff involved?

  - What is the timeline for this research?

  - What is the plan for obtaining approval to conduct research on human subjects?

  - What is the plan for displaying the results and disseminating the information found?

When in doubt, spell out all the details of your plan, since the clarity and comprehensiveness will indicate the credibility and feasibility of your research plan. Having written out the specific steps and details will also help you through the actual research. So long as you keep focused on the audience for your proposal, you will cover all of the elements that are required.

AUDIENCE AND POINT OF VIEW

For some new researchers, the hardest part of developing a proposal is preparing the proposal for a particular audience and developing the appropriate voice. That *voice* represents something different than the perspective or *point of view*. Voice represents the tone with which you present your proposal and the personality of the proposal; it refers to the stance that you take toward the topic of the research and the assumptions that you make about the inquiry, the participants, and the findings. The questions to ask about the voice are: Is it formal and very distant, written in the third-person point of view, or is it more informal and written in the first person point of view? Some formats suggest a more informal and first-person point of view—in that case, follow the suggestions. However, more commonly, proposals are written in the third-person point of view, which supports objectivity in the proposed research.

The perspective that you take in writing a research proposal can make a huge difference in the way in which it is reviewed. A formal and intimidating know-it-all tone and perspective may discourage your audience and incline them to reject your proposal since your voice may indicate that you are not aware of the difficulties in conducting serious research and you may be minimizing how difficult it is and how hard to ensure findings with real significance. (For more information about significance, see **Chapter 13, Analyzing Data and Other Information**.) A voice that is too timid and unsure may lead your readers to think you are not properly prepared to conduct the research and that the investment in your project should not be made.

Your perspective should be thoughtful, objective, and curious. You should write with confidence that you know about the field, you have done the preparation, and the project is important. Your voice should convey a mastery of the topic and the many aspects of the research project without overstating the plan. An assured tone that dismisses serious challenges will not help you; an insecure perspective that you are not sure you can conduct the research will not work either. Speak with some confidence and plenty of reasons about why the project should be undertaken and how it will contribute to industry knowledge and practice.

The perspective needs to be an impassioned, objective, third-party point of view. After all, the reader or readers want to be assured that you have a logical plan and that it has a very high likelihood of being successful in producing the findings and insights that you indicate. The plan should be professional looking and presented well so that it gets a fair reading based on the content of the proposal and is not undermined by a poor-quality presentation.

Just as a company or firm will present a proposal with a clear organization and structure, a research proposal should be organized in the same manner and focused on the audience to which it is being presented. The more that you know about the potential audience for your proposal—the persons who will actually read it and make a decision on the basis of the proposal—the easier it is to write or revise in light of the requirements of that organization (Baker 62).

Since research is designed to be objective, valid, and reliable, the proposal needs to carry that tone and voice. There is no room in a solid research proposal for the first person point of view; "I" is not relevant, and it detracts from what you want to convey—a carefully reasoned and comprehensive proposal. The third-person point of view encourages the objective review of the proposal and avoids making the proposal into a personal matter or a commentary on you as a person presenting the proposal. The same point of view needs to pervade the first parts—and for some, the only parts—of the proposal that a reader will encounter.

PREFATORY DOCUMENTS

At the beginning of most proposals, there is an explanation or a summary of that document. Some proposals require an *abstract*, a short version of the entire document explaining it to the potential reader. Others require an executive summary, typically a one- or two-page document that has several purposes, the primary one of which is to clarify for the reader what is included in the full proposal and to invite the individual to read or to make a decision about what to do with the report or proposal. Sometimes that decision is to refer it to the appropriate group or person to analyze it closely; sometimes, it is to put it on the individual's reading list. Often, it helps the executive know to whom to refer the proposal.

While different from an executive summary, an abstract serves the same function—to provide the reader with an overall view of the key points in the document and enough information to decide whether or not to read the document. An abstract provides a reader with a short précis or review of the focus and findings, where an executive summary gives the reader enough information to determine to what use the document should be put. Typically, an abstract is briefer than an executive summary and provides a quick and highly focused review of a particular article or report for a colleague, fellow scholar, or researcher. Since abstracts are normally written for articles and not research proposals, the abstracts are shorter as well.

In addition, the purposes are slightly different. For example, an abstract in front of a scholarly article will help a scholar decide how relevant that article is to his or her interests. An executive summary can be used in sorting research proposals in order to send them to an appropriate reviewer. In the case of a white paper or other document, the executive summary furnishes enough information to enable a reader to decide what to do with the document.

A reader of the executive summary should know what the study is about, why it is important, how it will be conducted, and what difference it is likely to make.

EXECUTIVE SUMMARY

An *executive summary* is a one-page description of a report, proposal, or other document that provides the reader with a short synopsis of the document in front of the individual and provides sufficient information to encourage the person to read the entire document. It should contain enough key ideas so that the person knows the range and scope of the document and will have some idea about what to do with the document. It provides a reader with enough information to know whether he or she should read the entire document or forward it to another person for more close examination. For good examples of brief executive summaries, read a current issue of the *Harvard Business Review*. Those summaries are written to provide sufficient information for the reader to decide whether to examine the article in depth or simply use the insights gathered from reading the summary. A reader of the executive summary for a research proposal should know what the study is about, why it is important, how it will be carried out, and what impact it can make.

The executive summary should review or capture the reason for the documents, the methods of investigation, the perspective, and the key points that you make in the report, proposal, essay, or article that you have written. It should reflect the tone, style, and point of view of the report. It should also be confined to a few pages since it is a summary and not an exposition of the key points; however, some executive summaries are longer, especially if they preface a long and detailed study or report. (In some cases, with long reports, an executive summary needs to be longer and more detailed, but it should be a brief and carefully focused document.) For example, the "The Greater Mekong Subregion Tourism Sector Strategy" document is 71 pages and prefaced with a seven-page executive summary ("Greater Mekong" 1). Sometimes reports do not include executive summaries. The proposal to hold the 2012 Olympics in New York City did not have an executive summary.

Executive summaries that serve their purpose cover all the essential points of the main document without overwhelming the reader with too much detail. That means that the document needs to be written, rewritten, edited, and revised several times to eliminate extraneous information and to focus on the audience. Good executive summaries are well written, comprehensive, tightly organized, and carefully focused.

CRITERIA FOR EXECUTIVE SUMMARIES

- Well-written
- Comprehensive
- Tightly organized
- Carefully focused

They do not include too many details, but they do need to encourage the reader to take the report or article or document seriously and enable the individual to determine what to do with the document.

TIPS FOR WRITING AN EXECUTIVE SUMMARY

When writing an executive summary, consider the key points in the report, paper, analysis, or proposal. Then write the executive summary in several paragraphs.

The first paragraph should be very succinct and to the point in order to help the reader focus on the purpose, point of view, or perspective of the entire document. It should capture the reader's interest, encourage the individual to read or examine some parts in detail, and explain the significance or importance of the report. Therefore, construct the paragraph to provide a context for the reader and indicate the significance of your report. What is it generally about, and why is it important? What difference does it make? Why should the study have been undertaken?

The second paragraph should explain the research methods involved, the sources consulted, and the techniques used to develop findings. Provide enough detail that the process is not obscure but do not fully explain the research methods. This paragraph should demonstrate the validity and reliability of the report and assure the reader that it contains sound insights and recommendations.

The third paragraph should indicate the findings, the insights from the study, and their implications. Sometimes, this paragraph also contains the recommendations of the report or the implications of the study. Other times, the findings constitute one paragraph, and the recommendations or applications fill another one.

Save the task of writing it until you have completed the study or proposal since it typically incorporates all the key elements of your document. Until you have completed the entire proposal, you are not sure what you want to say. The process of waiting is not appropriate for writing a literature review, however, which also carries an objective, third-person perspective.

Since the goal is to encourage the executive, manager, or professional reader to spend time with the entire document, it should be well written and carefully organized so that nothing detracts the reader from the information in the executive summary. The summary should also contain no errors of fact, style, or logic. Remember that the reader may have little background about the report; the executive summary has to orient the reader and encourage reading the entire document.

Other documents are also provided to enable the reader to make a good decision about the research proposal. They include a range of supporting documents.

OTHER SUPPORTING DOCUMENTS

For your proposal to make sense, you need to keep the report focused and clear and detailed so that it supports what you are trying to say in terms of your *research questions*, the insights from the literature review, and the research design. Whenever possible, use *appendices*, a collection of supporting documents that explain parts of the research proposal in more depth. Appendices might include budgets for the research project, background information about members of the research team, letters of support, permission to conduct research on human subjects, possible sample charts and diagrams of the research process, and a timeline, which shows what will be done while completing the project. There can be other documents as well, which may vary depending on the type or research being conducted and the requirements of the review process.

SAMPLE LIST OF APPENDICES

Budget for the project

Travel plans

Publication or dissemination of results plans

Timeline

Curriculum vita of the principal investigator

Permission to conduct research on human subjects

Letters of support from organizations and companies involved

Review of deliverables

Plan for disseminating the findings

Sample forms

Information about statistical methods to be used

Information about staff to be involved in the research

List of approvals

Annotated bibliography (sometimes included in an appendix and sometimes a separate document)

They will provide the reader with a chance to find and read the important details separate from the logic and coherence of your proposal. In any proposal, the details are included for credibility; they indicate that you have thought through all the pieces of the research design and will, in fact, be able to implement the design if it is approved, scheduled, or financed.

The most common reasons that proposals are not accepted include: unimportant purpose or problem, lack of match between purpose and design or procedures, lack of expertise or inadequate background of the principal investigator, and insufficient information about how the project will be evaluated or the data analyzed (Porte 20).

Not providing enough of these documents or giving the reader incorrect or incomplete documents shows that you have not really prepared the materials thoroughly nor thought about the information that the reviewer will need to make a careful decision. It also may communicate that you have not thought through all of the issues involved in conducting the actual research.

INTRODUCTION AND CONCLUSION

One of the areas that can make a difference in the quality of a research proposal is the introduction and conclusion. The introduction should orient the reader to the entire proposal and prepare him or her to read and review the various sections of the proposal. If done well, an introduction develops the reader's interest in the proposal and prompts some thinking about the topic, the purpose, and the research questions (Heath 150). In that way, the reader is more positively disposed to consider the proposal and remain open to the possibilities suggested by what you plan to do. Therefore, work on making clear what the proposal is about and why it is important: What are the reasons that it should be supported? How will it make a difference in the industry? What impact can it have on current practices? What might it suggest for future research efforts? Unfortunately, many proposals are not really clear about the goal of the research or the purpose (Porte 17).

The introduction should also offer a picture of the structure of the entire proposal so that it is clear where the reader can find specific information. Providing that overview also indicates that you have an overall picture of the proposal and how the parts fit together, an important aspect of convincing the reader of the credibility of the proposal and the likelihood of success, an important goal of your proposal.

At the end of the entire proposal, you should review the purpose statement and research questions, the research design—at least its key elements—and the expected findings and applications. That information will provide the reader with a brief review of the entire proposal and its likelihood of success. Reviewing a research proposal is not an easy task; the more that you can make it pleasant and intelligible, the better the response you will receive. Writing the entire proposal is not easy:

> *To write a good research proposal is a demanding task and requires high caliber writing skills, organization, and the intellectual capacity to critically analyze and evaluate research, both other people's and one's own. It also requires intellectual curiously on the part of the candidates, together with an intrinsic motivation to enhance their knowledge of the topic. Creativity and an open mind further help in looking at the research topics from novel and relevant angles (Heath 161–62).*

The conclusion to your proposal should convince the reader that you have a solid plan, a curiosity to find out the answers to your research questions, and the desire to share the results with others. That impression will help them give you a positive recommendation or decision. The criteria upon which they will base the decision are also important to consider.

CRITERIA FOR A GOOD RESEARCH PROPOSAL

When developing a comprehensive proposal, you can benefit from considering the criteria against which it is measured. At the same time, these criteria are the ones that you should use when assessing the merits of a proposal made to you as part of your work. Whether it is a research proposal or a consulting proposal, the elements are similar, and the criteria are the same (Heath 159–61). The seven criteria with which to evaluate a research proposal include: clarity, coherence, comprehensiveness, creativity, contribution, credibility, and feasibility.

Clarity is a question of the goal of the project. Does it make sense? Can you understand it, and does it make sense to you? Is there logic to the project that can be clearly stated and seen? Does the proposal have a focus that you can readily understand and explain to others? One of the key questions to determine clarity is the ease with which a person who has developed a proposal can explain its logic and focus. The clarity of the proposal will also help ensure that it is carried out successfully (Baker 74).

The criterion of *coherence* applied to a research proposal relates to the match and fit among the parts. Does the proposed research purpose statement fit with the design, or does it seem disconnected? Do the research questions or objectives match the overall research design? Does the sampling strategy make sense of the direction that the research is taking? Do the sampling strategies take into account the reality of the situation?

Comprehensiveness addresses the fullness of the proposal. Have you considered all the factors that will affect the research design? Have you developed a backup plan for unforeseen circumstances? Have you considered the difficulties in obtaining the data you need or access to the persons you want to interview, question, or otherwise find out information from? Do you know that you can access the data needed, and are that data valid and in usable or analyzable format?

CRITERIA FOR A GOOD RESEARCH PROPOSAL

Clarity	Contribution
Coherence	Credibility
Comprehensiveness	Feasibility
Creativity	

Have you created or collected any and all of the supplemental documents and other information necessary to explain the proposal? Without all of these parts, the proposal is incomplete and will most likely be rejected or at least sent back for considerable rework, something that you are trying to avoid.

Creativity is a question that can be applied to a research design because it is a matter of showing that you have considered several options in your plan and that you have brought an innovative approach to the topic, the purpose, or the research design. You may have an unusual method of collecting data, a plan to discover information a new way, an alternative way to analyze data that had already been collected, a renewed perspective to the topic of your research, or an inventive method of disseminating your research. Reviewers like to support creative research so long as it is carefully planned and well explained. Faculty committees like to support students undertaking creative research projects as well.

Creativity can be focused on the subjects of the research, the approach to the topic, the use of individuals, statistics, documents, or organizations. It can involve using observations of hotel lobbies to analyze servicescape, atmosphere, and ambience; the examination of stadium tours as a new form of tourism using participation in the tour and then interviews of participants; or content analyses of case studies already prepared (Countryman and Jang 534–35, Gammon and Fear 249–51, Xiao and Smith 746–48).

Contribution refers to whether a research proposal is worth doing. Will it make a difference to do this research in the way it has been suggested? Will it make a contribution to the scholarship on the topic or to industry practices? Is it worth spending the time and energy on this particular project, or would it be more useful to do something different? Although hard to consider when you have spent so much time considering your purpose and your research objectives, some research proposals do not look likely to make a difference. They seem that they take a lot of time and energy to find out something that is not really worth investigating. Finding out why people stay for one night at hotels located beside major interstate highways or what they look for in these hotels is probably not a topic worth studying since most tourists driving on those roads stop for one night and move on; there are not a lot of motivation questions.

Credibility is a matter of the balance and thoroughness of the plan. Does it look like it can work? Might work? Is it realistic, and do you have the background to conduct the research? Is it likely that you will be able to carry out the design in the time frame planned and with the resources available or requested? One of the problems with many grant proposals is the lack of foresight about unforeseen circumstances and the insufficient resources requested to ensure that the project is successful and that the findings will make the contribution expected. And the issue of credibility is critical whether you are writing a grant proposal, a contract, or a research proposal for graduate school (Porte 16).

Credibility of the proposal also relates to the feasibility of the research project. If you have thought through all the pieces and provided support for the importance and feasibility of the design, the reviewer will be more likely to support it. Some reviewers look for past experience in conducting research, or this type of research, since they want to trust you and your work if they approve it.

SUMMARY

This chapter has suggested ways in which to structure a research proposal in light of the audience who will read your document. It pointed out the reasons for a research proposal; the various parts of the proposal; and the importance of an impartial, third-person perspective for the audience who will read the proposal. It also explained the rationale for an executive summary and provided tips for writing one as opposed to an abstract. It concluded with the criteria most commonly used to assess the merits of a research proposal.

Now that you have all of this information, you are prepared to plan a coherent and carefully reasoned proposal. With luck, your readers will support it and you can implement it.

Good luck, and Godspeed!

KEY TERMS

Abstract	Comprehensiveness	Feasibility
Appendices	Contribution	Point of view
Audience	Creativity	Research questions
Clarity	Credibility	Voice
Coherence	Executive Summary	

WORKS CITED IN THIS CHAPTER

Baker, Michael J. "Writing a Research Proposal" *The Marketing Review* 1 (2000): 61–75.

Countryman, Cary C., and SooCheong Jang. "The Effects of Atmospheric Elements on Customer Impression: The Case of Hotel Lobbies." *International Journal of Contemporary Hospitality Management* 18 (2006): 534–35.

Davis, Gordon B., and Clyde A Parker. *Writing the Doctoral Dissertation: A Systematic Approach.* New York: Barron's Educational Series, 1979.

Gammon, Sean, and Victoria Fear. "Stadia Tours and the Power of Backstage." *Journal of Sport Tourism* 10 (2005): 243–52.

Heath, M., Teresa Pereira, and Caroline Tynan. "Crafting a Research Proposal." *The Marketing Review* 10 (2010): 147–68.

Locke, Lawrence F., Waneen Wyrick Spirdosuo, and Stephen J. Silverman. *Proposals That Work: A Guide for Planning Dissertations and Grant Proposals.* 4th ed. Thousand Oaks: Sage Publications, 2000.

Piantanida, Maria, and Noreen B. Garman. *The Qualitative Dissertation: A Guide for Students and Faculty.* Thousand Oaks: Sage Publications, 1999.

Porte, Michael. "Writing Effective Research Proposals." *Journal of Business Communication* 5 (1967): 13–20.

Punch, Keith F. *Developing Effective Research Proposals.* 2nd ed. London: Sage Publications, 2006.

"The Greater Mekong Subregion Tourism Sector Strategy." *Asian Development Bank* (2005): 1-71.

Xiao, Honggen and Stephen L. J. Smith. "Case Studies in Tourism Research: A State-of-the-Art Analysis" *Tourism Management* 27 (2006): 738–749.

Wolcott, Harry F., *Writing Up Qualitative Research.* 3rd ed. Thousand Oaks: Sage Publications, 2008.

Writing an Annotated Bibliography

INTRODUCTION

An annotated bibliography is an excellent reference document that provides summaries and comments of all of the sources consulted during a research enterprise. A well-written annotated bibliography can be a pleasure to read as well as a great future research tool. It always provides useful assistance since it contains information about the sources you have read and analyzed.

Often, we forget where we found certain ideas or do not correctly remember which source is the most valuable for what particular information. Since an annotated bibliography contains more information than just the details of the citation, an annotated bibliography can be the place where you go to solve this problem.

An annotated bibliography differs from a list of works cited because it contains information summarizing and commenting on each source. The rest of this document will explain the reasons for creating an annotated bibliography and some tips about how to do it.

PURPOSE

Any bibliography or list of works cited can provide details of the documents, interviews, and websites consulted in the process of conducting research. An annotated bibliography goes beyond that point by providing a summary and an assessment of each source. The comments provide a reference for what documents and sources were valuable in the current research and how they might be useful in the future.

There are several reasons for preparing an annotated bibliography. The most important one is the practice it provides you in examining the point of view of a document, website, report, interview, article, or book. Reading it carefully for the perspective, approach to a topic and scope helps you focus on what is being said and how it is being characterized. It also causes you to think more critically about what you are reading while you read it and forces you to make some evaluation of the merits of the source as you read it.

The second reason for developing an annotated bibliography derives from the encouragement it provides you to consider the article or book that you are reading as a whole. Whether reading an article, a review, or a book, your recognition that you will need to summarize and comment on it as an entity helps you keep that perspective on what you are reading. While you inevitably take notes on parts of an article, many students do not step back from what they are reading and consider the point of view, purpose, or scope of the document. Compiling comments for an annotated bibliography requires that you consider the perspective of the work and make a judgment about the relative value of what you are examining. It also helps you to keep focusing on the goal of your research and examining the adequacy of the range of quality sources you have consulted.

A third reason involves your credibility as a researcher. Showing that you are able to distinguish between valuable sources and ones that have significant limitations increases your readers' trust in your insights. Your ability to describe the sources that you use and their merits shows the reader that you are bringing critical thinking to your work and that you are able to keep a healthy skepticism about what you are reading and using in your research.

A fourth reason for an annotated bibliography is its future value, both to you and others. It can be a worthwhile gift to other people—students or other professionals—learning the area you have been investigating since it provides a road map to a new subject. For you, it can be a reminder about what sources are worth revisiting and reusing in the future. As you continue to conduct research in similar or related areas, having an annotated bibliography helps you remember which articles you read previously were worth reading again and which ones might have useful bibliographies that can propel your new research forward more easily and productively.

For these reasons, take every opportunity to create annotated bibliographies; the person who will benefit the most is you.

TECHNICAL DETAILS

Good annotations are well written and thoughtful. They include three types of information: the citation, a summary, and an assessment. They show that the author has thought about what he or she read and considered its value from a variety of perspectives. The following example points out the merits of a study and raises questions about its generalizability:

> *This study compared the responses for guest satisfaction from 281 hotel guests at first-class hotels in Korea with the responses of 259 employees. For cleanliness and courtesy of employees, both the guests and the employees valued these factors similarly. However, there were differences where the guests valued more service oriented factors such as quietness and handling of complaints, whereas the employees focused on complimentary items.*
>
> *The article was helpful to identify some areas of the hotel stay that can affect customer satisfaction. However, the study was conducted with first-class hotels in Korea and the results may not be able to be generalized to middle tier or economic properties.*

Each annotation should be completed, accurately, and thoroughly, in the appropriate bibliographical style—MLA, APA, or other, depending on your institution followed by phrases or complete sentences.

Each entry should be listed alphabetically and accurately so that you, or readers of your bibliography, can locate the source easily and effectively. Errors in the citation will make it difficult for you to return to the source or require you to search for it again using the search engines you found productive in your work.

The commentary in an annotated bibliography should be in the third-person, objective point of view. Although you have made the comments, your professional judgment is involved, and not just your emotional reaction to what you have read. In addition, you never know who will read this annotated bibliography; writing it in the third person gives you an easier time in sharing it; you will not need to go back and edit out certain comments or emotional reactions. It also provides credibility to what you are saying.

For clarity, separate the comments about each source from the listing of the source itself. For example, the following citation does not clearly indicate where the annotation starts and the listing ends. It also does not contain any assessment of the merits of the article:

Garlick, Rick. "Putting the Pieces Together: Using Research to Create Fully Aligned Brands." *Maritz Research* (2009): 1–5. Print. This whitepaper not only speaks about strengthening a company's brand but also how it affects the type of guest a company wants to attract. This article discusses employee teamwork and culture values, which were applicable to the seven principles of quality service. The data helped strengthen the reasons to select the seven principles of quality service due to the fact that they both encompass several of the same values.

A clearer layout might be:

Garlick, Rick. "Putting the Pieces Together: Using Research to Create Fully Aligned Brands." *Maritz Research* (2009): 1–5.

This whitepaper not only speaks about strengthening a company's brand but also how it affects the type of guest a company wants to attract. This article discusses employee teamwork and culture values, which were applicable to the seven principles of quality service. These data helped strengthen the reasons to select the seven principles of quality service due to the fact that they both encompass several of the same values.

This next example provides thorough and complete technical details of the source as well as a summary and commentary:

Palumbo, Frederick A., and Ira Teich. "Segmenting the U.S. Hispanic Market Based on Level of Acculturation." *Journal of Promotion Management* 12 (2005): 151–73.

Palumbo and Teich's research suggests that advertising to the Hispanic market in the United States requires a more complex approach due to the various national and cultural differences within the community.

The scholars suggest that the level of acculturation to U.S. culture is a key factor in determining how to best reach the Hispanic market. While the researchers argue that the Hispanic market can be fragmented, they also note that the Hispanic market as a whole does share common traits that can be leveraged in national campaigns.

The article provides much needed insight into the consumer preferences and advertising influences of one of the fastest growing segments of the U.S. population.

Both these examples indicate that there are various styles appropriate for an annotated bibliography, and you should feel comfortable writing them in the manner you want so long as the citations are accurate, the summary is clear, and the assessment makes sense. In addition, it is important to make some visual distinction between the citation and the annotation.

Some individuals write them as whole paragraphs and some write in short phrases. The following examples illustrate a wide range of possible styles and formats.

SAMPLES

Following are a number of samples provided by students (who have granted me permission to share them) with comments—*in italics*—about the annotations. This set of samples illustrates various ways to write an annotated bibliography while recognizing the two essential parts—a summary and an evaluation.

Baldacchino, Godfrey. "Total Quality Management in a Luxury Hotel: A Critique of Practice." *International Journal of Hospitality Management* 14 (1995): 67–78.

This article provides a definition and description of what TQM is and how it is applicable to the service industry. The research continues by incorporating several case studies on a variety of other luxury hotels including the Four Seasons. This article was chosen because it provided more insight on TQM as well as giving me the idea of using the Four Seasons as the case study for this particular paper.

Notice the first two sentences review the focus and scope of the article and the last one points out why it was used. The annotation does not evaluate the merits of the article even though it indicates why the writer wanted to use it. It also uses "me" which is not appropriate.

Cialdini, Robert B., Richard J. Borden, Avril Thorne, Marcus Randall, Stephen Freeman, and Lloyd Reynolds Sloan. "Basking in Reflected Glory: Three (Football) Field Studies." *Journal of Personality and Social Psychology* 34 (1976): 366–75.

One of the first studies into basking in reflective glory, this article contains some oft-cited results: fans are more likely to wear team colors the day after their team has won and fans often use the pronoun "we" when their team has won. Both of these findings underscore the phenomenon of basking in reflective glory and the relationship between sports results and perception of self-esteem.

This paper is one of the seminal studies of fan behavior, so it was important to read and cite, especially since several of the other studies also cited it. These insights have withstood the test of time and have impacted much of the research that followed it.

This annotation separates the summary from the assessment, making it easy to review and use the comments for future research. The summary is incomplete, and it does not provide as much evaluation of this particular article as it could.

Cruce, Ty M., and John V. Moore. "First-Year Students' Plans to Volunteer: An Examination of the Predictors of Community Service Participation." *Journal of College Student Development* 48 (2007): 655–73.

The researchers estimated the differences in first-year students' decisions to volunteer while in college by their demographic characteristics, as well as by the characteristics of the institution they attended. The findings demonstrated that the traditional student is least likely to volunteer (young, white, male). In addition, students who attended large institutions in urban areas were least likely to volunteer. Finally, learning-community membership was a key predictor of volunteerism during the first year of college. The study can be useful for the development of target programming to encourage the U.S. college students to participate in volunteer activities.

The explanation of the article is clear and focused. The commentary also show in what ways the article can be useful. Separating the summary from the commentary on the article would improve it.

Correia, Abel, and Esteves, Sandra. "An Exploratory Study of Spectators' Motivation in Football." *International Journal of Sport Management and Marketing* 2 (2007): 572–90.

The authors set themselves the objective to see the attributes of the sport experience that motivate spectators to attend a certain football game and explore if there are differences in the factors' influence between genders and age groups. The authors base their work on a huge number of studies, mainly because they faced a certain amount of uncertainty concerning what they were going to find in this specific setting, which is the Final of the Cup of Portugal played at the National Stadium, a specific, one-off event. They surveyed 156 spectators in the vicinities of the stadium seven hours before the match kickoff.

Even though the authors had some previous constructs about factors to be found, such as Perceived Options (event selection regarding other events, value, etc.), Sense of Self (team identification), Personal Intentions (task incentives, ego incentives, social incentives and extrinsic incentives), once the study was conducted they had to group the results in five different factors affecting the stadium attendance experience: Material Reasons (economics, ticket value, etc.), Team Affiliation (loyalty), Extras and Facilities (parking, gifts, etc.), Star Player, and Form of Entertainment (enjoy sports). They found, au contraire to other studies, that Material Reasons are the most important ones to fans, followed by Team Affiliation and Extras and Facilities. They also found that there are differences between women and men spectators: women are higher in Material Reasons and in Star Players than men. In terms of age group, younger spectators are more influenced by Material Reasons, Extras and Facilities and Star Players; young adults are not influenced by Star Players; and elders are influenced by Star Players.

Overall, a very good study that ascertains its limitation: that it was for a one-off event and cannot have the same replication for the regularity of games in Portugal.

This very comprehensive review of the article helps the reader understand both the focus of the article as well as some key elements. The separation of paragraphs also distinguishes aspects of the annotation. It also provides a quick review of the key research results.

Dolnicar, Sara, and Melanie Randle. "What Motivates Which Volunteers? Psychographic Heterogeneity among Volunteers in Australia." *International Society for Third-Sector Research* 18 (2007): 135–55.

The researchers constructed market segments among Australian volunteers based on their motivation to donate time. They determined six homogenous subgroups among volunteers on the basis of their psychographic and demographic characteristics. The research provides valuable insights regarding ways to develop customized marketing messages in order to maximize the impact of appeal to volunteers.

The explanation of the article is clear, but the summary is so general that it is not clear what they found. "Valuable insights" is so broad a term that it does not provide useful information for future reference.

Kowske, Brenda J., Rena Rasch, and Jack Wiley. "Millennials' (Lack Of) Attitude Problem: An Empirical Examination of Generational Effects on Work Attitudes." *Journal of Business and Psychology* 25 (2010): 265–79.

Through a case study, the authors describe how generational traits affect work attitudes of each generational segment in the workplace. The study further illustrates how millennials in particular are different from previous generations.

The comments provide a good review of what the article is about, but there is no evaluation of its merits or usefulness. The limited description of its content—what are the traits and how do they affect attitudes is not clear—diminishes its usefulness.

Kwon, Hyungil H., Galen T. Trail, and Donghun Lee. "The Effects of Vicarious Achievement and Team Identification on BIRGing and CORFing." *Sport Marketing Quarterly* 17.4 (2008): 209–17.

The article analyzes whether or not highly identified fans rely on basking in reflective glory or cutting-off of reflective failure to aid their fan experience. The authors found that CORFing (Cutting Off Reflected Failure) is a strategy favored by low identified fans. Highly identified fans are more likely to use BIRGing (Basking in Reflected Glory) strategies while less likely to rely on CORFing.

This article was useful to the discussion of coping strategies and the reactions of highly identified fans. It underscored some of the findings of the other research, which was helpful in establishing a pattern of BIRGing and CORFing behavior.

Although brief, the summary provides useful information about the article and an explanation of how fan behaviors can be differentially explained by these two processes. The lack of critical commentary weakens the annotation.

Wann, Daniel L., and Paula J. Waddill. "Predicting Sport Fan Motivation Using Anatomical Sex and Gender Role Orientation." *North American Journal of Psychology* 5 (2003): 485–98.

Examined the usefulness of anatomical sex, masculinity, and femininity in predicting fan motivation.

This citation is accurate but so brief as to be useless; it provides no new information and only reiterates the title of the article.

Wann, Daniel, et al. "Motivational Profiles of Sport Fans of Different Sports." *Sport Marketing Quarterly* 17 (2008): 6–19.

The authors set themselves the objectives to see what are the differences in motivations of consumption among sports fans of 13 different sports: figure skating, golf, professional wrestling, professional football, tennis, gymnastics, auto racing, professional basketball, college football, college basketball, boxing, professional baseball, and professional hockey. Those sports were also termed into categories of individual and team, aggressive and nonaggressive; and stylistic and nonstylistic. They follow the eight-point Sport Fan Motivation Scale developed by Wann in the study of 1995, and it follows up a similar study that Wann did in 1999. This study was only for sport fans of the 13 sports in a couple of universities in the Southwest, with an homogeneous student sample.

The eight factors that serve to explain motivations of sports consumers are: Escape, Eustress, Entertainment, Economics, Group Affiliation, Family, Aesthetics, and Self Esteem. The study finds that Entertainment is the motive that loads more highly for sport consumers, followed by Eustress (Euphoric Stress, desire to gain excitement). Those lower are Family and Economics. Escape motive does not differ in any sport type, and Aesthetic motives are higher for individual, stylistic, and non aggressive sports. As well, economics is a big driver in boxing and Escape in professional wrestling. Self Esteem is highly regarded in team sports for a sense of team identification developed when young. Eustress is regarded more highly in aggressive sports, and so is group affiliation, basically for the tailgating aspect of those sports. Finally, no significant differences were found between college and professional sports, contravening some findings in other studies.

This version is more detailed and provides an excellent summary of the article. The reader knows what is covered in the article and can connect this study with previous work that Wann did in the same area. Although a very comprehensive summary, there are no comments on the usefulness or validity of the study.

SUMMARY

Writing an annotated bibliography does not need to be difficult if you keep notes and make a short summary and assessment of each source as you read it. If you wait until the end of your research project, the task of preparing annotations can be challenging. Recording your evaluative comments as you go can make a real difference.

An annotated bibliography can be a gift to you for your future research and for others who ask for your advice about various sources. Therefore, take the time to think about what you write and write it carefully and clearly. Taking time now will save lots of time later.

Index